WIRED FOR
SOUND

D0351288

Also by the Author

Crazy Little Thing Called Love
Half A World Away
Rock and Pop Elevens (co-author)
We Could Have Been The Wombles
The Encyclopaedia of Guilty Pleasures (co-author)
Shopping While Drunk (co-author)
All in the Best Possible Taste

TOM BROMLEY
WIRED FOR
SOUND

SIMON &
SCHUSTER

London · New York · Sydney · Toronto · New Delhi

A CBS COMPANY

First published in Great Britain in 2012 by Simon & Schuster UK Ltd
A CBS COMPANY

Copyright © 2012 by Tom Bromley

This book is copyright under the Berne Convention.
No reproduction without permission.
All rights reserved.

The right of Tom Bromley to be identified as the author of this
work has been asserted by him in accordance with sections 77 and 78
of the Copyright, Designs and Patents Act, 1988.

1 3 5 7 9 10 8 6 4 2

Simon & Schuster UK Ltd
1st Floor
222 Gray's Inn Road
London
WC1X 8HB

www.simonandschuster.co.uk

Simon & Schuster Australia,
Sydney

Simon & Schuster India, New Delhi

A CIP catalogue copy for this book is available
from the British Library.

ISBN: 978-1-84983-393-6

Typeset by Hewer Text UK Ltd, Edinburgh
Printed and bound in Great Britain by
CPI Group (UK) Ltd, Croydon, CR0 4YY

For Joanna, my very own smash hit

'It's so clear that all we have now
Are our thoughts of yesterday . . .'

Strawberry Switchblade, 'Since Yesterday'

Contents

WIRED FOR SOUND

Side Two (1985–1989)

Intro

It's the late noughties, and in a small nursery school just outside of Salisbury my pregnant wife, Joanna, and I are attending the first of our antenatal evening classes. It's a strange gathering: a group of well-meaning but slightly nervous would-be parents brought together by their impending birthing experiences. The person running the course – unhelpfully and almost inappropriately attractive – has given out one of those 'ice-breaker' quizzes in the hope of relaxing everyone before she has to start talking about pelvic-floor exercises. The task itself is fairly straightforward: each couple must write down the attributes they hope their new baby will inherit from each other.

The other couples in the room – sensible, responsible people, such as teachers and charity workers – come back with the sort of answers you'd probably expect. Honesty. Drive.

1

Compassion. Thoughtfulness. One father-to-be, perhaps spoiling the mood slightly, announces that if his baby is a girl he hopes she'll grow up to have his wife's 'fantastic legs and breasts'. And then, finally, it's our turn. Joanna and I look at each other a little awkwardly and then down at our piece of paper. We haven't come up with any sort of emotional ability or particularly striking physical attribute we'd like passed on to our baby. The only thing we've written is 'a love of pop music'.

This book is the story of a musical childhood – not my eldest daughter's (she does like pop music, by the way; ABBA, if you're interested), but my own. For better or for worse mine was a childhood dominated by a love of music, a childhood that chimed with a sort of Police-like synchronicity with the era of the 1980s. This is a book about what it was like growing up listening to the music of that decade, and includes the stories of the bands, records and wider themes that helped shape it.

What it isn't is a definitive encyclopaedia of eighties music: if I was writing about every single band who had a hit during that decade we'd be here for about, well, probably about ten years. It also isn't some cool look back at all the hip bands who strutted their stuff at the time: as much as I'd like to tell you I was collecting obscure Wedding Present seven inches and was down the front when Pere Ubu came to town, these would be untruths. Would I lie to you? (As the Eurythmics once sang.) You'll have to take my word for it that, although I might be occasionally forgetful, I'm not deliberately an unreliable narrator.

2

Instead, this is an everyman story of music in the eighties from the point of view of a child growing up – the sort of child whose week was punctuated by the Top 40 countdown on a Sunday evening, *Smash Hits* coming through the letterbox every other Wednesday and *Top of the Pops* at 7.30 on a Thursday evening, just after *Tomorrow's World*. I was the sort of child who bounced on their bed listening to their first Walkman, spent all day glued to Live Aid and wasn't completely sure about Boy George's sexual orientation. The sort of eighties child (I'm guessing from the fact that you're still here) who was probably a bit like you.

Like a DJ who doesn't know when to put a sock in it, I can hear my producer (editor) shouting in my ear, telling me to finish up as I'm about to do what's known in the radio business as 'crashing the vocals'. I'd better go because if you listen carefully you'll hear that in the background the short introduction to our first song has started to play: a disco-speed drumbeat, some familiar funky guitar chords; and now, of all people, Roger Waters is about to start singing . . .

Side One

(1980–1984)

(1850-1884)

Track One

Another Brick in the Wall (Part 2)

The 1980s began with the last band you'd expect to find at Number 1. Pink Floyd, like Led Zeppelin, were one of those 'proper bands' who didn't do singles: 'We don't do singles,' they informed their producer Bob Erzin. 'So fuck you,' they somewhat unnecessarily continued to his suggestion that they expand one of their songs, which he felt had 'hit' written all over it.[1]

The song topping the charts was 'Another Brick in the Wall (Part 2)', which was the filling in a three-section sequence for their rock opera *The Wall*. This was the late seventies and, during his time spent in the New York studio next door to Chic, Erzin had heard enough of 'Le Freak' pumping through the wall to become a big fan of disco.[2] He persuaded Roger Waters to go clubbing and hear it for himself, and the result was that the band came up with this

Funk Side of the Moon groove. For the lyrics, Waters went back another two decades, recalling his 1950s boarding-school experiences.

There was just one problem: the song was only one minute twenty seconds long. In one of the rare instances of a progressive-rock band being asked to go back and make one of their tracks even longer, the Floyd colourfully rejected Erzin's suggestion to turn the song into something more radio friendly. Erzin, though, wasn't to be put off. With just one verse and a chorus to play with, Erzin came up with the fantastic wheeze of repeating the first verse all over again, but this time getting a group of schoolkids to sing it instead. The children chosen were from Islington Green, a gritty, grotty Grange Hill-type comprehensive school close to where the band were recording. The school boasted a maverick head of music in the shape of Mr Renshaw, a teacher who smoked in class, wore tight jeans and got his pupils to hit walls to see what sort of sounds they made. So when Pink Floyd came calling he was more than happy (and much more happy than the headmistress) to allow his class to sing about how crap the whole concept of education was.

I might be simplifying the song's message just a little there. In fact, the famous line about not needing no education is ungrammatical to the point of suggesting that the children *do* need at least a lesson or two in English. If you bothered to pay attention, Jones, rather than staring out of the window, you'd realize that the double negative actually suggests the kids would like at least a *bit* of schooling . . . However, such subtleties are soon lost. All anyone hears are a load of anti-teacher, anti-authority lyrics, a feel reinforced by the song's Gerald Scarfe video. This stars a cane-wafting schoolmaster whose pop-eyes mutate into hammers, which in turn proceed to march along in unison as if the world is about to be taken over by a Soviet version of B&Q (the video also features a different group of children to those on the record: they didn't have Equity cards so a selection of stage-school kids got the gig instead).

Bob Erzin's instinct about the song proved to be correct. For the first time since 'See Emily Play' reached the Top 10 in 1967, Pink Floyd released a single – and were rewarded with five weeks at Number 1. Slightly better rewarded than the Islington Green singers, it has to be said, who got a flat fee of £1000 for their contribution. At least they could tell their children and grandchildren that they'd sung on the first Number 1 of the eighties. The single was no doubt there legitimately, but it's worth adding that in those days no one could quite be arsed to compile the charts in the week between Christmas and New Year and thus the list from the week before was just reprinted instead.

The Top 10 as the eighties began was undoubtedly something of a mixed selection. Sitting in Pink Floyd's slipstream were two of the biggest singles bands of the time, ABBA ('I Have a Dream') and the Police ('Walking on the Moon'). ABBA, by this stage, were beginning the descent towards the end of their career. They still had a couple of Number 1s left in them ('Super Trouper' and the quite magnificent 'The Winner Takes It All') but their main contribution to the eighties would be their final, brooding album *The Visitors*: a sleek, melancholy record that didn't sell to the 'Dancing Queen' hordes but was by the far the best thing they ever did. The Police, meanwhile, were heading in the opposite direction, taking giant steps towards their own world domination – even if internal band disharmony was approaching ABBA proportions. Drummer Stewart Copeland's irritation with Sting was famously shown by writing the words 'Fuck', 'Off', 'You' and 'Cunt' across the tom-toms of his drum kit.

Presciently, that first eighties Top 10 also boasted 'Rapper's Delight' by the Sugarhill Gang. This might not have been the first rap song but was certainly the first one to cross over and make it high in the charts. Here, too, was the influence of Nile Rodgers and Chic again, with a song based around a sample of their hit 'Good Times'. Not only did Wonder Mike, Master Gee and Big Bank Hank give a flavour of what would become one of the dominant musical trends later in the decade, but the song's opening line coined the phrase 'hip hop' to boot. The Top 10 also offered glimpses of the (then) future in the shape of the Pretenders' gorgeous 'Brass in Pocket', on its way to Number 1, and Annie Lennox and Dave Stewart's pre-Eurythmics band the Tourists, with their cover of Dusty Springfield's 'I Only Want to be with You'.

That first eighties Top 10 wasn't all fantastic. Several rungs down the disco ladder from Chic were the Gibson Brothers, who, judging by the way they shout the lyrics to 'Que Sera Mi Vida', should really have stood closer to the microphone during recording. There were the Three Degrees, the Philadelphia group whose name was appropriated by the then West Bromwich Albion manager, 'Big' Ron Atkinson, to describe his trio of black players, Cyrille Regis, Laurie Cunningham and Brendon Batson. This being the festive period, there's Paul McCartney in full Fab-Macca-Wacky-Thumbs-Aloft mode with 'Wonderful Christmastime', the sort of saccharine guff to which, had the Beatles still been going, John Lennon would have taken a pair of blunt scissors.

This being the British charts, there's also the obligatory one-hit wonder thanks to the folking awful Fiddler's Dram and their 'Day Trip to Bangor (Didn't We Have a Lovely Time)'. Even the title of the song is annoying. *What* is with those brackets? Either the song is called 'Day Trip to Bangor' or it's called 'Didn't We Have a Lovely Time': you can't be indecisive and go with both. It's a record so preposterously out of kilter and cheerfully irritating that one could imagine the children of Islington Green Comprehensive groaning 'Hey! Nonny nonny! Leave those chords alone!'[3]

I was seven years and a couple of weeks old at the start of the decade – Pink Floyd, as it happened, went to Number 1 on my birthday. The eighties, then, very much dovetailed with my childhood, and my transformation from the spotty, awkward kid at junior school to the spottier and even more awkward teenager at sixth form. These were my formative years, and my affection for them remains strong – to the point that (I would readily admit) my opinion of their cultural importance is no doubt subjectively skewed. For anyone writing about the era they grew up in, being able to comment objectively is tricky because everything resonates so strongly; it's hard not to be seduced by its Ready brek glow of over-importance.

It was pretty much impossible to be a small child at the start of the 1980s and not like the sentiment of 'Another Brick in the Wall'. With its depiction of 'the kids' standing up to a miserly schoolmaster and, if Gerald Scarfe's video was to be believed, his plan to grind us all through some kind of child mincer like a Roald Dahl villain, it was impossible not to feel galvanized into classroom defiance. It was no doubt equally difficult to be a teacher at the time and not loathe the song in equal measure as yet another class of previously well-behaved pupils turned round and told you where to stick it.

My own schooling, I have to say, did not reflect the nightmare vision of education that Roger Waters had come up with. The only teacher I encountered who was stuck in the 1950s was the one I had for PE at junior school. He had the sort of temper you didn't want to get on the wrong side of, but I avoided getting into trouble on account of being a member of his football team – not, I should hasten to add, because I was any good at football, but because I was just about the only child in my year who was left-footed, and could thus play at left wing (a position that I have stuck to politically ever since).

My schooling (a term that makes it sound far grander than it actually was) all took place in the suburbs of York, as if in a *Sesame Street* episode brought by the letter H: I lived in leafy Heworth and went to Hempland Primary School and what was then called Huntington Comprehensive School. The latter goes under the name Huntington School these days, though it is still a comprehensive. However, no one ever consulted me on that fact, and I have continued to call it Huntington Comprehensive School – to make the point on my CV in a slightly chippy northern way, and just in case anyone mistakes it for a minor biscuit-tossing private school.

It's a slightly affected badge of honour because I am about as middle-middle class as they come: that's what happens when your father is a doctor and your mother a teacher. Keeping up the family tradition, my brother is also a doctor and my sisters both teachers; it's only me who lets the side down by spending his life messing about writing books on eighties music. It's also the case that the only reason that I ended up going there was because York was in the process of getting rid of the Eleven Plus: I was the last year to take the exam (I passed) but, rather than find out what happened when a grammar school merged with a secondary modern, my parents opted for a nearby comprehensive instead. Even then they weren't entirely convinced. When the teachers' strikes hit in the mid-eighties – a glorious period in which we got sent home every lunchtime and had at least one after-noon off a week for a couple of years – they were sufficiently worried that they considered sending me to a private school. However, I refused to even look round the place, let alone countenance swapping.

That was less to do with some stirrings of early left-wing principles and more because I liked the school I was at. Being OK at football, or being left-footed at least, went a long way towards making my school years easier. I cottoned on early that an interest in sport was important in avoiding getting your head kicked in by the harder kids from the estate. What took me a little longer to figure out was that an impressive statistical knowledge of the Division Four table was not always sufficient to attract the attention of the fairer sex. I use the phrase 'attract the attention of': my main goal was getting them to acknowledge my existence beyond 'Can anyone else smell that?'

The way to impress girls, I discovered, was to know about pop music. Music plays a big part in the course of anyone growing up, and particularly so for me. Its effect on a childhood is subtly different to other types of culture: television, as I discussed in an earlier book (*All in the Best Possible Taste*, still available in all good bookshops[4]) is more about family. It's something that you watch at home with your mum and dad, switch off from when you are old enough to go to the pub, and return to when you have children of your own, as small compensation for the fact that you're never going to leave your house for an evening out ever again.

Music is different. Records were something you listened to on your own, locked away in your bedroom: a teenage rebellion against your parents' (lack of) taste. What you watched growing up was determined by who had control of the family remote control – i.e., your dad. What you listened to, by contrast, was influenced by your friends. Those early musical choices are, until you know better, all about peer pressure: wanting to be cool, wanting some of that pop-star glamour to rub off on you, and wanting to define your identity. In the eighties that meant wearing a stolen VW badge round your neck to show how much you liked the Beastie Boys, or attaching the top of a bottle of Grolsch to your shoes to prove you really 'hearted' Bros. In the pecking order of school and making friends, who you listened to was who you were.

If that was me at school – a slightly gangly individual with red hair, a functional left foot and a head full of *Smash Hits*-assisted music trivia – what were some of the eighties pop stars like at the same age? Looking back at the early years of the likes of Duran Duran, Wham! and Spandau Ballet, it's noticeable that they were a pretty eclectic bunch. If you put them all together in one room you'd probably need the cane-waving antics of Pink Floyd's disciplinarian teacher to keep them in check.

The teenage alpha male in this particular class was probably Andrew Ridgeley. At Bushey Meads School near Watford in the mid-seventies, Ridgeley was just about everything I wasn't: good-looking, stylish, sporty and a Top 10 hit with the ladies. He was the cool, confident kid boys wanted to be friends with and girls wanted to go out with. 'He looked good, he dressed good, and he *thought* he was a good footballer,' George Michael recalled in his autobiography, *Bare*: even at that early age, 'he wanted to be famous. He didn't care if it was a football player or a pop star or whatever – he just wanted to be famous.'[5]

Andrew Ridgeley's ambition was matched in Birmingham by a young boy called Nicholas Bates. Bates (who'd later go by the stage name Rhodes) was ten when he told his parents he was going to be a pop star. When he started at Woodrush High School in the mid-seventies he reiterated his intentions to his art teacher: 'Nicholas knew what he wanted to do at an early age and was one of the few schoolkids who've said to me, "I want to be a pop star" and actually achieved his ambition'.[6] Bates and Ridgeley are similar, too, in having each befriended their respective class ugly duckling – ugly ducklings who later turned into two of the eighties' biggest musical, er, swans. For Nicholas Bates that duckling was the lanky Nigel Taylor, a boy who had worn glasses since the age of five and liked to spend his spare time painting small toy soldiers and playing war games.

For Andrew Ridgeley the friend in question was Georgios Panayiotou. Georgios was 'the embodiment of adolescent awkwardness, a podgy, gangling figure whose intimidating height was immediately rendered irrelevant by the comic shock of curly hair and the thick-rimmed spectacles which perched precariously on his nose'.[7] In the school playground Ridgeley goaded Georgios into a game of 'king of the wall': this essentially involved a preening Ridgeley sitting on top of said wall and showing off his athletic prowess by pushing off all challengers. If you were a betting boy you wouldn't have put your Panini stickers on Georgios, but to everyone's amazement he unseated Ridgeley to become 'king'. Ridgeley, rather than attempting revenge and reclaiming his crown, instead insisted that Georgios sat next to him in class and the pair became the closest of friends.

A short car ride down into North London, meanwhile, were two young brothers with an early taste of the stardom Ridgeley craved. Martin and Gary Kemp were both members of the Anna Scher Theatre and found themselves appearing in TV shows such as *Jackanory*, *Dixon of Dock Green* and *Rumpole of the Bailey*. They were having a better time of it than nearby Tony Hadley, who, having passed his Eleven Plus to go to Dame Alice Owen's Grammar School, found himself struggling and getting into trouble. (Not the greatest idea he ever had was to have a hosepipe fight with a friend in the middle of the science block. So badly did they drench the corridor that water seeped through to the dining room below and caused the wallpaper to peel off; the damage repair ran into thousands of pounds.)

Joining Tony Hadley in detention would undoubtedly be young Adam Clayton. Clayton had been born in Oxfordshire but moved to Dublin when his father, a pilot, got a job with Aer Lingus. Clayton got into and was then removed from the private St Columba's College. He was bright but no doubt infuriating to teach: when he didn't want to play a cricket match, he resolutely sat down for the duration of his fielding duties; he also thought nothing of turning up to school wearing sunglasses, Arab headdress and billowing caftan (come on, we've *all* done it . . .). When he ending up at the local comprehensive, Mount Temple, Adam's same disregard for authority continued: he'd drink coffee in class from a flask he'd brought with him

('I'm having a cup of coffee, sir,' was his polite explanation to his exasperated teacher); he was also prone to streaking along the corridors (though presumably not at the same time as the coffee drinking – that could have been dangerous). Before he was removed from school for a second time, Adam had at least, along with Dave Evans and Paul Hewson, answered the message that the drummer Larry Mullen had pinned to the school noticeboard about wanting to form a band.

Across the Irish Sea in Liverpool, Holly Johnson gave a prescient taste of his future band's shock antics by writing 'sex' and 'shit' on the primary-school blackboard. Such profanity was a world away from the apparently angelic boy who sang the solo to 'Once in Royal David's City' for the church choir. Holly, like Tony Hadley, found himself getting into grammar school and not enjoying it. He couldn't pursue his interest in art, because art was taught only to those boys in the bottom streams, so instead ended up acting the class clown.

Steven Morrissey found himself up against a similar culture-free environment at St Mary's Secondary Modern in Manchester. He liked reading, music and drama, but music and drama weren't on the St Mary's syllabus and there wasn't even a school librarian. The young Morrissey was relatively athletic and could have run and jumped with the best of them, had he so desired. Sport, though, wasn't exactly his bag (he insisted on batting one-handed when playing cricket). Throughout all of this, Morrissey's love of music remained undimmed: in June 1974 the *NME* published the first of several letters by 'Steve Morrissey', this particular one in praise of the new LP by Sparks.

George O'Dowd, meanwhile, didn't have the best time at school: 'Eltham Green School was like a back-street abortion – it happened, I wish to forget it ever did.'[8] In the years before George entered the school it had enjoyed, if that's the word, a poor reputation. The new headmaster, Peter Dawson, declared that 'discipline was the only way to bring it under control' and his authoritarian rule rippled throughout the school. George describes being made an example of by his PE teacher, who offered him the choice of 'hand or backside' then hit him so hard he bled (George's mum was a dinner lady at the school and later gave the teacher a piece of her mind).

But it was with the school's headmaster that O'Dowd would go on to have his biggest run-in, eventually describing him in his autobiography as a 'resident Hitler lookalike'. (A slightly more sympathetic drawing of Dawson is offered by Michael Frayn, who based the character Brian Stimpson in *Clockwise*, played by John Cleese, on him.) At Eltham Green, O'Dowd's decision to dye his hair bright orange might have made for a cool look but it also made it fairly obvious to spot when he was skipping school. After one showdown too many Dawson expelled O'Dowd with the words: 'You'll never make anything of yourself, O'Dowd. You're a fool.' A few years on, however, George was one of the biggest stars on the planet. Dawson (by then head of a teachers' union) hadn't softened his attitude towards him. O'Dowd was 'a classic example of the word "misfit"', he declared, claiming his schooling had been a 'waste of time'. 'He couldn't understand how I'd become success-ful,' George noted, looking on in bemusement as the *Times Educational Supplement* letters page filled with correspond-ence debating whether a headmaster should speak publicly about a former pupil's education.

This small constellation of eighties stars at school shows a wide variety of attitudes towards not needing no education, but all these early lives had in common a single, unifying feature: music. And not just any old music, either – for almost to a Mr T they were turned on by more or less the same, small select band of seventies artists.

Nicholas Bates/Nick Rhodes had his world turned upside down when he bought David Bowie's *The Rise and Fall of Ziggy Stardust and the Spiders from Mars*. Together with Nigel Taylor – Nigel *John* Taylor, as I'm sure you've guessed – Rhodes went to Birmingham Town Hall in 1974 to watch Bowie's former sidekick Mick Ronson touring his debut solo album (*Slaughter on 10th Avenue*), then soon after to see Roxy Music at the Birmingham Odeon. So keen were they to watch the latter that they turned up at the box office hours before the venue opened to ensure they got in. And so enamoured were they with Roxy Music's perform-ance – somewhat more than the *NME*, who mocked Ferry's Spanish cowboy outfit as 'more gauche than gaucho' – they spent the next day hanging around the Holiday Inn in the hope of speaking to the band (they eventually had to make do with chatting to the group's violinist).

ANOTHER BRICK IN THE WALL (PART 2)

For Holly Johnson, T. Rex's *Electric Warrior* was 'the record [that] changed my life [. . .] Marc Bolan was the only charismatic character around, as far as I was concerned.'[9] David Bowie soon joined this select list, with Johnson's 'obsession' reaching fever pitch with the release of *Ziggy Stardust*: 'this record had a huge effect on kids of my generation [. . .] bisexuality became a fashionable pose, along with the idea of androgyny in fashion'.[10] Holly describes in his autobiography how together with his best friend he'd record *Top of the Pops* each week with a microphone held up to the TV, and then dress up as Bolan or Bowie, creating their own dance routines. Morrissey, too, was a big fan of these early-seventies stars: he would sketch pictures of Bolan in his exercise book during lessons, and saw T. Rex live at the King's Hall; when Bowie played Manchester's Free Trade Hall in June 1973, Morrissey and friends were not only present but also visited the hairdresser first to get themselves an approximation of a Bowie haircut.

Gary Kemp also followed this first-Bolan-then-Bowie route. Having persuaded his mum to buy him 'Get It On' on a Saturday-morning shopping trip, Kemp's wait to hear the record was extended when they stopped off to buy saveloy and chips on the way home. By the time they got back, the hot chips had, to Kemp's horror, warped the single: 'as the needle bobbed like a boat on the high sea the sound left everyone in earshot feeling nauseous. I suffered the indignity on behalf of Marc, and in between gobfuls of the now cold, shameful saveloy, I sang along anyway.'[11] Five months after Morrissey had seen Bowie play in Manchester, Kemp was fortunate enough to see him play at the Marquee Club in Soho for an American TV special, *The 1980 Floor Show* (by this point Bowie had 'retired' from live performance). 'At some magical moment during the night,' Kemp recalled in his autobiography, 'he reached down, looked into my eyes and accepted one of my bangles as a gift.'[12]

George O'Dowd – Boy George – was introduced to David Bowie by his elder brother, Richard: *The Man Who Sold the World* was the first Bowie record he owned. A few weeks before Morrissey saw him in Manchester, George saw the same Ziggy Stardust tour in Lewisham. Rather than getting a hairdresser to give him a Bowie haircut, George attempted to do it himself: 'it was a disaster – I looked like Dave Hill from Slade'.[13] The concert, meanwhile, had a huge impact on young George: 'it was the most exciting thing I'd ever seen [. . .] no concert I have seen since has had the same effect'. Inspired by the experience, George would sometimes get on the bus to Beckenham and join the other fans hanging outside Bowie's house. He didn't get a glimpse of his idol there, but was instead treated to Angie Bowie leaning out of the window and telling them all to 'Fuck off'. He did see Bowie a few years later, however, in May 1976, when he was in the crowd at Victoria Station to witness Bowie returning from Berlin and giving his fans the infamous Nazi salute.

In fact, among this constellation of would-be stars, the only ones listening to anything noticeably different were Tony Hadley, Andrew Ridgeley and Georgios Panayiotou. Hadley liked David Bowie, but was a real fan of Elton John and Queen as well as crooners like Frank Sinatra and

Tony Bennett. Panayiotou – or George Michael, of course – started his record collection with three singles: two by the Supremes and one by Tom Jones. By the seventies, like Hadley, it was Elton John and Queen that he loved – two acts with whom he'd later go on to have Number 1 duets.

All these stars grew up around the same time so were inevitably listening to the same sorts of records – that's one element. Even so, the specificity of their musical interests and the effect this had on them feels instructive. These were young teenagers who fell in love with the glitz and glamour of Bowie, Roxy and Marc Bolan – not just their music, but also their fascination with style and the hints of sexual ambiguity. This wasn't a generation of would-be musicians enthralled by the Beatles and the music of the sixties or drawn in by the virtuosity and complexity of the progressive-rock bands. Instead, there was an instinctive, shared love for a very fashion-conscious, very English style of music. If early-eighties music was a stick of seaside rock it would have Bowie and Roxy written all the way through.

The first Number 1 single of the eighties now seems symbolic, not for suggesting that the eighties were facing annexation by the prog-rock rulers of the seventies but in highlighting just how significant – or, rather, how not entirely significant – punk had been. It is something of a given in music writing that punk changed everything. To read *Melody Maker* or the rival *New Musical Express* in the 1980s an easily led young music fan could be forgiven for seeing 1976 as some sort of Pol Pot-type Year Zero, where anything recorded before that date had been to all intents and purposes erased from memory. Punk, with Johnny Rotten wearing his 'I Hate Pink Floyd' T-shirt, had killed off the supposed 'dinosaur bands'.

I'm not for a second saying that punk wasn't important or crucial in giving a kick up the backside of what was undoubtedly a rather staid and sorry music scene in the mid-1970s. What I am saying, however, is that its influence has perhaps been overdone over the years, and that the neat simplicity of its supposedly game-changing nature ignores what in fact is a subtler and more blurred picture. What punk gave to teenagers and young musicians was self-belief: just as the Beatles had challenged the songwriting hegemony of Tin Pan Alley back in the sixties, and shown artists that they could come up with their own material, so punk demonstrated that you didn't need to be a prog-rock virtuoso to join a band – a rudimentary three chords and you were away. That was undoubtedly key in capturing people's imagination: time and again there are stories of eighties stars having seen bands like the Sex Pistols play – but if everyone who claimed they were at the Pistols' 1976 gig at Manchester Lesser Free Trade Hall had really been there there'd have been an Old Trafford-sized crowd in attendance (actually watching were only thirty-five to forty people[14]).

The attitude that punk brought undoubtedly had an impact. But in terms of its musical influence punk's legacy is markedly more limited. If punk inspired teenagers to pick up their guitars, it didn't inspire them to play punk music itself. For many of the bands that dominated the charts in the early 1980s the reference points came from the music they'd listened to back at school: earlier-seventies, pre-punk music, and in particular the 'glamour twins' of David Bowie and Roxy Music. These were the acts this generation had watched on *Top of the Pops*, whose creativity, talent and colour made them stand out against the brown-and-beige background of the rest of the decade.

Punk not only had less musical influence than it some-times aspires to, but it faded quickly in terms of its ethos too. There's a great book from the time by the music writer Dave Rimmer (recently brought back to life thanks the delights of digital publishing). In this, Rimmer looks at what he called the 'new pop' bands – the Spandau Ballets, the Duran Durans, the Wham!s – and casts his eyes and ears over their lifestyles and the sounds they were making by the mid-eighties: 'swimming in jewellery, swanning about in limousines, swilling champagne and swaggering into each other's parties, they created a new rock establishment. It was [. . .] like punk never happened' (a phrase Rimmer used to title his book). The fact that the first Number 1 of the eighties was by Pink Floyd, then, was a useful marker for what was to follow.

Track Two

Vienna

My own musical journey begins in a way that couldn't be less rock and roll if it tried. I'd love to tell you a story about how I used to gurgle along to 'Life on Mars?' and 'Virginia Plain' in my pram, how my first words were 'dirty fucker' after watching the Pistols with Bill Grundy, and how my parents once caught me attempting to put my nappy pin through my nose in homage to Sid Vicious. That, though, would be a figment of my imagination – or, as Imagination the band might have put it, futuristic funk gladiator garb and all, just an illusion.[1]

Instead, let's set the dial on the literary DeLorean back to 1980 and show you what is – as a singer with rolled-up jacket sleeves might croon – true. We're in York. Not cool and happening New York, with CBGBs and Studio 54, but old York, the original one, whose equivalent was the back room of the Spotted Cow and the sticky-floor experience of Ziggy's nightclub. Not that I was old enough to know what these sort of places were; I was seven years old and the only thing that I knew about pubs was gleaned from the sarcastic comments my mother made when my father came back from one on a Friday after a 'swift' half of Double Diamond.

It is a Sunday evening, about twenty past six, and (I am ashamed to say, even now) I am already bathed and in my blue-check pyjamas and dressing gown ready for bed. It is pathetically early, I know, but as a parent myself I can now appreciate that, having entertained, refereed and riot-controlled small children all weekend, getting the little buggers off to bed at the earliest possible opportunity is essential for your sanity. I might have made a bit more of a fuss about it but, fortunately for my parents, they had an ally in helping keep me sweet.

Sunday evening in our house always followed the same routine. Mum would bath the children while Dad mopped the kitchen floor. Having sluiced it down, he'd then lay pages of the *Guardian* as soggy stepping stones for us to walk around on – cheery articles about rising unemployment and Russian tanks rolling into Afghanistan. Then he'd retire with the rest of the family to the sitting room, seduced by Gordon Giltrap's Spanglishy theme tune to the *Holiday* programme, where Cliff Michelmore and his team would warm up winter evenings with reports of summer cruises and Mediterranean adventures (not, for all the drooling, that we ever went on such holidays; we always ended up in Swanage instead).

I didn't join my family round the fire (and we did have a fire in those days – a proper one with a coal shed in the garage and everything). Instead, I remained in exile in the cold of the kitchen. I'd then fix myself a drink. Not *that* sort of drink: the only alcohol in the house was a half-bottle or two of sickly sweet Liebfrau anyway, but of course there was none of that for me – just straight *milch*, in the days before Bob Geldof had made a 'lotta bottle' sort of cool with his hilarious 'You're . . .? Yeah, shattered . . .' adverts.

But, for all my almost aching unhip-ness, there was one glint of cool to add to proceedings. For in this middle-class kitchen, sipping milk in my pyjamas, there was, in the corner, a radio. It was an old Roberts radio, the original sort with a grill on the front and two chunky knobs on the top, one for the volume and one for tuning. My dad had, as with so many gadgets in the house, got his blue masking tape out; in this instance, small triangles of the stuff denoted where certain stations could be found on the dial. However, there wasn't much twiddling to be done as the radio was pretty much permanently set to 88-91, on what these days we'd call FM but back then went under the name VHF.

That frequency, as today, is the home of Radio Two. But that's not what I was listening to. Because, for three hours a week, this VHF stereo setting was handed over to Radio Two's younger, brasher (and, in the case of several DJs, hairier) sibling. Usually Radio One crackled away on medium wave at 1053/1089 KHz (or 275/285m), but for those few Sunday-evening hours it could be heard on the Radio Two FM frequency. Up and down the country ('England, Scotland, Ireland, Wales ... the United Kingdom!' as one jingle helpfully and inaccurately reminded) there were people like me – six to seven million of us, in fact – huddled round our radios, listening excitedly as the 'sensational' tones of Tony Blackburn counted down over the backdrop of 'Rockall' by Mezzoforte. And I'd make a careful note that 'Feels Like I'm in Love' by Kelly Marie was a 'climber', that it had gone up two huge Top 40 places from last week's Number 3 to be this week's brand-new (cue jingle) 'Number 1!'

The singles chart in the UK began back in November 1952, bang in the middle of that sixteen-month period between the death of George VI and the coronation of Queen Elizabeth II. It was set up by the *New Musical Express*, who, in a move the about-to-be conceived Peter Mandelson would have been proud of, had just rebranded itself, junking its original title of *Musical Express and Accordion Weekly*. Accordions, after all, are just *so* 1940s it's not true. In the days of shillings and half-crowns there was nothing quite so decimal as a Top 10. Instead, the original 'Record Hit Parade' comprised a Top 12.[2]

By the time I was listening, in the early 1980s, the Top 12 had become the Top 40; and instead of ringing round a dozen or so shops on a Monday morning the British Market Research Bureau (BMRB) electronically collated the sales from 250 stores (randomly chosen from 6000 across the country). It's easy to overlook but the charts were, essentially, sales charts. And not just sales charts but sales charts of singles – singles that were then primarily a promotional tool used by record companies to shift albums. And not even just a sales chart of a promotional tool, but one created by the *NME* with the express purpose of selling more copies of their magazine. In terms of capitalism it doesn't really get much more unfettered.

Yet at the time the charts never came across as grubby like that. Instead they felt exciting, and fresh, and like something you needed to know about. The *NME*'s original idea had taken a creative activity – making music – and turned it into a competition that, for those golden years, captured the young imagination. A single is a cultural entity in exactly the same way that a novel or a film is, yet bestseller lists or box-office Top 10s have never taken the nation in the same way. The fact that the singles charts were known simply as 'the charts' said everything about their significance. No explanation as to which charts they were was necessary: they were *the* charts.

These days the music charts have gone the same way as all these other bestseller lists. When was the last time that you listened to the Top 40? Do you even know what's Number 1 right now? I have to confess, I usually don't know either.[3] Back in 1980, not knowing what was in the charts would have been unimaginable to my seven-year-old self. That early evening ritual was my own form of Sunday service. I'd sit there each week and religiously write the charts down in a notebook I kept for such important information. In the early eighties the Top 40 was hosted by a bit of a revolving door of presenters; but, whether it was Tony Blackburn,

Tommy Vance or Simon Bates, it seemed the charts required a DJ with a deep voice who could inject proceedings with the requisite mixture of excitement and dignity. Later in the eighties the show was handed over to the likes of Mark Goodier and Bruno Brookes, and that seemed to sum up the era's more frivolous nature.

I didn't really know why the charts were important. I just knew that they were. Before I grew to begin to appreciate music properly I learnt to love the charts, and I was far from unique in that. Most men, and particularly most young boys, have an autistic streak to them that given half a chance will come to the fore. Sitting there in the kitchen, writing out the charts in my notebook, is symptomatic of that. I remember well the late-night conversation at university, years later, when I discovered that several of my friends had done exactly the same thing – one, I jealously noted, had even used different-coloured pens for songs that went up and down (why hadn't I thought of that?). In terms of my being a young boy growing up, then, my behaviour was both a bit odd and perfectly normal at the same time.

What was equally odd (and equally normal) was the way I would imbue these chart placings and positions with a relevance and meaning that, I can happily admit now, didn't really exist. Back then, if a song didn't get to Number 1 it was because it didn't *deserve* to get to Number 1. A straight-in-at-Number-1 entry was such a rarity it was to be relished and admired when it occurred. I would devour chart facts – facts like how David Bowie's 'Loving the Alien', released at the same time as Paul Hardcastle's

'19', became a non-mover . . . at Number 19! Man, that freaked me out. Or how the Tourists' version of 'I Only Wanna Be with You', which featured in that first eighties Top 10, peaked at Number 4 – *exactly* the same number as Dusty Springfield's original *and* the Bay City Rollers' cover! Whoa. I had to sit down as I took that in. For years I had a party trick of being able to say exactly which position a song in the eighties had reached: *DeBarge? 'Rhythm of the Night'? Number 4, 1985* . . . (I'm ashamed to say I did that one from memory.) It's been suggested that this might be a sign of an eidetic memory, though I've generally heard it described in rather ruder terms – usually when I've used it to win a bet in the pub.

As well as building my collection of handwritten Top 40 rundowns I saved up and spent most of my pocket money on singles. In 1980 these still cost just under a pound, at a child-friendly price of 99p (an album, by contrast, would set you back £4.69). I was far from alone in my buying habits – during the early eighties the British bought just under eighty million singles a year, making the country the second-highest market of seven inches in the world (first was the United States: in 1981 the US accounted for one third of all records sold). This was a golden era that wasn't to last: from 1985 onwards British singles sales started to slide and by the end of the decade were back to middling mid-seventies levels. A decade later this was down to the low forty-million mark; by 2010 the number of physical singles sold in the UK was just two million.

The early additions to my record collection were not exactly marked out by their quality. The first record I ever bought – and I must stress I was five at the time – was 'Pretty Little Angel Eyes' by Showaddywaddy. No, I'm not really sure why either. I do remember watching them on *Top of the Pops*, mistaking their Teddy Boy suits for pyjamas and thinking that this was somehow subversive (it wasn't) and hilarious (it also wasn't). I then bought – and you do have permission to kick me at this point – 'Hot Shot' by Cliff Richard, his rubbishy rock-and-roll follow-up to his guilty-pleasure classic 'We Don't Talk Anymore'. I'm also the (less than) proud owner of 'Ain't No Pleasing You' by Chas and Dave, 'My Camera Never Lies' by Bucks Fizz and 'This Time (We'll Get It Right)' by the England World Cup Squad. None of these singles are even the worst in my collection, a (dis)honour that goes to my ownership of Paul McCartney and the Frog Chorus' 'We All Stand Together'. I got that as a birthday present without actually asking for it, so really it's there only by default.

A ray of light among these early embarrassments is Adam Ant's 'Stand and Deliver'. There were other big stars at the start of the eighties who I liked – Madness for their sense of fun and wacky videos, the Welsh Elvis that was Shakin' Stevens – but Adam Ant was by far the most colourful and charismatic. Ant's journey to pop stardom had been an unusual one. His first brush with music fame had been via his mother, who in the mid-1960s had been Paul McCartney's cleaner. Adam – or Stuart Goddard, as he was then – would go with her, gaze in amazement at the

Pop Art style and Höfner bass leaning against the wall, and take McCartney's sheepdog Martha for a walk (the Martha in the Beatles' 'Martha My Dear'). Goddard's own musical taste began with a love of soul, Tamla Motown, Al Green and Freda Payne's 'Band of Gold' (which he listened to, poor Mrs Goddard, 'over a hundred times' in 1970).

From here, Goddard sang in a succession of seventies bands, my favourite being the B-Sides, so called because they 'only played the B-sides of singles that hadn't been a hit'. In November 1975 Goddard watched a new group playing their first ever gig at St Martin's Art School: the Sex Pistols. It was watching them play that gave Goddard the idea to become Adam Ant, a name whose wordplay I have to confess escaped me for years. It's a name, too, that feels more sixties than seventies to me; a little bit Beatles, perhaps? Certainly, it chimed with what Adam Ant ultimately was – an old-fashioned entertainer but with an eighties twist.

Adam and his band, now christened the Ants, became a cult success, without ever threatening to break through – a fact probably not helped by the decision to turn down a £100,000 record contract from Polydor in the expectation that they'd come back with a bigger one (they instead withdrew the offer). Adam then turned to Malcolm McLaren, the mastermind behind the Sex Pistols, and paid him £1000 to act as a sort of consultant for the band, offering his ideas as to the music they should be playing and the fashion they should be following. What followed was a melting pot of ideas: Adam was reading books on American Indians and African tribes, and picking up fashion ideas from them; Malcolm McLaren's partner, Vivienne Westwood, was looking at eighteenth-century fashions, which led to McLaren becoming convinced that the pirate look was the next big thing. There are differing views on who came up with imitating the 'Burundi Beat', a drum-heavy African tribal music: maybe McLaren heard it during his time spent in Paris; maybe Adam had been listening to 'The Jungle Line' on Joni Mitchell's 1975 album *The Hissing of Summer Lawns*, which also used these rhythms. What is beyond dispute was that something distinct had been created, and that McLaren promptly persuaded the rest of the Ants to ditch Adam and use the sound for a new band under his stewardship (this became Bow Wow Wow).

Adam, meanwhile, hired himself a new colony of Ants. It was this distinctive double-drum sound – part African, part glam rock – that was soon thumping its way out of transistor radios everywhere: 'Dog Eat Dog', 'Antmusic' and 'Kings of the Wild Frontier' were Top 5 hits, 'Stand and Deliver' and 'Prince Charming' both Number 1s, all in less than a year. Adam's look was equally as striking: part Apache, part gypsy warrior, he wore Morris Dancer-like knee bells, David Hemmings's jacket from the film *The Charge of the Light Brigade* and painted his trademark white stripe across the face.

Looking back on Adam now, I'm reminded in a strange way of two of the biggest comic turns of the decade. The first of these is Blackadder – the Richard Curtis/Ben Elton character followed Adam Ant, of course, but there's a similarly playful sense of romping through history: here's the 'dandy highwayman' in 'Stand and Deliver'; here, in a suit of armour borrowed from the film *Excalibur*, is the Arthurian knight for the (not really very good) 'Ant Rap'. Adam's success also echoes that of comedian Kenny Everett. By which I mean that Adam Ant was a one-off, a standalone star rather than part of a bigger trend. In the same way that Everett's programmes were primetime (just about) family entertainment, so Adam Ant's act was equally all in the best possible taste. There's no doubt that there was a pinch of pantomime to Adam Ant: how could there not be, with songs like 'Prince Charming' and 'Puss in Boots'? When the band was invited to perform at the Royal Variety Performance there was Adam in the line-up next to Lulu, bowing to the Queen in his black tie. There, too, was Adam on *The Cannon and Ball Show*, 'because it had seventeen million viewers'.

All of which was part of the reason that I liked Adam: his act was child-friendly enough to appeal to pre-teen types like me. Yet, at the same time, even he sounded a bit frustrated by the squeaky-clean image: 'I'm sick and tired of being told that because I don't drink and smoke I'm a goody-two-shoes,' he told Paul Morley in an interview for the *NME* – a comment he promptly adapted to write 'Goody Two Shoes', his third Number 1. Adam might have avoided the drugs and the booze, but he more than made up for that in the shagging department: 'sex was available every few feet' was how he described the girls he encountered on tour. Among Ant's many conquests were a young

Amanda Donohoe, future Cherie Blair guru Carole Caplin, Jamie Lee Curtis, Vanity from Prince's girl group Vanity 6 (who, if Prince had had his way, would have had the stage name of Vagina), and Heather Graham – all of whom, with the exception of Caplin, I would also go on to enjoy relationships with later in the decade. Though admittedly in a slightly more one-sided manner.

One of the incongruities of the charts is how they can throw together random battles between the unlikeliest of artists. In 2005, Coldplay's 'Speed of Sound', failed to become the band's expected first Number 1 when it was beaten by a tuneless, ringtone-ribbeting amphibian called Crazy Frog. A similar chart battle was played out in the spring of 1981. In the credible Coldplay corner of things were Ultravox. Ultravox – or Ultravox! as they were originally called – had been actually been around since the mid-1970s without ever particularly 'troubling the Forty'. By 1980 they'd dropped the exclamation mark and swapped original lead singer John Foxx for Midge Ure. Unlike the rest of the band, Midge knew what chart success was like, having enjoyed hits with his previous bands Slik and the Rich Kids.

Midge ('Mij') is Jim said backwards, by the way. Jim/ Midge was given the name in an earlier band, when it was decided that having two Jims in the same outfit was just going to be *too* confusing for all concerned. Midge wasn't just a name but also a metaphor for a man buzzing the eighties from all directions: other accolades included playing guitar for Thin Lizzy on their American tour, having a hand in Steve Strange's Visage (the band, not literally palming the poor man's face), and co-writing 'Yellow Pearl', the Phil Lynott song that was the *Top of the Pops* theme tune in the early 1980s (the one with the flying saucer exploding pink records). Ure got £350 every week it was played, a nice little earner. And, of course, there was Band Aid.

On board for Ultravox's fourth album, Midge got the initial inspiration for the title track and hit single from a misheard lyric. Brenda Hempstead, wife of his former manager, told him 'what you need to write is a song like that "Vienna" . . . You know, the Fleetwood Mac song.' If you aren't familiar with the Fleetwood Mac song 'Vienna', you won't be alone. What Brenda actually meant was 'Rhiannon': if you listen to the song, you can sort of hear how she might have thought that. With the greatest respect to Brenda's musical advice, I'm not sure that what Ultravox (or, indeed, the world) needed was for the band to turn themselves into a sort of New Romantic Fleetwood Mac: a slowed-down, synth-heavy version of 'Don't Stop' feels more of a 'Don't Start' to me. But no matter: Brenda's place in musical history was assured. She'd lodged the word 'Vienna' in Midge's head, and the following morning he'd come up with the chorus for the song.

'Vienna', according to the never-wrong Wikipedia, 'takes its inspiration from the 1948 film *The Third Man*. In Midge's autobiography, *If I Was . . .*, he remembers it rather differently. Here he admits that 'we lied about it at the time. In interviews with the *NME* I talked for hours about the Secessionists and Gustav Klimt, all the stuff that was going on in turn-of-the-century Vienna. That was all rubbish designed to make us sound interesting.' In fact Midge wrote the lyrics around the idea of a holiday romance, about being back home in the day job and failing to convince yourself that the foreign fumblings meant nothing. Not (it should be added) that Midge was exactly writing from experience. As he cheerfully admits now: 'the whole idea was made up. I'd never been to Vienna, never had a holiday romance.' I think that's OK, though, because I'm not sure anyone bought the record thinking they were getting an electronic version of 'Farewell My Summer Love'.

The photo on the 'Vienna' record sleeve is of an iconic grave from Vienna's Zentralfriedhof Cemetery. The grave, which features a statue of a man kneeling down in front of it with his head in his hand, is a monument to Carl Schweighofer, a famous nineteenth-century Austrian piano-maker. I don't know if that is a deliberate attempt to pay homage to a longstanding keyboard tradition, but that's where the song sits: 'the sound of the eighties is the synthesizer', declared *Melody Maker* in 1980, and 'Vienna', with its whirl of electronic keyboards and sprinkling of piano on top, is the sound of keyboard past, present and what then felt like the future. There aren't many songs that can start with the drumbeat as the riff to draw the listener. But that's exactly what happens here, with its heartbeat bass drum and electronic snare going off like an explosion in the distance: from the moment you hear that, you're drawn in. To add to the mood, there's even a viola solo halfway through – which was, in order to get the ambience right, recorded in the studio toilet.

'Vienna' was a song that Ultravox's record company needed their arm twisting to release. Heading towards six minutes in length, the song was seen as too slow and long for the radio. Ultravox won that battle, and then faced a similar one over the video. Contractually, the record company had to make videos for only two singles per album, and Ultravox had used these up in their previous two, unsuccessful releases. But further pressure was applied, and in came Russell Mulcahy to direct. Mulcahy's original idea for the video was perhaps not his best – 'I can see it now . . . Gondolas, bridges, boats' – but once the Australian director was given a brief European-geography lesson he produced one of the first of his many great eighties videos: a moody, *Third Man*-style number that was – and if you look carefully you'll see this – actually filmed in Covent Garden (those hilarious mime artists were presumably edited out). To save money, the filming in Vienna was reduced to a flying visit, and the discovery that if you turn up to the Austrian capital out of season not only is it bloody freezing but half the city's main tourist attractions are mothballed for the winter too. Despite this, the video captured the mood of song. I'm still not really sure what that white horse wandering through the opening shot is about, with the mysterious blonde in the long twenties dress and the fur coat running after it. Likewise the presence of Midge, hiding behind a pillar, with his razor-sharp sideburns and pencil-thin moustache.

'Vienna', then, should really be the story of a great early eighties success. Here was a band, after several albums and numerous singles attempts, finally having the hit song they deserved. Here was a group who had gone about it the hard way, eschewing the rules about what a single should be. Here was a four-piece who used two of the touchstones of early-eighties music – keyboards and videos – to devastating effect. 'Vienna' would go on to be the fifth-bestselling single of 1981 and win Best Single at the Brits.

And yet, in chart terms, the song found itself in one of those incongruous battles that only the British Top 40 can throw up. For, rather than getting the Number 1 that of all the above seemed duty bound to bestow upon it, in February and March 1981 'Vienna' stayed limpet-like to the Number 2 spot. And the song that kept it from Number 1 was not an even better one, nor a release by one of the big early eighties names such as the Police or Blondie or the Jam, nor a song that, overall, would sell more copies. Instead, Ultravox found their best song up against, and losing to, the modest charms of archetype one-hit wonder Joe Dolce (Joe Dolce Music Theatre, if you are feeling particularly pedantic) and his song, 'Shaddap You Face'.

Joe Dolce was an American turned Australian who ran a small revue in Melbourne of assorted comic characters: a sort of backroom-of-the-pub version of Harry Enfield. One of those characters was an Italian chap called Giuseppe, whose 'Shaddap You Face' song encouraged the audience to shout 'Hey!' The song was picked up by a local DJ and became a record and Australian Number 1. Before long, the ditty was spreading across the world like the yoyo craze in the playground. There was even an Elton John-instigated version of the song, sung by Andrew Sachs in full Manuel

'Que?' mode, to counter which 'Shaddup You Face's release in the UK was speeded up. So you could argue that, if not for Elton, Joe Dolce's song would have been released later and Ultravox would have had their Number 1.

For what have must have felt like three excruciating weeks, Joe Dolce (or Joe 'Bloody' Dolce, as Ultravox drummer Warren Carn was still calling him twenty years later) with his mandolin, pork-pie hat and hilarious hammed-up Italian mannerisms kept 'Vienna' from the top spot. It wasn't as if the British public were deliberately depriving Midge of his accolade, going out to buy the record in the way that Rage Against the Machine stopped *X Factor* winner Joe McElderry getting the 2009 Christmas Number 1. Yet depriving him they were. Quite why is one of those music unfathomables; my guess is that it is a combination of the British liking the plucky underdog combined with a streak of gooey bad taste – the sort of instinct that these days manifests itself in forwarding videos of kittens on YouTube, or keeping John Sergeant in *Strictly Come Dancing*.

These chart battles and their sheer unpredictability is one of the reasons that following them became such a compelling spectator sport. Back then, in the British charts, every record was equal, every sale of a single a vote for that particular artist. It was, in a way, democracy in action, except that sometimes it was the equivalent of the Monster Raving Loony Party who got elected.

Somewhere along the line, between the eighties and today, the Top 40 lost its way: it stopped being 'the' charts, so definitively important that it took the definite article, and slid in significance to become just another chart – the sort where the Christmas Number 1 is the only race of passing interest. It wasn't just people like me growing up that were no longer interested: it was also the people who used to be the prime singles markets: teenagers. The end of *Top of the Pops* in 2006 was the day that this particular interest in the music died.

The charts are bit like a currency. For a long while they were very much the gold standard: a sound investment, if you'll pardon the pun, that maintained its value. Getting to Number 1, as Ultravox and Midge Ure knew, was a big deal. A Top 10 hit was significant; even getting into the Top 40 could be a big deal for an up-and-coming band. And the weight of this importance was shown by how few records went straight in at Number 1. When that happened (and, as someone who used to sit down and write out the charts, I know) it was a rare and exciting thing.

In the 1980s it happened just fourteen times. And even that was moderately profligate compared with the previous two decades. In the 1970s just four songs achieved this accolade. In the 1960s the number was just three.[4] So how many singles went straight in at Number 1 in the 1990s? Twenty? Thirty? The answer is, in fact, 117. By the late 1990s around thirty songs a year were going in at Number 1; in 2000 the number hit forty – or, to put it another way, there were only twelve weeks that year during which a song *didn't* go to Number 1.

This can be put down to the fact that the record companies simply got too good at marketing their records. They would sell the singles in different formats, with different songs on each, in order to ensure the fans bought them all. They would start releasing the records to the radio stations earlier, so that the songs would be in heavy rotation for several weeks before the single was out. And they would combine all of this with reducing the price of the single for the week of release. This meant a walloping first week's sale . . . And then, more often than not, bugger all afterwards. By then we'd all heard the song to death for well over a month, and also the single was now back to a less enticing full price: the nation knew if they didn't buy the single that first week they'd end up coughing up double. In the process, the record companies at a stroke killed what had been fun about the charts: their spontaneity, their predictability.[5] As with any currency, once it is devalued its worth starts to sink. If Number 1 records are ten a penny, they're less of a big deal. And once they're less of a big deal, fewer people take an interest and the process becomes less of a shared cultural event.

All of which makes a seven-year-old boy, sat in his pyjamas on a Sunday evening, listening to the radio and writing down that week's Top 40, something of an anachronism (and yes, probably an 'anorakchronism' too). I feel sad for that, and not just the sentimental aspect of looking back on a younger, more innocent version of myself who knew no better than to spunk his pocket money on a Showaddywaddy single. I feel sad, too, that this way 'in' to discovering music, and the love of pop it created in me, is now closed to the generation my own children belong to. Cultures change, of course, but even so, I can't help wondering whether yesterday's sense of belonging hasn't been succeeded by a search for longing instead.

Track Three

Fade to Grey

Philip Larkin, in his poem 'Annus Mirabilis', famously suggested that sexual intercourse began in 1963, between the lifting of the ban of D. H. Lawrence's novel *Lady Chatterley's Lover* and the Beatles first long-playing record, *Please Please Me*. When Larkin said 'sex' what he really meant was the change in attitudes to it: that heady rush towards a more liberal and permissive society – the real start, in other words, of the sixties. Larkin could see that with the clearness of a poet's eye, even if, as the poem ruefully acknowledged, he was just too old to be part of it himself.

So where did the eighties – or more specifically, given the subject of this book, eighties music – begin? There's any number of starting points to choose from. Rather than going forward a couple of years, as Larkin did, there's a strong case to argue that the eighties really began in 1979.

That was the year when music seemed to shrug off the seventies, punk was assimilated into the more mainstream-friendly post-punk and new wave and standout acts like the Jam, the Police and Blondie. Singles sales soared thanks in no small part to a plethora of top-notch releases: 'Hit Me With Your Rhythm Stick', 'I Will Survive', 'Ring My Bell', 'Are "Friends" Electric?' 'Pop Muzik'.

There are a couple of events from that year that also feel equally eighties prescient. There was that year's General Election, held on 4 May, when Jim Callaghan cleared out of Downing Street and Margaret Thatcher became Prime Minister with a Conservative majority of forty-three. Then there was the day when the Blitz wine bar on Great Queen Street in Covent Garden opened its door to Steve Strange's 'Club for Heroes' night. With Strange on the door, letting in only those people he liked the look of, and Boy George taking your coats in the cloakroom, this was the exclusive starting point of the New Romantic movement, a prawn cocktail of outrageous dressing and David Bowie and Kraftwerk on the turntables. It was a compliment Bowie was smart enough to return when he co-opted the crowd for his 'Ashes to Ashes' video in 1980 (even if he couldn't resist a dig about the scene with the lyrics to 'Fashion').

This group of clubbers who went there got called various things in the press – the Blitz Kids, New Dandies and Futurists among them – but the name that stuck was the New Romantics. Looking back on the New Romantic scene now, it's worth noting how its mythological status became so much bigger than the scene itself. Club for Heroes, for example, had a capacity of only 350 people – not exactly an enormous crowd. Rather than being the supposed melting point of intellectualism, according to Tony Hadley, 'the idea that everyone was discussing Nietzsche and Jean Paul Sartre was laughable. The Blitz was more about dressing up, drinking Schlitz beer, taking speed and meeting girls.'[1] Equally, the amount of bands to break out from this particular scene was not huge. Putting Culture Club to one side, as they didn't really come together until a couple of years later, the acts who went directly from the Blitz to *Top of the Pops* could be counted on a couple of digits: essentially Spandau Ballet and Visage.

For Spandau Ballet the journey to pop stardom was as long as the list of names they went through on the way: first they were called the Roots, then the Cut, then the Makers, then the Gentry. It was Robert Elms, then a journalist, who suggested the name Spandau Ballet, which he'd seen graffitied on a toilet wall in Berlin. The group liked the sound of the name, and went with it for that ('preposterous but edgy; arty but aggressive' was Gary Kemp's take[2]). It did, however, have other potential connotations. The full piece of graffiti apparently read: 'Rudolf Hess, all alone, dancing the Spandau Ballet'. Hess, a leading Nazi and deputy to Hitler in the Party, was imprisoned at Spandau following the Nuremberg Trials and by the late 1970s was the jail's only prisoner. None of which especially made the original meaning of the term any clearer, but left the band open to insinuation: at an early gig in St-Tropez a combination of the name and a poster showing a sort of S&M jackboot led to suggestions that the band's image was flirting with fascism ('posing for publicity shots [. . .] dressed like storm troopers' in front of a war memorial probably didn't help either).[3]

By 1977 the band were getting reviews in the *NME* ('An everything you've always wanted but never thought you'd hear band') and *Sounds* ('energy and beautifully cut hair'); but, while everyone else they knew were getting signed, they were being left alone. With the arrival of the Blitz, the band decided on a different tack: rather than persuade an A&R man to come to see them in the back of the pub they started playing gigs in odd places, which they made exclusive and difficult to get into. These events included the Blitz itself in December 1979, the Scala cinema (backed by an art-house film with subtitles) and HMS *Belfast*. This line of attack was far more effective and the longed-for deal finally arrived, albeit at the cost of being called elitist by the music press.

Spandau's first single, 'To Cut a Long Story Short', came out in November 1980 and was the first New Romantic song to properly make the charts. It was, offered *Melody Maker*, 'a forgettable piece of self-regarding fluff' but it quickly rose to Number 5. In provincial places like York, which didn't exactly have its own Blitz scene, the band looked and sounded different: floppy fringes, frilly shirts and tartan (tartan?) seemed to my eyes as though the band had been beamed in from an episode of *Doctor Who*. The song itself, that contrasting mix of Tony Hadley's old-school crooneresque vocals against a backdrop of synthesizers, sounded very *modern*, but wasn't, it turned out, very Spandau Ballet.

By this point the action had turned north, or at least as far north as Birmingham. Here Nick Rhodes and John Taylor had teamed up with singer Stephen Duffy, who was a student at Birmingham Polytechnic with Taylor. Rhodes by now had a Wasp synthesizer, a rather basic early keyboard that had black and yellow markings, and the group's early sound oscillated between 'a hotchpotch of influence – early Human League one minute, Lou Reed or Syd Barrett the next'.[4]

The name the trio chose for the group (after rejecting RAF and Jazz) was Duran Duran. It comes from the character Durand-Durand in the cult sixties sci-fi film *Barbarella*, which they'd watched on TV and which had also given its name to the Birmingham club they used to go to.

With Rhodes playing keyboard and drum machine (on a stand made out of Meccano), Taylor on guitar, Duffy on vocals and fellow student Simon Colley on bass, the band's early gigs included a puppet theatre with a slide-show projection behind. Just as Spandau Ballet played the Blitz, so Duran Duran played Barbarella's (supporting Fashion, the local band who everyone assumed was going to make it). 'I think we were all wearing women's clothing,' Nick Rhodes remembered. 'Stephen stepped up to the microphone and in his most fey voice eloquently announced, "This next song was influenced by F. Scott Fitzgerald." '[5] Despite this, the band went down well. There's a reason for that and it's because the songs were good: Duffy and Rhodes returned to these early songs and re-recorded them to make an album, *Dark Circles*, as the Devils in 2002. Including songs like 'Lost Decade', the first song the group wrote together, the sound is a bit more spacey and basic than the Duran that got into the charts, but you can hear the key combinations of their signature sound: the mixing of keyboards, guitars and memorable melodies.

Stephen Duffy, though, wasn't to end up as Duran's famous lead singer: he eschewed the synthesizers and then left the group for a more Dylanesque band, Obviously Five Believers (Duffy's subsequent career, via solo hits like 'Kiss Me', folksy band the Lilac Time, and collaborations with Nigel Kennedy and Robbie Williams, is a book in itself). Meanwhile, the classic Duran Duran line-up began to shape. In came drummer Roger Taylor, whose previous bands included the oddly named Crucified Toad. Andy Taylor joined after answering an advert in *Melody Maker* for a 'livewire guitarist': not even in his twenties, Andy Taylor had already been gigging round Europe for various bands and brought with him both buckets of experience and a more 'rock' sound. This would help both in terms of the band's ultimate success in America and in creating the band's key dynamic – his guitar shapes against Rhodes's synth sounds – as well as its musical fault line. Last in was singer Simon Le Bon: his girlfriend at the time was a barmaid at the Rum Runner, the Birmingham club that had by then replaced Barbarella's as the Duran hangout of choice. She told him that the group were looking for a singer, so he put himself forward. For his first meeting with Nick Rhodes, Simon wore a brown suede jacket and pink leopard-skin trousers: Rhodes thought he had the attitude they were looking for, even before he heard him sing.

Duran Duran were supporting Hazel O'Connor on her 1980 tour when the offers of record contracts started coming in, and the debut single, 'Planet Earth', was released in early 1981, a couple of months after 'To Cut a Long Story Short'. Like the Spandau single, it still sounds fresh to me, though it got a kicking in the music press at the time. 'Fop music,' dismissed *Smash Hits*. 'This isn't just dull. It's an old style of dull.' *Smash Hits*, though, were quick to reverse their opinion. It didn't take much for listeners to join the dots between Spandau and Duran, not least because Duran also got out the frilly shirts and Simon Le Bon had shoehorned a line about New Romantics into the lyrics.

The thing with any music scene is that its shelf life is inherently short, as the music press look for the next big thing. The smart bands, then, find a way of taking the initial publicity and, as with Duran Duran, find a way of disassociating themselves just as quickly. If you don't, then you can find your career tied in to the scene and ending just as quickly. Take for example Visage, perhaps the only other successful, properly New Romantic band, who couldn't have been more associated with the scene if they'd tried – after all, the Blitz night was lead singer Steve Strange's club. A cynic might say that that was exactly why they got a record contract. But a cynic might not have heard 'Fade to Grey': nestled between the Spandau and Duran debut singles, Visage's only Top 10 hit is, for the supposed sound of a celebratory club-land scene, surprisingly dark, and with an unexpected sliver of sadness.

Perhaps that came from the fact that in October 1980 the Blitz club shut its doors for the last time: the New Romantic scene was over before it had even properly begun. Other bands tried and failed to make their way out of the scene: signed with a lot of fanfare were Blue Rondo à la Turk, a preposterously named Latin-funk concoction whose minimal contribution to musical history was to spawn Matt Bianco and be blown off stage by the Smiths (who supported them in their first-ever gig). Japan, meanwhile, managed to sound both fey and lumbering at the same time: it is no coincidence that their one proper hit, 'Ghosts', was conspicuously drum-free.

'Ghosts' is what these various bands became: spirits doomed to watch a pop banquet they weren't quite good enough to attend.

For me, in terms of what I properly remember, eighties music begins with the death of John Lennon. I was a week short of my eighth birthday when the former Beatle was shot by Mark Chapman in New York on 8 December 1980, and without really understanding I could still sense the significance of the event. I remember vividly the report on John Craven's *Newsround*, the pictures of people putting flowers down in the New York park. I remember, too, the reaction of my mother, the tears at the television.

Lennon's death was the eighties equivalent of the JFK assassination, the Princess Diana of its day. Each of these figures were not just world-class famous but also carried a sense of hope, of humanity with them. It's a combination of that and the rupturing nature of their deaths – not by illness or old age but by bullet or speeding car – that makes them so shocking, allowing them into that select group of historical moments for which you know exactly where you were when you heard about them.

My mother's reaction to John Lennon's death was typical for her generation. She had been to see the Beatles in the days when 'seeing' a band was an apposite description, so loud were the screams and so crap was the PA. The soundtrack to her university years comprised *Sgt. Pepper's*, *Pet Sounds*, Simon and Garfunkel and Bob Dylan. My parents had married in 1971 and I was their first of four children, born the following year. Settling down for my parents had been a musical as well as a physical thing. The sounds of the seventies meant little to them. In fact, as far as I could work out, the only contemporary bands in their record collection (and I use the word 'collection' most loosely) were greatest-hits albums by ABBA and Blondie. I'm not even certain that my father's interest in Blondie was entirely honourable.

The shock of John Lennon's death quickly translated into the charts being chock-full of his records (in tribute, I'm sure, his record company shipped 600,000 singles and albums into the shops within three days of him dying). Lennon's then current single, '(Just Like) Starting Over', which was on the slide after peaking at Number 8, jumped back up to Number 1. 'Imagine' followed suit for four weeks in January, followed by 'Woman'. With 'Happy Xmas (War is Over)' climbing back up to Number 2, there were several weeks where Lennon had three of the Top 5 singles. In fact, there was only one record to hold a candle to Lennon in this period – in another of those incongruous chart battles, St Winifred's School Choir took the Christmas Number 1 spot with their saccharine single, 'There's No One Quite Like Grandma'.

For eighties music, John Lennon's death was on one level not significant. The truth was that all the best parts of John Lennon's solo career happened in the instant-karma aftermath of the Beatles: 'Imagine', 'Cold Turkey', 'Power to the People', 'Working Class Hero', 'Jealous Guy' – all were written, recorded and released by 1971. I think there's a case for arguing that, in terms of death influencing the way music panned out during the decade, Joy Division singer Ian Curtis's suicide six months earlier was markedly more important: here was someone at the cutting edge of where music was actually *at*, at the time, and whose death cut down someone on the *up* rather someone on the creative downslope.

Where John Lennon's death mattered, musically, was in finally shutting the door on the 1960s. That other great sixties icon, Elvis Presley, had died in less than flattering circumstances in 1977: with John Lennon no more, that long-mooted Beatles reunion could also be laid to rest. Lennon's death sealed the sixties and preserved the Beatles music: there was to be no going back, no testy comings together like the Simon and Garfunkel reunion in front of half a million people in New York's Central Park in 1981.

Success creates a shadow. Success on the level that the Beatles achieved creates a long one indeed. Lennon and

McCartney on their own could never quite get away from being compared with Lennon *and* McCartney. The seventies, too, could never quite escape the sixties: the so-called *Red* and *Blue* albums released in 1973; the seven Beatles singles re-entering the Top 40 in 1976; the *Live at the Hollywood Bowl* album reaching Number 1 a year later. The nation still loved the Beatles, and with good reason to, of course.

John Lennon's death marked the end of all this looking back. As wonderful as the Beatles were, it allowed everybody else space to breathe – allowed public and musicians to look forward: indeed, even as Lennon single after Lennon single hit Number 1, there in the same Top 10s were 'To Cut a Long Story Short', 'Planet Earth' and 'Vienna'. For the generation my parents belonged to, it marked that moment when they were cut loose from the tide of modern music, left behind to sail happily on the good ship *Swinging Sixties*.

If the beginning of the eighties for me was the death of John Lennon, the other half of its Philip Larkin-type origins happened six months later on the other side of the Atlantic. The eighties equivalent of the Beatles releasing their first album happened just after midnight on 1 August 1981, when a new American television station called MTV launched by playing the Buggles' 'Video Killed the Radio Star'.

I wasn't particularly aware of this cultural event at the time. In fact, I knew little about MTV until several years later, when Sting guested on Dire Straits' 1985 hit 'Money for Nothing' (the first song played when MTV Europe was launched in 1987). And even then I didn't get the significance or reference of Sting's line – that 'I want my MTV' was actually the slogan from the TV channel's original advertising campaign, in which the likes of Mick Jagger and David Bowie encouraged young Americans to ring up their local MTV-free cable supplier and shout down the phone the line that a not-entirely philanthropic Mr Sumner would himself croon a few years later.

In 1981, the chances of our family television being able to pick up a twenty-four-hour cable music station were, frankly, laughable. British TV was still more than a year away from having what then seemed like the revolutionary advent of a fourth television channel. Indeed, it is a curiosity of eighties music in Britain that one of its most significant moments took place out of reach and abroad. For a whole host of British bands, MTV was the crucial catalyst that turned their modest success into global superstardom. Part of the reason for this was that British bands had taken to music video while many American artists had yet to truly understand its potential. The concept of music video itself was far from unique to the 1980s: the late 1940s saw the launch of the Panoram 'Soundie', a sort of video jukebox; a decade later, the French Scopitone machine upgraded the idea into glorious Technicolor. Yet neither really caught on, and the nearest the sixties got to exploring music and video together was probably the made-for-TV band the Monkees.

Although a smattering of bands went down the occasional-video route (the Beatles shot accompanying films for

'Penny Lane' and 'Strawberry Fields Forever', for example), the moment when the idea properly lodged in the public consciousness was 1975, when Queen decided to put together a promo for 'Bohemian Rhapsody'. Director Bruce Gowers took his inspiration from the cover of the earlier album *Queen II*, which features the band in that familiar four-headed diamond against a black background. From here, he used special effects to match what was going on in the song: 'when there was echo thrown on the vocals, we'd throw "echo" on the visuals by trailing multiple images on the faces, and so on.' The video wasn't expensive to make (total cost $7000) and didn't take long to put together (four hours of filming, another day farting around with editing) but the effect was a thunderbolt-and-lightning moment: the video stood out on *Top of the Pops* as something different to a Pan's People dance routine, and spared Queen having to put up with another hilarious Dave Lee Travis cameo halfway through (as he did when they performed 'Seven Seas of Rhye'). While it's impossible to dissect how much of 'Bohemian Rhapsody's nine weeks at Number 1 was down to the genius of the song itself and how much was the result of the video, the latter certainly had a role. From this point on, the British music scene started to take videos seriously. For young, fashion-conscious bands, videos felt avant-garde and exciting: an artistic extension of who the band was, rather than a promotional chore.

American music was in a somewhat different place as the eighties began. One could sum up everything that was wrong in three letters: A (for album, or possibly adult, or maybe even air guitar), O (for oriented, which isn't really a proper word, is it?) and R (for rock, or, to give the correct spelling, 'rawk'). Unlike in the UK, where most people tuned in to the unifying sound of the 'nation's favourite' Radio One, seventies American was proliferated with regional FM radio stations called things like WNK and KRP and B-LLKS (I might not have got all those letters entirely correct there). Being commercial ventures, these stations wanted to maximize their audiences in order to charge advertisers the highest possible premium to run ads on their shows. What followed was an extensive amount of market research, the leaders in the field being radio consultants Kent Burkhart and Lee Abrams, who by the end of the decade conducted research for more than 100 different stations. What these consultants looked into was not what listeners wanted to hear, but what they *didn't* want to hear: these were the tunes and artists that would cause people to 'touch that dial'. The resultant formula was what known as 'passive programming': based around playing songs that people might not necessarily love but like enough to keep listening and not switch over.

In terms of maximizing audience and income, the conclusion was to appeal to the largest, homogenous social group going. In seventies America, that demographic was white. The type of music this group would listen to without switching over was, essentially, rock in a limited variety of flavours: heavy metal, hard rock, progressive rock, classic British rock and LA studio rock. What bands and record companies cottoned on to pretty quickly was that if you mixed together the key components of these – a heavy-metal power chord or two, a sixties-type harmony, some slick LA production and the epic feel of progressive rock (though with slightly fewer goblins) – then you'd be guaranteed a lot of radio airplay.

The result was a succession of bands so bereft of imagination that when choosing a name they couldn't get beyond where they came from: groups like Boston, Chicago and Kansas (Journey, who hail from San Francisco, were originally called the Golden Gate Rhythm Section). These are the sort of names which might sound kind of cool when looking over from the other side of the Atlantic, but bear in mind that it's the equivalent of calling your band Birmingham. Or Warrington. REO Speedwagon chose a truck for inspiration, while Grand Funk Railroad (who were neither grand, nor funk, nor, indeed, a railroad) relied instead on their signature song, 'We're an American Band', to ram home their identity. Such distinctions needed marking out in AOR: Foreigner were so called because – gasp – some of their members were not from the United States.

These were bands who, it's fair to say, spent more time practising their guitar scales than working on their appearance. A typical AOR look would consist of a blue and black hooped singlet, low cut enough to display a bulge of chest hair, and tight white trousers (short shorts were optional for drummers). Moustaches were to be encouraged – to the point that it seemed almost compulsory for at least one member of an AOR band to have one (preferably of a different colour to their hair). Here the cuts of choice were the mullet or perm, leaving each group looking less like a rock band and more like the back four of a relegation-threatened German football team.

So tried and tested was the radio-playlist formula that it was difficult for any new music to break through, and consequently record sales were in sharp decline. The AOR scene knew what it liked and liked what it knew. When the Knack and their quite wonderful single 'My Sharona' were launched on a wave of publicity, AOR fans decided they weren't 'real' and wore 'Nuke the Knack' T-shirts in response. The burgeoning disco scene, meanwhile, had the temerity to have black, gay and sometimes even black *and* gay influences. The AOR reply was the infamous Disco Demolition Night in July 1979, when a packed Chicago baseball stadium chanted 'Disco sucks! Disco sucks!' and cheered as thousands of disco records were blown up in a huge explosion.

Given all this, it's not a huge surprise that the AOR scene didn't exactly welcome the advent of video with open arms. Sartorially challenged, and all about the music in their minds, the result was a somewhat standoffish approach. 'A lot of bands that were established before we came along looked at [MTV] with scorn,' recalled Def Leppard's Joe Elliott. 'Bands like Journey, Kiss, Styx . . . They were like, "Why do we have to shoot videos?"/"We never had to do this before . . ." They reluctantly shot videos, and consequently they didn't make very good ones.'

It seems so obvious now that 'Video Killed the Radio Star' by the Buggles should be the first song to be played on MTV.

So obvious, in fact, that one wonders what would have been chosen had it not existed. The Buggles song wasn't chosen for being an amazing video, or for being a particular popular song: while it had been Number 1 in the UK two years earlier, the single spent one solitary week in the American Top 40, at Number 40. But I don't think that mattered. If anything, I think the song's lack of chart success in America actually helped MTV: it meant that they could appropriate for themselves the song and its rallying-cry title.

The origin of the song was the J. G. Ballard short story 'The Sound Sweep'. Ballard's tale tells of a world without music, and a young boy going around vacuuming up rare tunes wherever he can find them, and chancing on an opera singer hiding underground. The song picks up on this theme of something disappearing: this lost world of music. Its focus is on the elbowing out of the radio age – there's lots of fuzzy reminiscences about the growing up listening to the wireless – but it doesn't take much to see this as making a wider point about the usurping of sound by vision, music by pictures. With the arrival of the video age, being a pop star was about the whole package: not just musical talent, but looks, fashion sense and appearance too.

The Buggles video itself, meanwhile, is probably best described as an early example of the genre. It starts with a young girl in a red dress listening to one of those old-fashioned wirelesses that look like a chocolate-brown washing machine. This particular version glows on cue to the 'O-Wa! O-Wa!' of the backing vocals before it's given the 'disco demolition' treatment and blown up. The young girl, meanwhile, is transformed into a fully grown futuristic-looking woman (i.e., wrapped in BacoFoil like an extra from *Blake's 7*) and is transported in some sort of giant test tube to what I assume to be the video age to watch the Buggles sing their song.

Where MTV's choice of opening song is especially apposite is in its bringing together two of the most influential figures in the way that music developed. The Buggles was the brainchild of Trevor Horn (giving it the proto-Ben Elton look in the video, with his large white glasses and shiny silver suit), who formed the group with Geoff Downes. Trevor Horn's main role in the eighties, though, would not be as a singer but as the producer *du jour*: ABC's *Lexicon of Love*, Spandau Ballet's career-saving 'Instinction' and Frankie Goes to Hollywood would be just some of his credits.

What Trevor Horn was to the sound of eighties music, video director Russell Mulcahy was to how it looked. As well as 'Vienna' and 'Video Killed the Radio Star', among his many other videos were Duran Duran's 'Rio' and 'Hungry Like the Wolf', Spandau Ballet's 'True', and that freaky children's choir in Bonnie Tyler's 'Total Eclipse of the Heart'. Out of all the directors in this fledgling industry, Mulcahy was the most influential in setting out how videos would look. Mulcahy had been making films from an early age in his native Australia, and by the late seventies found himself in the UK. His style, which others would go on to emulate, was a mishmash of Hollywood homage, Magritte, and fashion photography. When Mulcahy shot the video for

'Vienna', for example, he was not only infusing a *Third Man* air but also for the first time cutting off the top and bottom of the picture, to give it that Cinemascope feel. He put to use his several years of studying surrealism, too: his video for Duran Duran's 'Is There Something I Should Know?' included lots of Magritte-style bowler hats and mysterious red triangles.

But it was from fashion photography that Mulcahy perhaps got his most recognizable cue: slow-motion shots of splashing water, breaking glass and furniture being smashed that would quickly become video staples. Everything that Mulcahy was doing was in some ways no different to what an advertising director got up to: the techniques that worked there worked in music videos, too: it was just that Mulcahy had Duran Duran to sell, as opposed to Shake 'n' Vac. It is perhaps no coincidence that the British-based rise of the music video happened in tandem with the golden era of British advertising, when firms like Saatchi & Saatchi became global leaders to rival the 'mad men' of New York.

MTV's beginning wasn't just low key in starting at one minute past midnight on a Tuesday night in August. It was also a quiet start in the areas it was broadcasting to. The US cable network is divided up into different regional suppliers; for the grand launch, the key East Coast and West Coast areas were absent: the launch of MTV might have been broadcast from New York, but even if you lived in New York (let alone old York) you couldn't watch it.

For its first few months, MTV broadcast to a curious patchwork of more central, less glamorous states. But it didn't take long for its reach to grow, from an initial five million subscribers to twenty million within a year. The channel's claim to offer 'music like you've never seen it before' struck a chord, and not the hard-rock power strum of AOR either. MTV desperately needed good videos, and lots of them. They found them in the UK. Here, bands and record companies were ahead of the US in understanding the importance of videos. The result was what was dubbed the 'second British Invasion'. Whereas the first was spear-headed by the Beatles in the early sixties, this early eighties incarnation took its cue from the likes of Duran Duran, the Police, Culture Club and A Flock of Seagulls. The latter, with lead singer Mike Score's Dairylea Triangle of a haircut, made it in America in a way they never achieved in the UK. This surge in British success reached its peak in July 1983, when six out of the Top 10 and seventeen out of the Top 40 in the American charts were by British artists.

To an American teenager, seeing all these new bands (and seeing is the key word here) must have felt the equivalent of a door opening. Suddenly there was a whole new range of sounds out there to listen to, with which they could identify and that they could claim as their own. The fact that it went against the established order of American bands, with their staid, sewn-up FM radio schedules and dislike for videos, served only to tick all the right rebellion boxes. This was a generation that had never even thought of having their hair cut like A Flock of Seagulls. They probably never would again, but for that brief moment such a look was the height of cool.

WIRED FOR SOUND

The success of music video led to the even greater success of music video. What had once been a begrudging contractual obligation was now a recognized part of the process. Because of the success of British bands in America the video budgets went up, which meant the films became bigger and glossier and more of a must-see. As increasing numbers of homes got video recorders, so the sale of music videos began to grow too: there was excited talk of selling video versions of singles, even of bands releasing entire video albums, where every track had its own film.

MTV, then, saw a shift not only in the way music was consumed but also in the type of music that was being produced. The vibrancy and colour of the new wave of British bands gave American teenagers their ownership of music back and a distinctive new sound for the decade. How far it served to overcome old-fashioned stereotypes of the AOR era is open to question: on one level, this was a bunch of badly attired white bands being replaced by a load of better-looking foreign white bands with sillier hair; these in turn were replaced by a new group of better-looking American bands with even bigger hair – the Bon Jovi generation. It also became the shop window for a whole bunch of stars who could not only sing but dance and perform as well: Michael Jackson, Madonna and Prince.

While 'Video Killed the Radio Star' is an obvious choice with which to launch a music station, it's a curious one at the same time. It isn't a celebration of the video age, but rather a nostalgic look back at the end of a previous one: whether that's taken to be the original wireless star, stars of radio in general, or the ultimate trumping of sound by vision. Killed is the key word: we're not talking about radio handing the baton over to a new generation, but about something more brutal.

With a similar lack of sentiment, video has ended up the same way as its predecessor. MTV is now most famous for its reality shows, such as *The Osbournes* and *The Hills*, and the 'M' in its name largely redundant. The music video, which once seemed to be the future – like the wireless in the opening line of the Buggles song – is now a cultural artefact from an earlier era.

Track Four

Computer Love

You might have thought that confessing to owning records by Showaddywaddy might have been the point when the bottom of this particularly sorry barrel finally got a scraping. I'm afraid to say that worse is still to come. The only way I will achieve closure on this particular period of my life is to also confess which musical instrument it was my choice to take up.

That's 'choice' in the Jack Bauer sense of the word. By which I mean that in almost every episode of the Kiefer Sutherland TV series *24*, Kiefer's character would come up against a situation that was so patently ridiculous the only way round it was to utter the immortal line 'We don't have a choice.' Which is the writer's shorthand for: 'Yup, viewer, I know the plotline is complete horseshit – but I can't think of anything better to get round it.'

COMPUTER LOVE

My parents had come to the not unreasonable decision to make something of my love of music. It was time, they concurred, to formalize things and turn my incessant playing of records into the playing of tunes. It was time to pick up an instrument other than my regulation cream-and-chocolate-brown Aulos descant recorder. The choices to my young mind seemed almost endless: did I have the thumbs to match the slap-bass skills of Level 42's Mark King? Should I learn to 'give it some stick' like Chas and Dave's drummer Mick? Should that great eighties staple, the saxophone, be my calling card? Or were the six-string skills of Andy Summers going to be my inspiration?

Helpful as ever, my parents decided to help me through this particular musical minefield by choosing the instrument for me. One day I came home from school to find a small, black rectangular music case on the breakfast-room table. Goodness, I thought to myself, how do you manage to fit a guitar in there? The answer – as I found out when I clicked open the box – was that you couldn't. What my parents had bought me instead, I discovered, picking up the three metal tubes that slotted together into one humiliating whole, was a flute.

The history of the flute in rock and roll could be the title of one of those hilarious World's Shortest Books. Perhaps the only rock flautist anyone has actually heard of is Ian Anderson, erstwhile crazy-haired singer in proto-prog rockers Jethro Tull, who insisted on playing the flute while standing on one leg. The instrument has also popped up here and there (generally there) in pop music: 'California

69

Dreamin'" by the Mamas & the Papas, 'Nights in White Satin' by the Moody Blues, 'Moondance' by Van Morrison and 'The Revolution Will Not Be Televised' by the late great Gil Scott Heron are pretty much all the hits that have been graced by a bit of flute action. The eighties would add only one significant addition to this short but exhaustive list: Men at Work's 'Down Under', which, with its one-hit-wonder mutterings about Vegemite sandwiches, did not exactly deposit much in the credibility bank.[1]

The Moody Blues and the Mamas & the Papas might have been my parents' era, but that wasn't the reason behind their desire to hear me play the flute. That, I think was down to the only other flautist anyone has actually heard of: Belfast's James Galway, the modestly nicknamed 'Man with the Golden Flute' (who, to be fair to him, *did* actually have a golden flute). Galway was a big name at the time, scoring a Top 3 hit in 1978 with his instrumental cover of John Denver's 'Annie's Song', a sort of Kenny G's 'Songbird' for the seventies. Also among Galway's repertoire was 'Danny Boy', the popular Irish ballad based on the tune of the Londonderry Air, as were several hymns, including 'O Son of Mine', which my parents had sung at their wedding. My parents' desire for me to play the flute was therefore born: they wanted this son of theirs to be able to serenade them with the Londonderry Air.

All of which might be a sweet little story, but the upshot was that I got stuck with learning the prissiest instrument in the orchestra, the sort played only by men with beards or uptight young girls. There's a do-goody reason why the producers of the later film *American Pie* thought a flautist would make a perfect school square. This was an instrument so un-rock and roll that James Galway could openly record an album of cinema classics called *Quiet on the Set*. Any dreams I had of musical stardom seemed over almost as soon as they had begun.

If my parents had been less stuck in the sixties and more up on the eighties they would have realized just what a wide range of instruments were available to the budding young musician. Perhaps more than any other decade, the eighties was a musical era defined by its instruments. What has happened, for example, to that large pool of saxophonists whose solos graced every other single going? Then there was the synthesizer: British Rail adverts of the day might have claimed this was 'the age of the train', but for a few years in the early eighties this was very much the age of the keyboard.

In its funny way, synth-pop, or New Romanticism, or new pop, or 'British haircut bands' – as termed by mullet-wearing Americans with no discernible hint of irony – was the logical conclusion of the punk revolution of 1976 and 1977.

'This is a chord,' ran a famous article in the punk fanzine *Sideburns*. 'This is another. This is a third. Now form a band.' In 1976 all you needed was an A, G and E and a bucketful of attitude to get on *Top of the Pops* (not that you'd actually play *Top of the Pops*, because that would be, like, selling out). It was liberating stuff undoubtedly, but, to borrow a phrase, the wheel was still in spin. The guitar, however rudimentary and distortedly played, was still a guitar. This was the mainstay of music since the later 1950s, and remained part of the tradition instead of breaking with it.

The arrival of the synthesizer, however, was something different. Here was a whole new set of sounds that was set apart from what people's parents had been brought up on. Instead of looking to the past for inspiration, as punk did, this strand of music took its cue from the imagined sound of the future. Instead of throwing those classic rock shapes that everyone recognized – the masculinity of the guitar as a sort of symbolic penis extension – standing behind a keyboard offered far more mixed and ambiguous sexual signals. Rather than involving a whole afternoon's effort to learn three guitar chords, here was an instrument that in the late seventies was so primitive you couldn't even play a chord on it: prior to the arrival of polyphonic synthesizers, a few years later, monophonic keyboards could play only one note at a time. And for all punk's talk about doing it yourself, you didn't actually get more DIY than buying a musical instrument that arrived in a flat-pack kit, like a piece of IKEA furniture, that you had to put together yourself.

Keyboards and synthesizers weren't a new thing at the end of the 1970s. Stalwarts like the Mellotron and the Moog had been knocking around since the late sixties, but such devices were so exorbitantly expensive that they were out of reach to pretty much everyone bar prog-rockers like Rick Wakeman. But, as the technology improved and the costs came down, so synthesizers become affordable; whereas before they'd cost tens, even hundreds of thousands of pounds, you could now find machines like the Transcendent 2000 in the small ads in the back of *Melody Maker* for a couple of hundred quid.

In self-assembling these kits, albeit to fairly rough-and-ready effect, the budding young keyboardist was following in some pretty hallowed footsteps. Although the eighties touchstones of Roxy Music and David Bowie had both had their synthesizer moments (the latter on his Berlin-era albums; the former via Brian Eno and the switchboard-like VCS-3 machine), two other influences loomed large over the scene. The first of these was the soundtrack to Stanley Kubrick's film adaptation of Anthony Burgess's *A Clockwork Orange*. Written and performed by Wayne (later Wendy) Carlos, the music was played entirely on synthesizers – producing a sound that felt cutting edge and futuristic and sparkled with the associations of glamour and fashion and violence that the film portrayed. The fact that the film was banned, too, could only add to the soundtrack's kudos.

The second influence was German, and came particularly from Kraftwerk. The band hailed from Düsseldorf, where members Ralf Hütter and Florian Schneider grew up: a city whose industry dominated the landscape. Hütter and Schneider were classically trained musicians – Schneider, it warms the cockles of my heart to hear, played the flute. Early experiments involved mic-ing up and messing around with his instrument, though the course of music is probably thankful that they switched to keyboards instead. Into the mix came Karl Bartos and Wolfgang Flür and the four-some began recording, in their Kling Klang studio, using a mixture of very early synthesizers and their own creations: Kraftwerk didn't like the available drum machines, for example, so simply made their own. The result was a unique, and uniquely electronic sound.

One band to be inspired by Kraftwerk were the Human League – or, as they were originally (and appositely) called, the Future. The band came from Sheffield, a city that, like Düsseldorf, was defined by its industry. Sheffield is all about steel, with factories and towers dotting its scenery. The proximity of these fixtures creates an atmosphere that must surely affect the music created there – indeed, one could write a whole book on the relationship between music and landscape. But for Sheffield, which had once been an industrial powerhouse, the economic difficulties of the 1970s and the recession of the early 1980s turned this vibrant local economy into something else: as redundancies came and the factories fell silent, the buildings hung in there casting their eerie shapes and shadows over the city.

Growing up there, singer Phil Oakey read Burgess's *A Clockwork Orange*, Philip K. Dick and (as per Trevor Horn's inspiration for 'Video Killed the Radio Star') the work of J. G. Ballard, whose dystopian tales of high-rises and car crashes chimed with the Sheffield of the seventies. Looking every bit the lead singer, Oakey was invited to join the Future by founding members Martyn Ware and Ian

Craig Marsh. His unique, asymmetrical hairstyle was one he'd spotted on a girl on a bus – she was a hair model and it was a 1960s Vidal Sassoon cut.

Oakey loved the band's sound but hated the name. The Human League came from a science-fiction war game called StarForce, in which said league fought intergalactic battles with the Pansentient Hegemony (which is probably not such a good name for a band). Oakey also brought to the table a love of pop music – the Human League sound was intended to be a concoction of Kraftwerk and ABBA. This works better on a theoretical level (combining electronic sounds with soaring pop sensibilities) than a literal one (a clipped robotic voice creepily singing a slowed-down version of 'Lay All Your Love On Me').

Perhaps appreciating that the band's stage show was not the world's most exciting – Marsh and Ware standing behind keyboards, Oakey nervously stationary, a tape recorder with the bass and drums on it – the group brought in art student Adrian Wright as 'Director of Visuals'. Wright put together a suitably strange concoction of slide projections to play out on a screen behind the band (everything from rockets to erotica, flowers to scientific diagrams). This was the height of punk, and the Human League looked and sounded different. Not that they were alone in doing so, it should said. In fact, all around the country, there were little pockets of similar bands starting up, experimenting with cheap DIY keyboards in the same way: in Essex there was Depeche Mode; in Liverpool there was Orchestral Manoeuvres in the Dark, for example. Organically might be an odd word to use for a synthesized movement, but that's how a scene and a sound were developing.

The Human League, though, were the ones who were picked up, got the record deal and, well, nothing. Early singles like 'Being Boiled' (about silkworms) and 'The Dignity of Labour' (an EP of instrumentals about the Russian space programme) did not threaten to nudge 'Dancing Queen' off the nightclub DJ's turntable. The group's biggest claim to fame was being mocked by the Undertones in their Top 10 single 'My Perfect Cousin'. In the song, a swotty, nerdy character called Kevin decides to take up the synthesizer, which his mother bought for him on the advice of the Human League.

The Undertones were not the only ones to respond to the Human League like this – for them, as for many bands, teenage kicks were all about guitars rather than keyboards. But at least they were responding, unlike the record-buying public. Listening to the Human League's early recordings now, one suspects the reason for this is the coldness of the music. The danger of electronic music is that synthesized sound doesn't seem real, that there's no emotion there for the listener to latch on to. This wasn't something that only the Human League struggled with: for example, as influential as they were on a select group of musicians, Kraftwerk were not setting the charts alight either.

It wasn't that the record-buying public were immune to such music. In 1979 the British synthesized sound had its first big hits in the shape of Gary Numan's 'Cars' and 'Are "Friends" Electric?' Numan, a more traditional musician by nature, had come across synthesizers by chance: a Minimoog keyboard had accidentally been left behind in a recording/rehearsal studio he'd booked. Numan started playing around with it and instantly fell in love with it. What he did differently to the Human League was to put these striking new sounds on top of his more conventional rock-band ones – he still had drummers, bass players, guitarists and so forth. The combination of the two made it more palatable for the listening public: intrigued by the electronics, but reassured by the more familiar rock shapes behind. With his striking looks – white make-up and a short, sharp shock of blonde hair – and science-fiction-inspired lyrics, Numan followed the same musical formula as the Human League but found a way to make it work.

For Phil Oakey, however, things were about to get worse before they got better. The band spilt in two, with Martyn Ware and Ian Craig Marsh leaving to set up the band that would become Heaven 17 (another *Clockwork Orange*-inspired band name). Oakey was left with his haircut, the band's name and a Director of Visuals. To borrow a term from the new craze in Space Invader computer games, it seemed to be G A M E O V E R. It was here, though, that the Human League found their human touch. When he assembled a new line-up for the band Oakey included two young female backing singers, Joanne Catherall and Susan Ann Sulley, whom he'd chanced upon not in a cocktail bar but in Sheffield's Crazy Daisy nightclub. The girls, who'd originally met at Showaddywaddy concert in Christmas 1976, were Gary Numan fans and dressed accordingly:

at the time, they didn't even like the Human League that much.

What the girls' introduction did bring, however, was a softening and warming of both the band's image and music. These days Elbow are often championed for their connection with their fans as the 'people's band'. What the Human League did by bringing in two regular, provincial girls was proper people's-band stuff: bridging the gap between group and audience by bringing two of the latter on to the other side of the mixing desk; introducing into their music, as more than one commentator has noted, the sound of the crowd. Complementing the new line-up and approach was the band's new producer. Martin Rushent might have most recently worked with the likes of the Stranglers and the Buzzcocks, but his background was in classic pop and big voices, everyone from Shirley Bassey to T. Rex.

It might not be the most obvious musical comparison, but the Elbow reference is worth making again. Sometimes the best albums are forged out of adversity. Elbow's *The Seldom Seen Kid* came out of the band losing close friends and record contracts; by having nothing to lose, the group suddenly found they had everything to gain. The same was true for the Human League: *Dare* was one of the great pop albums if not *the* pop album of the eighties. For years Queen had proudly declared 'No synthesizers' on their album sleeves; *Dare* equally revelled in the fact it was played on nothing else. The band credits on the album sleeve are listed as follows:

COMPUTER LOVE

Ian Burden – Synthesizer
Jo Callis – Synthesizer
Joanne Catherall – Vocals
Philip Oakey – Vocals and Synthesizer
Susan Ann Sulley – Vocals
Philip Adrian Wright – Slides and Occasional Synthesizer

Gary Numan might have introduced the listening public to synthesizer sounds, but *Dare* was the album that went the whole way.

What *Dare* also had was warmth. Gary Numan, for all his killer synth riffs, was singing lyrics based on an unfinished science-fiction book he'd been writing. The 'friends' in 'Are "Friends" Electric?' are part of a futuristic world in which everyone is unisex and you can hire cyborg beings by the hour for whatever purpose you like. *Dare*, by contrast, focused on good old-fashioned romance with real people, rather than on sex with robots. Mostly, anyway: the inspiration behind the 'Love Action' part of 'Love Action (I Believe in Love)' was the film *Emmanuelle*.

Dare spawned four monster hits in the shape of 'The Sound of the Crowd', 'Love Action', 'Open Your Heart' and most memorably 'Don't You Want Me' which held off Julio Iglesias ('Begin the Beguine'), Cliff Richard ('Daddy's Home') and perhaps most symbolically ABBA ('One of Us') to spend five weeks at Number 1 in December 1981 and January 1982. The song, featuring alternate verses sung by Philip Oakey and Susan Ann Sulley, has echoes of Oakey's initial meeting with the girls and his plucking them from obscurity. Its actual origins, however, were from a story Oakey was reading in a women's magazine: 'It was called "Intimate Romance" or something, an American import. It wasn't actually a waitress in the story, it was, "I was working in a bus station" or something, and somehow they summed up a person's whole life in a sentence. And it was really good, so I pinched it.'[2]

What was also really good was the accompanying video, directed by Steve Barron. The promo oozed class, not least because Barron blew the budget on using cinema-quality 35-millimetre film, rather than the standard 16-millimetre or video that everyone else was using. The film not only looked cinematic but was inspired by the big screen too: 'I was very influenced by that François Truffaut film *Day for Night* . . . I thought, "We've got 35-millimetre. Let's do a film within a film like the Truffaut film."'[3] I don't know how many people got those references, but whether you did or not it was difficult not to be taken in by the moody glamour of the video and Barron's focus-switching camera shot from Philip Oakey to Susan Ann Sulley.

'Don't You Want Me' shifted almost one and a half million copies in the UK (making it the twenty-fifth-best-selling single of all time) and topped the American charts for three weeks the following summer. It was the classiest Christmas Number 1 for many a year, but the Human League were by no means the only synth-led success story of the time. Hitting Number 1 a few weeks before were Soft Cell, with Marc Almond and David Ball's cover of Gloria Jones's Northern Soul song 'Tainted Love'. Then there was

Orchestral Manoeuvres in the Dark, who were so fascinated by Joan of Arc they had not one but two hit singles about her. Depeche Mode, meanwhile, enjoyed their first Top 10 hit in September 1981 with 'Just Can't Get Enough'.

Perhaps the most telling hit, however, came a month later. Kraftwerk, the band who had inspired all these British musicians in the first place, found their re-released double-A-side 'Computer Love/The Model' pushing Shakin' Stevens off the Number 1 spot. The group who had been ahead of their time now found that the world had finally caught up with them: by 1982, computer love was catching; their synthesized sound was the model for everyone to follow.

The Undertones weren't the only ones who were less than enamoured with the new keyboard sounds. The Musicians' Union took the threat to its members' livelihoods so seriously that it argued for some sort of ban on keyboards, with their use restricted to a rationed amount within a few agreed studios. The Union's London branch was particularly concerned about the effect on West End productions, with the vision of a bulging orchestra pit being replaced by a Thomas Dolby-type in the corner.

A ban on synthesizers might sound far-fetched, but the clout of the Musician's Union in those days was not to be underestimated. Such was the Union's power that for many years every band appearing on *Top of the Pops* did the following little dance. The day before a *Top of the Pops* appearance, each band was required to turn up at a studio where, under the watchful eye of a Union representative, they would record a live version of the song to be mimed to the following night. Getting the song to sound the same as the original recording in one afternoon was no easy matter, which is why, with a nod and a wink, the original master would be slipped to the *Top of the Pops* producer instead. Occasionally, if a new band didn't know the rules, or if they managed to piss off the Union rep, they would find themselves miming to their dirgy afternoon recording instead. 'Keep Music Live' was the Union's campaigning slogan, which some synthesizer bands responded to with their own logo: 'Keep Music Dead'.

It was one thing for the likes of Freddie Mercury and Fergal Sharkey to dislike synthesizers because they didn't like the sounds they produced and preferred their music to be played on more established instruments – on the grounds that this was somehow more 'real'. But the suggestion that these instruments removed the need for musicianship, and that all you had to do was press a button, was somewhat misleading (even if early Human League concerts did involve the band walking over to the tape player positioned where the drummer would have been, and making a big show of pressing 'play'). The early keyboards were, by today's standards, so primitive that it took a huge amount of skill and knowledge to tease out their sounds. Some early models were essentially a box of wires and clips to be fiddled with, and every change or tweak of a knob would alter the sound that came out. Then there was the problem of syncing all these different instruments together, with all of them operating on their own time

systems. It might not have been musicianship in the traditional sense of learning scales and being able to play long and
complicated Rick Wakeman-type solos, but to suggest that
there was no skill involved is wrong. Technology on its own
is never enough: it's what people do with it that makes the
difference, and gives it that human element.

So what were the instruments and bits of kit that defined
the sound of the eighties? The Linn drum machines, both
Linn LM-1 and its successor, the LinnDrum, were all over
the charts of this era: that's where all the rhythm sounds on
Dare come from, for example. The LM-1 was different at
the time, because it was both programmable (rather than
being limited to pre-set patterns) and used digital samples
of actual drummers for its different sounds (whichever
LA session musician originally played these has probably
appeared on more hit records than any other musician).
Each individual drum sound could then be messed around
and played with until the desired effect was discovered.
What the machine couldn't do was add in an actual drummer's individual style – everything was digitally bang on
the beat, rather than having that natural bit of swing. It also
couldn't look exciting to play – hence the dusting down of
those hexagonal drum pads for television appearances.

The keyboards of the eighties can be divided into monophonic and polyphonic ones: in other words, those that
could only play one note at a time, and those that could hold
down whole chords. The earlier affordable keyboards, such
as the Minimoog which Gary Numan happened upon in the
studio, were all monophonic ones, hence the proliferation

of all those basic-sounding single-note solos: it wasn't that people couldn't play anything more complicated, it was that the technology wasn't there to allow them to do it. As the technology improved, polyphonic synthesizers became the norm. The Roland Jupiter 8, so called because you could play eight notes at the same time, was perhaps the most popular, the instrument of choice of Duran Duran's Nick Rhodes, for example.

Another hugely influential machine was the Fairlight, a combined keyboard and computer kit that allowed the user to upload sound samples as well as using the preset ones, and then painstakingly programme drums, keyboards, the lot. The computer screen on the machine glowed green and black, and instead of a mouse, came with an electronic pen that directed proceedings by touching the monitor. The early versions could also give a not entirely healthy dose of radiation, and users could find their fillings getting hot after a particularly long session. Peter Gabriel was one of the first purchasers, and other early advocates included Kate Bush (the 'breaking glass' sound on 'Babooshka' is a very Fairlight sound), Tears for Fears and Trevor Horn. The Art of Noise's 'Close (to the Edit)' is almost a showcase for what the machine can do.

For all their grumbling about technology, guitarists found themselves far from immune to their charms. Effects hadn't particularly changed since the late sixties, when sounds like distortion, flange and wah-wah pedals were lapped up by the likes of Jimi Hendrix. Digital technology, however, opened up a whole new box of tricks. Roland developed its hugely popular range of Boss foot pedals: its chorus pedal was one that no aspiring Goth or indie guitar player could be without. The digital delay effect, where a note could be repeated at a chosen delay or attack was perhaps the most striking, as used by U2 on 'Where the Streets Have No Name'. Indeed, the Edge's knowhow of pedals, rather than his skill with a flashy solo, made him the archetypal eighties guitarist.

Back in York, it was to be the Edge's footsteps that I would decide to follow. I practised and played my flute like the well-behaved child I was, but my heart wasn't in it. I think the nadir for me was when I was entered for my grade 3 exam (which sort of sounds impressive, except that's the level flute players usually go in at). These took place at the Quakers' meeting house in York, in the corner of a huge cavernous hall, where the examiner would listen to you play tunes accompanied by piano, and then put you through your paces with scales and singing back notes at various intervals. I was nervous at taking the exam, but felt that my opening pieces had gone well. As the pianist tidied her music together to leave, she turned to me with a sympathetic smile, and said, 'Never mind.' The confidence that had thus far carried me through disappeared, my scores collapsed in the second half of the exam, and I failed.

It turned out that I wasn't destined to be the new James Galway after all. I was less the Man with the Golden Flute and more the Boy with the Bad Breathing Technique. My musical adventure, however, was only just beginning. York had, as did most towns, its second-hand shop full of musical instruments and paraphernalia (the sort of place you go when you've just had something nicked, in case this is where it's ended up). One day my dad returned from a visit there with a second-hand acoustic guitar, which he'd bought for fifty quid. I might not quite have joined the synth-pop revolution, but musically it was a start.

Track Five

Wired for Sound

This chapter begins in the woods of St Moritz in Switzerland. It is February 1972 and, as the snow falls on this winter-wonderland scene, a man is going for a walk with his girlfriend. The man's name is Andreas Pavel, a German-born inventor who grew up in Brazil. On this particular day, on this particular walk, Pavel has one of his inventions with him: an electronic device shaped like a chunky set-square. The machine has a slot for an audio cassette, and sockets for two sets of headphones: one for himself and one for his girlfriend. He is about to press 'play' on what he has decided to call his Stereobelt: the world's first prototype personal-cassette player.

The first song ever played on this device was 'Push Push', the title track of an album by jazz musician Herbie Mann. Mann's instrument of choice – and this would have been useful information for a young York teenager years later – was not the classic jazz staple of the saxophone or the trumpet but the flute. (If only I'd known this particular piece of eighties-music trivia I might not have been so embarrassed about learning the flute myself.) The album cover of *Push Push* shows very much that Herbie was all Mann. There he is, 'flauting' it in full naked seventies hairy torso, glistening with sweat. With his thick 'tache compensating for a receding hairline, Mann stares confidently out, his flute hooked over his shoulder like a worker with his spade after a hard morning's labouring. *That's right*, the image appears to be saying. *Just back from some serious heavy-duty flute playing. Got so hot with those arpeggios out there, I had to take my clothes off. Hope that's not a problem, ladies . . .*

'Push Push' seems a curious choice of track for an event that would go on to have such subsequent significance. It's more of a groove than a song, a mildly grinding early-seventies jazz-funk number, with Herbie push-pushing it over the top. If you listen carefully, I swear you can hear that luxuriant Selleck of a moustache tickling away at the embrasure. All of which would be in keeping if you found yourself in some Eastside dive after midnight, but frankly feels somewhat out of place in the middle of the Swiss countryside. But perhaps, in a way, that was exactly the point: this was, after all, the first time that anyone had listened to a song on a personal stereo, and the incongruity between the music and setting served only to emphasize the machine's ability to transform the mood of the surroundings. That's certainly what Pavel felt: 'I pressed the button, and suddenly we were floating. It was an incredible feeling, to realize that I now had the means to multiply the aesthetic potential of any situation.'[1] (That's a great line to remember the next time someone asks you to turn your MP3 player down: *Sorry, but I really don't want to divide my aesthetic potential . . .*)

Andreas Pavel had hit on one of the key music innovations of the 1980s. Unfortunately, it was 1972 and nobody was interested in his idea. Grundig, Philips and Yamaha were just three of the music-electronics firms who listened to Pavel's device and couldn't quite imagine people buying a machine that allowed them to listen to sweaty naked flautists wherever and whenever they wanted to. The companies' instinct was one that chimed with the times. Pavel moved to New York and when he went out with his Stereobelt people thought he was mad: 'People would look at me sometimes on a bus, and you could see they were asking themselves, why is this crazy man running around with headphones?'

This, as it turned out, was not a question unique to Pavel. When Sony launched their Walkman, a few years later, one of the concerns about its potential for success was whether people would feel a bit weird wandering about listening to music on their own. That's why early versions of the Walkman echoed Pavel's Stereobelt in having two headphone sockets; in addition there was a 'hotline' – a microphone device that allowed the two listeners to talk to each other without having to take their headphones off. Both Pavel and Sony saw their devices as a 'stereo' rather than a 'mono' experience: something to be shared between friends, family or partners.

WIRED FOR SOUND

Andreas Pavel's Stereobelt ended up going the same way as Charles Babbage's Victorian computer: the right idea, just a couple of years too early. If that foresight counted for nothing, another bit of foresight on Pavel's part was ultimately to be rewarded. He patented his Stereobelt in 1977; and when Sony's Walkman later took off he filed a suit for royalties. In 2004, after a long and protracted legal battle, Sony finally agreed a settlement believed to be in the region of several million euros. All of which seemed a world away from that bright winter's day, when a young inventor pressed 'play' on a new way of listening to music.

Andreas Pavel was right and the companies who turned down his Stereobelt were wrong. When Sony launched its Walkman, it sold a remarkable 200 million worldwide within the first two years. The Walkman, perhaps unsurprisingly, is an idea that lots of people claim to have had a hand in. It might have been Akio Morita, founder of the Sony Corporation himself, who had the idea when out for a walk in New York. Or it might also have been Akio Morita wanting something to do on those long business flights between Japan and the US. It could have started the day co-founder Masaru Ibuka wandered in to see Morita with a dictaphone and pair of headphones. Or it could have come about from a more prosaic reshuffling of departments within Sony, with the tape-recorder division having had radio cassette recorders taken from them, and in need of a new idea to maintain the 'prestige' of their section.

WIRED FOR SOUND

Wherever and whoever the idea originated with, Sony was a company whose roots were founded in the aftermath of the Second World War. In May 1946 Morita set up the firm under the slightly less user-friendly name of Tokyo Tsushin Kogyu Kabushiki Kasha (or Tokyo Telecommunication Engineering for short[ish]). The company changed its name in the 1950s to Sony, from the Latin *sonus*, which means sound: it was chosen partly as the pronunciation was the same in any number of languages, and also to give the company a more global, non-Japanese feel.

The original success of Sony came about because of an earlier music-led invention. One of the reasons that Japan became such a powerhouse for electronic goods was that, after the war, the victorious Americans banned the manufacturing of arms there and Japan's large and successful manufacturing base needed to turn its hand to making something else instead. That something else was electronics. Sony succeeded in buying from American firm AT&T the rights to some transistorized electronic components they'd invented. AT&T were happy to take Sony's money, as they couldn't see how the transistors could be used to make anything except hearing aids. Back in Japan, however, Akio Morita and Masaru Ibuka used the components to create the world's first transistor radio.

So when it came to converting a piece of kit meant to be used for one thing to another, Sony had previous. The Walkman idea was much the same. Sony already made a device called the Pressman, which was – as the name suggests – a dictation machine, designed for journalists, which could record and play back cassettes. Technologically, therefore, the Walkman was not an advance but was actually a simpler machine: it could only play cassettes, not record them. But simpler also meant cheaper, which meant it was in the price bracket for ordinary consumers as opposed to being aimed at professionals. Not everyone was immediately convinced by the idea: why, ran the counter argument, would anyone want a cassette recorder that couldn't even record? Sony, though, were convinced they were on to a winner, and pushed to launch the product as quickly as possible (within six months, as opposed to the usual two-year development time).

What the product needed was a name. The first idea was to adapt 'walkie-talkie' – Sony's machine didn't offer any facility for talkie, so the 'Stereo Walkie' became the original choice. Unfortunately, rival firm Toshiba had already registered 'Walky' as a name. But by this point a logo had already been drawn, which everybody liked, with the 'A' of 'Walkie' being given a pair of feet and walking along (which now looks somewhat dated and naff). The idea came about to switch from Walkie to Walkman, thus matching up with the Pressman, and allowing not one but two walking 'A's in the logo. Concerns remained, however, as to whether the world beyond Japan would go for the ungrammatical Japanese-English of 'Walkman'. So, to begin with, the machine was marketed under different names in different countries: in the US it was sold under the name Sound-About; in Sweden consumers could buy a Freestyle; in the UK, meanwhile (and I'll leave you to decide what this says about what the

Japanese thought about the British), the original name was the Stowaway.

The launch of the product belied Sony's concerns that the world would need persuading that people actually needed a Walkman. They gave away a hundred stereos to travelling musicians, whom they thought might appreciate being able to listen to music on the go: members of the visiting Berlin and New York Philharmonics were given Walkmans in the hope that they would spread the word back home. Meanwhile journalists were sent invitations to the launch on cassettes rather than cards. They were taken to Tokyo's Yoyogi Park to watch teenagers rollerskating around listening to Walkmans. Sony also paid couples to walk through the capital's Ginza shopping district listening to Walkmans together, again to show how they envisioned the device being used.

Much emphasis was put on the shared experience of listening to a Walkman together: early advertising posters again featured happy couples smiling and nodding away together. The expectation was simply (as per Andreas Pavel's earlier experience) that listening to music alone would be seen as a bit strange: the behaviour of an alienated, isolated individual. To begin with the negative voices were proved correct. In the first month after the Walkman's release in July 1979, only 3000 machines were sold. But then the Walkman took off and by September the entire 30,000 run had sold out. From then on there was no stopping the Walkman.

The Walkman was the iPod of its day: everyone wanted one, and well beyond the young whom Sony assumed would be the sole audience. People out and about doing keep fit – joggers, cyclists, walkers, rollerskaters – all took to the machine, which served to give the Walkman an unintentionally sporty glow: this was a device for young, healthy people, as the subsequent marketing was quick to enforce.

One person who was certainly well beyond the Walkman core demographic yet became one of its early champions was Cliff Richard. In the late seventies, too, Cliff had undergone something of brief renaissance, and been given a slick, glossy *FM*-style makeover. These days, songs like 'Devil Woman', and 'We Don't Talk Anymore' are the archetypal guilty pleasures, but back then, in the pre-irony eighties, they were just pleasures.[2] In 1981 Cliff continued this run of songs with his paean to the Walkman, 'Wired for Sound'. In fact, the song is a general celebration of music, and there's not much he doesn't dig. From tall speakers to small speakers, Cliff likes the lot (that's speakers, by the way, not 'people', as my wife routinely hears). It's the freedom of putting on those headphones and wandering around that really gets Cliff feeling like a young one again. In his then trademark look of leather jacket and bright-yellow T-shirt, glossy mane and large, Mike Read-style glasses, Cliff is out and about with his headphones, walking and skating around the eighties concrete architecture of Milton Keynes for the accompanying video, loving the tunes while a succession of bright young things in leotards rollerskate around him. If there's a more eighties video than that, by the way, I'd love to see it.

There are moments when Cliff looks a little bit wobbly on his skates and, yes, perhaps watching the video back it's possible to think, 'Sony were right: this *is* a young person's thing.' But, at the same time, Cliff's endorsement helped me (and I suspect children up and down the country similarly) persuade my parents to buy me a Walkman. Like many parents, mine were suspicious of the Walkman. There were worries about headphones, and rumours among their network of liberal friends that you'd be deaf by the time you turned thirteen. There was also felt to be something almost ostentatious about wearing a Walkman in public: a show of wealth that went against their middle-class leaning; a one-upmanship that would be repeated years later with the iPod's white headphones. There were worries, too, that a Walkman could warp a child into an alienated individual, stripping them of their ability to socially interact: couple this with playing computer games and it would be only a matter of time before their flute-playing son turned into a crazed, psychopathic killer.

With Cliff's support my parents relented and I was finally allowed into the Walkman club. The WM-22 came in three colours – electric blue, vivid red and pearl white – and I chose the red, personalizing it with a large sparkly 'Thomas' sticker I'd got for my birthday (it was either that or my mother attempting to sew a name badge on it). I dug it out of a box in the attic when writing this book – and it's interesting how what then seemed so small and light now feels so heavy and clunky.

There is no doubt that the Walkman chimed with the eighties in a particularly resonant way. This was a decade defined in large part by the politics of Ronald Reagan and

Margaret Thatcher. The individualism that espoused the 'there's no such thing as society' mantra by which they ruled allowed a looser if not free rein on the nation's more selfish streak. The Walkman, in many ways, symbolized that: a materialist moniker for people to carry around, an object that nobody needed but everyone wanted, an object that removed the user from their surroundings and from interaction with other people: the train, instead of being a single shared public space, became a carriage full of private bubbles. The decade before, the idea of people behaving like that didn't make much sense. In the eighties it did: out went the shared listening experience and twin-headphone sockets, and in came a world that – like Nick Heyward leaving Haircut One Hundred, Limahl exiting Kajagoogoo or George Michael parting company with Andrew Ridgeley – was all about going solo.

My Sony Walkman added an eighties twist to the music equipment on offer in my house when I was growing up. At times it felt as though we lived in a museum for musical artefacts. From the sixties there was my mother's old Dansette record player, which my parents had dusted down in the attic – I think to keep my fledgling singles collection away from the sitting room. The Dansette was an early-sixties version of a ghetto-blaster: it had a handle to carry it around, and an inbuilt speaker. It was old enough to have speed settings of not only $33\frac{1}{3}$ and 45 rpm but 16 and 78 as well. Its most innovative feature was its facility to stack and play a load of singles, one after the other, the record needle by the end wobbling somewhat precariously on top of what looked like a cake made out of vinyl.

The seventies, meanwhile, supplied the music option in our sitting room where, on the shelf underneath the television, my parents kept their 'music centre'. The difference between a music centre and its successor, the hi-fi, can usually be detected in terms of height. While an eighties hi-fi stacked its moulded shiny black plastic features one on top of the other, like a block of apartments except with a record player on top, the music centre went for a single-storey, bungalow approach. Spreading itself out in its fake-wood livery, the cassette deck would sit next to the stylus, playing tapes in a lying down instead of a bolt-upright sitting position.

In the early eighties, the music centre was the only piece of equipment in our house to have both a radio and a tape player. This was the machine on which I would record the Top 40 every Sunday night (while I sat listening live in the kitchen) on my cassette of choice, the C90. I did try to record these on a C120 tape for a few weeks, but the extra length came at the expense of thinner tape, which inevitably led to disastrous spool unravelling (a pencil, quaintly, was the weapon of choice to try and wind it back in such circumstances). About halfway through the decade I finally got my own hi-fi system. I'm not sure whether the words 'hi-fi' or indeed 'system' are entirely consistent with whatever knock-off Far-Eastern manufacturer had produced this particular machine. It did, though, boast a turntable, radio and rudimentary graphic equalizer and, best of all, two cassette decks. This was every teenage music fan's dream, and every record-company executive's nightmare: the power to record not just from record and radio, but also from tape to tape. By the end of a decade, just to give the record executive a further shudder, I spent the summer working in a Gateway supermarket to upgrade again: this time for a stereo whose tape-to-tape decks boasted high-speed dubbing, allowing me to copy music twice as fast.

There is one final piece of eighties-listening kit I should mention, and that is the compact disc. Early prototypes of these varied in size and length: one was as big as a normal vinyl LP and could hold thirteen hours of music; the version that was settled on was a smaller, twelve-centimetre affair that could squeeze in seventy-four minutes of tunes: according to Louis Barfe's excellent history of the record industry, *Where Have All the Good Times Gone?*, the length was chosen because of the classical leanings of Sony's deputy president, Norio Ohga; he liked Beethoven's seventy-four-minute Ninth Symphony, and wanted the disc to be able accommodate the whole thing.

For me, in the eighties, the CD was something I watched excitable *Tomorrow's World* presenters spread jam on to to prove its indestructibility. In the early days, they felt the preserve of yuppies and Dire Straits fans. By contrast, I was more than wedded to my cassette collection and my love of vinyl. By the late eighties, so much did I adore the latter that I was convinced that there was something warmer about the 'analogue' sounds of a real record than the cold 'digital' sound on a CD. It wouldn't be until well into the 1990s that I finally relented and made the switch.

It says much of how widespread and prevalent home-taping was in the 1980s that it was never an issue in our house. By 1984, out of the UK's adult population of 43.8 million people, it was estimated that 24.1 million were home-taping, either off the radio or from records and cassettes (and that's not including the many millions of children like myself). This habit was fuelled by the purchase of blank cassettes, which by the mid-eighties were selling around 100 million a year: in 1983, research suggested that the British were recording 466 million hours of music a year (this compared to sales of about 100 million hours of recorded music). The (several) million-dollar question was just how many sales were being lost as a result. 'The record industry certainly does not claim that every home recording means a lost sale,' said the *BPI Yearbook 1985*, '[but] it happens that some 16% of album taping sessions *do* result in a lost sale. Lost sales, at the very minimum, are put at £300 million of retail sales.'

The record industry's suggested response was for a levy to be put on the sale of blank cassettes, with home-taping being made legal in return. Research carried out in 1988 found that 60 per cent of those polled would be happy to pay a proposed 10p tax per blank tape. Although similar schemes had been put into practice in a number of European countries, including France and West Germany, the Conservative government decided not to follow suit and removed the relevant clause from the 1988 Copyright Act at the last moment. The record industry was furious, but this was a tax-cutting administration, after all, and one that saw the state as a burden as opposed to a solution.

Instead, the record industry had to make do with their ineffectual 'Home Taping is Killing Music' campaign. This featured a Jolly Roger-style logo, with a blank cassette replacing the skull of the skull and crossbones. Which doesn't really work, when you think about it: a cassette and a pair of bones? If anything, this campaign highlighting the illegality of home-taping served only to give the activity credibility among young people such as myself. Unlike with later issues, such as downloading and file sharing, where there were high-profile cases and musicians such as Metallica on the anti-piracy side, home-taping was neither something that the police seemed to actively pursue nor something that musicians were coming out against. I remember a story that did the rounds at secondary school about someone who'd been stopped by the police for cycling without lights, had his bag searched and his home-taped cassettes within confiscated. I don't know whether that incident actually occurred or, even if it did, whether the officer was enforcing the law or just thought, 'The new Amazulu? I think I'd better take this.'

One band who came out in favour of home-taping were Bow Wow Wow, the pet project of former Sex Pistols manager Malcolm McLaren. Their debut single, 'C30 C60 C90 Go!' was a typical bit of McLaren wind-up, even if it caused more of a stir in the record industry than among the public at large.

With lyrics extolling the virtues of recording off the radio instead of that so old-fashioned habit of buying records, the 'cassingle' came with the gimmick of a blank B-side for people to do just that. But, for all McLaren's gift for mischief-making, the single reached only Number 34. Maybe this lowly chart placing was because fans were following the advice of the song's lyrics and taping it off the radio instead.

Bow Wow Wow were a curious concoction of a band, and one whose history touches on two of the biggest names in early-eighties music. In the aftermath of the end of the Sex Pistols and the subsequent court cases, McLaren's first move had been to set up a similarly uncontroversial project: a 'soft-core rock-and-roll costume musical for kids'. *The Adventures of Melody, Lyric and Tune* featured the exploits of three underage girls shagging their way around Paris. Strangely, McLaren failed to find anyone to offer financial support for the project.

One person who *was* offering McLaren money was, as we saw earlier, Adam Ant. The McLaren-inspired Ants were a revelation: they looked good and sounded great – every bit pop stars for a new decade. In fact, so good and great did they look and sound that McLaren decided to have them for himself, and persuaded the Ants to leave Adam behind and form a new band with him. Adam was offered the derisory role of the new band's hair stylist; he rejected the position and instead went on to recruit a new group of Ants and garner huge success on his own terms.

In Adam's place was a young – very young – teenage singer whom McLaren had discovered working in a dry cleaners. Myint Myint Aye was a striking-looking fourteen-year-old, born in Rangoon to a Burmese father and English mother. 'He had a chat with my mother, and asked her – well, he didn't ask. He said, "We need her for this band." ' McLaren took Myint under his arm and renamed her Annabella Lwin. He then came up with a somewhat unconventional way of getting this young teenage girl to gel with the rest of the band: 'McLaren even persuaded the guys that the problem was her virginity [. . .] one of them had to do the dirty and deflower the underage singer. Reluctantly, the band drew lots, and guitarist Matthew Ashman was dispatched to perform the task. He failed.'[3]

Having passed up on one early eighties music star, McLaren then briefly hooked up with a second. For the band's early gigs, Bow Wow Wow came with a second lead singer: the former Blitz cloakroom attendant and about-town trendsetter Boy George. George joined the group in the guise of Lieutenant Lush, backing up Lwin and, like Adam Ant, believing that hooking up with McLaren was going to be his ticket to the pop stardom he craved. Once again, however, McLaren let the bigger prize slip through his fingers, and George found himself dropped (though the exposure and gigging experience can't have hurt his cause).

Bow Wow Wow were not the overnight success story that McLaren had hoped for. The failure of 'C30 C60 C90 Go!' was followed up by another tape-themed release: 'Your Cassette Pet' was released on tape alone, featured six songs and was sold at half the price of an LP. This time the song didn't even make the Top 40: indeed, it wasn't until a year later, in early 1982, that the band finally had a bona fide hit with 'Go Wild in the Country', which was followed into the Top 10 by a cover of 'I Want Candy'.

McLaren's penchant for controversy continued. The band's debut album, which was the wonderfully named *See Jungle! See Jungle! Go Join Your Gang! Yeah! City All Over! Go Ape Crazy!* featured the band mimicking Manet's painting *The Luncheon on the Grass*, with the band picnicking by the river and a still-underage Lwin posing nude. This time, McLaren found he had met his match in the shape of Lwin's mother, who demanded that the sleeve be withdrawn. One can only imagine what she thought when she heard 'Sexy Eiffel Tower', a song in which her daughter appears to get, well, extremely excited about a famous French landmark.

Back in the early eighties, the idea that one day we'd all have machines the size of credit cards that could contain every song you ever owned would have seemed like something out of *Star Wars*. Streaming websites, where you could listen to pretty much anything you wanted to, would have seemed equally preposterous. Yet, for everything we have gained via iPods and iTunes, Spotify and Last.FM, there remains that nagging doubt for many that something has got lost along the way. For all the digital delights of modern music, that tangible quality of earlier formats – the ability to have and to hold – has disappeared.

Some formats are more fondly remembered than others. I don't think there'll be many people feeling too bereft when the compact disc eventually bites the dust. Vinyl, by contrast, remains revered by its fans in almost religious terms: the hallowed ritual of lowering the needle, sitting back in anticipation as the crackle gives way to track one, side one. The humble cassette is never going to be remembered in quite those terms: it's too plastic, too disposable, too chunky for that. Yet the affection it retains is stronger than you might first think.

That's because of two things. Firstly, the cassette was, for the first time, music on the move: this was the format you could listen to anywhere; the bus or train taking you to one destination and your ears transporting you to another. Secondly, the cassette was the format that let you leave your own individual stamp on the music you liked. It allowed anyone to make mix-tapes of their favourite tunes: tapes to get ready to go out to, to wallow in when down, tapes to give a boyfriend or girlfriend to show just what they meant to you. 'I've made you a playlist . . .' just doesn't have the same romantic ring to it. Yes, it might boast better editing and substantially less hiss than a compilation tape and, yes, it might feature umpteen more tracks than you can squeeze on a C90, but an emailed link to a website is never going to have quite the same meaning as a lovingly crafted cassette.

Track Six

Do You Really Want to Hurt Me

My week, like that of many a young music fan, was punctuated by music. Sunday evenings was the Top 40 show on Radio One. Every other Wednesday I waited for the latest edition of *Smash Hits*. And 7.30 on a Thursday evening, right after *Tomorrow's World*, was the television highlight of the week: *Top of the Pops*.

The start of the show remains seared in my memory. Gone was the 1970s 'Whole Lotta Love' theme tune (always an odd choice, given that Led Zeppelin never released a single), and in its eighties place a brand-new sparkling number by Phil Lynott and Midge Ure called 'Yellow Pearl'. Alongside electronic drumrolls, soaring synths and TARDIS-style *whoosh*ing noises, the graphics showed a selection of brightly coloured records flying through the air like flying saucers, neon numbers flashing

on and off the screen. In between, with a *swoosh*, would be
the magic words. Top . . . *swoosh* . . . of the . . . *swoosh* . . .
pops. A shocking-pink disc would settle in the centre of the
screen before – with a da-da-da-da-da, da-da-da-da-da of
the drum pads – exploding into a thousand pieces.

Top of the Pops had been a Thursday-night staple since
Jimmy Savile introduced the first show back on New
Year's Day 1964 in a converted church in the sort-of-
aptly named Longsight, Manchester. (I met Jimmy Savile
once. I say met, I was doing a [not so] fun run dressed
as a gorilla. As I overtook the gold-tracksuit-bottomed
DJ he said to his phalanx of co-runners, 'Oh look, there
goes a shaggy dog.' To which I replied, 'I'm not a shaggy
dog. I'm a gorilla.') *Top of the Pops* quickly took over from
ITV's *Ready Steady Go!* as the show everyone wanted to
be on, though sadly little footage of those original shows
remain. In those days the BBC thought pop music far too
fleeting to be worth keeping and wiped all the tapes. The
only recording left of the Beatles on the show is via an
episode of *Doctor Who* in which the Doctor goes back in
time to the early 1960s and the Fab Four are playing on a
TV set in the corner.

By the start of the 1980s the show had gone from its
black-and-white beginnings via its 1970s variety-show feel
into somewhere between an American political convention
and a giant children's party. Balloons and party streamers
were everywhere as glamorous young things gathered and
gyrated around the central diamond-shaped stage. This
was the disco equivalent of 'doughnutting', that television

practice in the House of Commons where a ring of support-ive MPs surround the speaking one, to make the chamber look full. Had the cameraman pulled his shot back by just a few metres you'd have seen the emptiness of the studio around. That's the magic of television for you, and I was completely taken in. Even the dancing itself was not all it seemed to be: the BBC hired professional dancers to mingle with the audience and act as 'cheerleaders' (those steps to 'Agadoo' don't learn themselves). The ordinary members of the audience were also subject to 'encouragement' from the DJs: 'We were on with Simon Bates,' Glenn Gregory of Heaven 17 recalled, 'and he never stopped shouting at the kids in the audience. He was like a bloody teacher, yelling, "Shut up! Move over! Clap!"' [1]

The Radio One DJs, at least in their own heads, were the stars of the show. 'The DJs acted as though they were on the same level as us,' remembers Graham Gouldman of 10cc. In the seventies this manifested itself in hilarious pranks: when Queen performed 'Seven Seas of Rhye', Dave Lee Travis dressed up as a caretaker, sweeping with a broom, before jumping on stage and playing air guitar to Brian May. By the eighties some of the DJs were dusting down their own instruments: 'The Specials were on *Top of the Pops*,' said Jerry Dammers, 'and we went into the canteen and nobody was talking. All the artists were just staring at the ground. Mike Read was sitting on a table with an acoustic guitar, singing "Lucy in the Sky with Diamonds", and nobody dared laugh because he was so powerful.' [2]

Steve Wright, meanwhile, put his mother's cooking over

Madonna's perfectionist streak: 'Madonna kept doing take after take [. . .] I went over and said, "Look, love, mum's doing me a shepherd's pie, could you please hurry up?" She looked at me as if I was insane.' When the old guard did get the boot, in 1988, the raft of new presenters who came in – such as Anthea Turner and Andy Crane – often made things worse, rather than better: 'Mmm, lovely on a hot summer's day,' commented Simon Parkin on REM's 'Orange Crush' (the orange in question actually being Agent Orange, the controversial chemical used by the US army in Vietnam): 'This is the Wedding Present,' Anthea Turner equally crunchingly introduced. 'I'll have a toaster please!'

The only presenters who had any sense of decorum were the late John Peel and his sidekicks David Jensen and Janice Long. 'I'm the bloke who comes on late at night and plays records by sulky Belgians,' Peel explained to a confused younger audience on his return to the show in 1982 after a fourteen-year absence. In hosting the show, Peel refused to suspend his disbelief at some of the tunes he was listening to: of Keith Harris and Orville he said, 'That record was the best thing since Napoleon's retreat from Moscow'; of Aretha Franklin and George Michael's 'I Knew You Were Waiting for Me', he suggested that 'Aretha Franklin can make any old rubbish sound good, and I think she just has'; Big Country he somehow got away with describing as 'the band that put tree into Big Country'. On one memorable occasion, Peel reduced Janice Long to hysterics by saying of Pete Wylie's 'Sinful!', 'If that doesn't make Number 1,

I'm going to come round and break wind in your kitchen.'
(It didn't.)

The programme also took a while to catch up with the shifting social mores of the time. It wasn't until 1983 that the show had its first-ever female presenter, in the form of Janice Long. Attitudes towards sexuality were not always the most enlightened. In 1980, for example, the Who's Roger Daltrey guest-hosted the programme with Tommy Vance. 'Do you like disco, Roger?' Vance asked. 'No,' Daltrey replied, 'I hate it.' 'Oh that's a shame,' Vance said, 'because here's the Village People with "Can't Stop the Music".' 'Backs against the wall!' Daltrey hilariously advised.[3]

For the first half of the decade at least, most of this passed me by. Julie Burchill might rightly have described Simon Bates as looking like 'a Conservative councillor supervising a local youth club', but I was at a young age when the thought of going to a youth club, even one run by Simon Bates, seemed intoxicatingly exciting.

The greatest edition of *Top of the Pops* almost happened in late September 1982. I say almost, because in two consecutive weeks two of the show's most iconic eighties moments happened, one after the other: on 23 September Boy George and Culture Club made their debut performance, singing what would become their first Number 1, 'Do You Really Want to Hurt Me'; the week after that, Dexys Midnight Runners performed their cover of Van Morrison's 'Jackie Wilson Said' complete with Jocky Wilson backdrop. Had those two things happened on the same show it would have been difficult to claim that any other edition bettered it (though there was a pretty special show right at the end of the decade, which we'll come back to).

The only reason that Culture Club appeared at all was that Shakin' Stevens was ill: he was scheduled to sing 'Give Me Your Heart Tonight', nestling just outside the Top 10. One man's cold, however, is another's career opportunity: Culture Club, whose single had only just scraped inside the Top 40 at Number 38, were in a position too low to have normally been considered for a call-up (the usual rule of thumb was that only those records in the Top 30 were considered). But, after everything else that the band had been through, they probably deserved their break.

As already mentioned, from the Blitz Club, Boy George had ended up briefly in Bow Wow Wow, where McLaren's big idea was for him to be Lieutenant Lush, a character in a song he'd written called 'The Mile High Club'. The song was about the touching subject of 'children getting gang-banged by animals on an aeroplane'[4], with George/Lush as the pilot. George played a couple of gigs with the band, at the Rainbow Theatre in London and at Manchester University, but his arrival midway through the set felt out of kilter, and didn't go down well with Bow Wow Wow's more punk-friendly fans. George found out he'd been let go when he read about it in the *NME*.

So he set about putting his own band together, first meeting bassist Mikey Craig at Planets, a club George where was DJing. He first bumped into drummer Jon Moss on the King's Road. Guitarist Roy Hay agreed to leave his previous band, the New Romantics Russian Bouquet, to complete the line-up. The original name for the band was not the particularly Radio One-friendly Sex Gang Children. Other names on a clubby shortlist were Can't Wait Club and Caravan Club. Instead, they settled on Culture Club because of their different backgrounds: 'Jon said, "Look at us. An Irish transvestite, a Jew, a black man, an Anglo-Saxon." That's how I came up with the name.'[5] The band's first performance was at Crocs nightclub in Southend, in October 1981: Crocs was famous for being the home ground of Depeche Mode, and indeed singer Dave Gahan was there to watch them. As, so it happened, was someone from Virgin Music, who signed the band.

Even now, though, the musical gods hadn't quite finished toying with Boy George. The band's first two singles, 'White Boy' and 'I'm Afraid of Me', failed to get into the Top 100. Culture Club toured, supported by Musical Youth, who they watched head up the charts with 'Pass the Dutchie'. Perhaps most infuriatingly of all, singer Jeremy Healy, whom Boy George knew well, had formed a rival band, Haysi Fantayzee. Stylistically similar to Boy George, with the same sort of 'hat and dreadlocks' vibe, the group scored a Top 20 hit with 'John Wayne is Big Leggy'. Just to really rub it in, Boy George found himself being stopped by someone with a Haysi Fantayzee single who asked him to sign it.

'Do You Really Want to Hurt Me', however, had two things going for it. The first was emotion: Boy George had something to write about in the shape of Jon Moss. Their fractious relationship would be the core of the band over the next few years, for better or worse. Second, for the first time the band had brought in singer Helen Terry to do the backing vocals. All the best bits of Culture Club are a combination of these two voices: Boy George's purer, almost Tamla pop sound; Helen Terry's blast of more earthy soul. On its release the song became record of the week, though not on Radio One. The station, like children's TV programme *Swap Shop*, didn't want 'that kind of person on our show'.[6] DJ David 'Diddy' Hamilton played the song repeatedly on his Radio Two show, though – support enough to get the song in the charts and on to *Top of the Pops*.

Different recollections of Culture Club's performance put the viewing figures somewhere between eight and twelve million. However, many of those watching (like me) were asking the same question: is that a boy or a girl? My father's response, after a careful analysis of Boy George's hands, was that he was a bloke. I wasn't sure, though, and was by no means alone: in his autobiography Boy George claims that most people thought he was female.

What Boy George did differently to, say, Haysi Fantayzee, was to not sex his image up. Haysi Fantayzee's style was all crop-tops and pull-ups – 'Dickensian Rastas, with the emphasis on dick', as Boy George put it.[7] His transvestism was almost asexual in its non-threatening nature: that plus comments about how he preferred having a cup of tea to having sex got him into places that a more provocative image would have ruled out; certainly in the more conservative US such an image would have stopped the band being the big deal they were about to become. This squeaky-clean image slipped somewhat when the band won a Grammy Award for Best Newcomer, though: 'Thank you, America,' Boy George said. 'You have taste, style, and you know a good drag queen when you see one.' Then he blew a kiss to the camera.

For two years, between autumn 1982 and autumn 1984, Culture Club and Boy George were huge; the band scored seven successive Top 5 hits. I personally preferred them when they moved away from the reggae and did something with more oomph – 'Church of the Poison Mind' is for me by far their best song. Their most successful song, and the one that drove me up the wall, was 'Karma Chameleon'. I wasn't alone in that – when Boy George first sang it to the band their response was 'fits of laughter [. . .] Roy and Jon banged kitchen pots and slapped their butts, "Yeehah, Cowboy." '[8] In his autobiography Boy George suggests that Roy's 'insipid' guitar line was his revenge for having to record a song he hated, although he also notes that Roy didn't go as far as returning the royalty cheques.

One of the reasons that 'Karma Chameleon' was so irritating was that it was so successful. Because it was so instantly catchy, it didn't take long for it to sound overfamiliar, and that process took a lot less that the six long weeks it spent at Number 1. A similar sort of fate befell Dexys Midnight Runners a year earlier with 'Come On Eileen'. It might be that even reading that title you feel a small groan come over you. So ubiquitous did the record become over the summer of 1982, and so much did it become a staple for every party and disco you went to for the next few years, it's easy for its original charm to get lost beneath the weight of overfamiliarity. Strong is the fan whose liking of the lyrics overcomes that moment, at two minutes forty-five, when the song stops, starts again slow and then speeds up and up as the entire dance floor jumps about, fists in the air.

In singer Kevin Rowland, Dexys boasted a true musical original. This was a man who insisted his band go jogging together in the early morning in order to foster a spirit of group togetherness; a man who at one point banned the press from his concerts, refused to do interviews and instead paid for full-page adverts in the music press in order to give his side of the story. This was a man who didn't feel the band were getting enough money for their debut album, and took the master tapes home with him until the record company agreed to renegotiate the contract.

This was a man, too, who came up with three of the best pop albums of the decade, each with a different style and sound: the first incarnation produced *Searching for the Young Soul Rebels*, a foot-on-the-floor stomping soul record that included the band's rollicking first Number 1, 'Geno'. From a Northern Soul dockers' look, the band returned with *Too-Rye-Ay* wearing an odd combination of dungarees, neckerchiefs and black plimsolls and filled the music with banjos and fiddles. Three years later and it was all change again: *Don't Stand Me Down* went for a preppy American look, no singles and no sales; it's still brilliant, though, in its own awkward, obstinate way.

DO YOU REALLY WANT TO HURT ME

Back in 1982, Dexys Midnight Runners were following up 'Come on Eileen' with 'Jackie Wilson Said'. That's Jackie Wilson as in the 'Reet Petite' soul singer, as opposed to Jocky Wilson, the big-boned darts player. However, as the band mimed along for their *Top of the Pops* performance, there in the background was the unmistakeable image of Jocky's face, grinning out from a large screen. The assumption was that this had been a mistake by the BBC – some wally in the production staff ordering the wrong picture from the stills department. However, Kevin Rowland later claimed it was his idea, and they asked the BBC to do it for a joke: '[The producer] said, "But Kevin, people will think we've made a mistake." I told him only an idiot would think that.'[9] As if on cue, Mike Read had a go about the error on his breakfast show the following morning.

Top of the Pops, with its almost perverse delight in playing a proper band like the Jam next to a one-hit-wonder like Toto Coelo, played a crucial part in my musical education. It wasn't the only music programme on television: Channel 4's *The Tube*, hosted by Jools Holland and Paula Yates, was the first live music programme on British TV since the 1950s. ITV, meanwhile, offered up *The Chart Show*, a one-hour presenter-free programme of music videos, complete with VHS-player graphics (including 'pause' when the adverts came on and 'eject' at the end of the programme). *Top of the Pops*, though, had the history and pedigree that made it a must-watch weekly event.

There was one major difference between the *Top of the Pops* of the eighties and that of previous decades, and that was the arrival of the music video. While the promo was doing its best to gun down the radio star, another group of much-loved individuals found themselves caught in the crossfire: the female dance troupe. This tradition had begun back in the late 1960s with the launch of Pan's People. The group cavorted their way through the glam years until they were replaced by Ruby Flipper in 1976, an attempt by choreographer Flick Colby to introduce male and black dancers into the mix: 'Bill Cotton [seventies producer] called me in to the BBC and said the British public didn't want to see black men dancing with women.'[10] They lasted about six months, succeeded by the all-female Legs & Co.

These dance troupes provided two functions on the programme: firstly, to fill the gap with one of their literal routines when a band couldn't play; and secondly, in their skimpy costumes, to offer something for the dads to ogle (this being a show for all the family). But, with the arrival of video, there was no need for the dancers to come up with a literal interpretation of, say, Shakin' Stevens's 'You Drive Me Crazy' (I'm no dance expert but even I could choreograph that title, word for word). If Shaky couldn't make it to the studio, *Top of the Pops* could show the video instead: Shakin' Stevens could be on the programme without him needing to be on the programme. What's more, however much the archetypal dad might grumble about where those nice girls had gone, the nation actually *wanted* to watch the videos: quite often, they were more exciting than watching the bands mime away half-heartedly in the studio.

Legs & Co. weren't quite the last of the dance troupes. That was Zoo, a multicultural collection of male and female dancers. Zoo, though, had a different line-up for each performance (there was a pool of about twenty dancers), and they were used only sporadically during their brief tenure. The lineage of dancers really ended with Legs & Co.'s last performance, in October 1981. It would be nice to think that this fondly remembered *Top of the Pops* tradition ended on some fitting high note. Ottawan were in the Top 10 that week with 'Hands Up (Give Me Your Heart)': the 'Legs' could have done wonders with that. Dave Stewart and Barbara Gaskin's cover of 'It's My Party' might also have had a little added meaning. Instead, keeping with the *TOTP* formula of mixing the sublime with the ridiculous, Legs & Co. headed out on the latter: their final routine was to 'The Birdie Song' by the Tweets.

Track Seven

Too Shy

When it comes to Scandinavian influence on pop, Denmark has always seemed a bit of a poor relation. Sweden, of course, has long been the market leader thanks to the FABBA Four of Benny, Björn, Agnetha and Anni-Frid, whose chart career ended with 1981's *The Visitors*. By the end of the decade, the Swedish influence in the charts returned in lesser form in the shape of Roxette, a flat-pack piece of peroxide power pop. In between these two Ikea bookends, Norway held up the Scandinavian presence in the charts thanks to Morten, Mags and Pål, the two Nordic hunks and one can of dog food that made up a-ha.

But what of Denmark? I have some inside knowledge of this burgeoning music scene in this otherwise oft-neglected musical backwater of the era. In the days before social media and Skype and all those other modern ways of shrinking the world into one large, overcrowded walnut, the only way for someone growing up to contact people from around the world was to get a pen pal. The scheme I took pat in was set up by my school, and to my teacher's chagrin, *every single one* of my classmates opted for a pen pal from the United States. The thought was that if we got an American pen pal maybe they'd send us an advance videotape of the next series of *Knight Rider*. So our teacher made us put down a second country on the form.

For reasons that are sadly lost in the dry ice of time, I decided to put down Denmark as my non-American choice. Which meant that as well as getting the American pen pal I actually wanted (Chris from Kentucky, with whom I'm still in touch), I started getting airmail letters from a young chap called Stig. Stig hailed from Aarhus, the Danish city that Madness famously sang about in their Top 10 hit. It seems a touch churlish to criticize the quality of Stig's English, given that it was substantially better than my Danish, but it did rather limit our ability to communicate. As a big music fan, I told Stig all about my latest purchases and asked who his particular favourites were. Stig responded with a single-line response: 'I have the one record by the Hot Eyes.'

I had never come across the mysterious Hot Eyes. The only hot things in the chart, as far as I was aware, were of the frothy-chocolate 'It Started with a Kiss' variety or the Level 42 water type. It wasn't until the 1984 Eurovision Song Contest that I finally clapped my own eyes on the Danish duo of Kirsten & Søren. Their number 'Det, Lige Det' was known in Denmark as 'the Swimming Pool song', on account of Kirsten throwing Søren into a swimming pool at the end of the song. Unfortunately, what would have been a memorable Eurovision moment to rival the great Bucks Fizz skirt-rip-off was stymied by the lack of a swimming pool in Luxembourg's Grand Theatre, and Hot Eyes were soundly beaten by the Swedish entry, 'Diggi-loo, Digg-ley'.

Musically, Hot Eyes sounded like they took inspiration from the theme tune to *Going for Gold*. Compared to the musical delights of Duran Duran, Wham!, Spandau Ballet and the Human League, Stig's taste in music seemed somewhat backwards. Stig, however, was as proud of his country's music as I was of mine. To borrow the classic explanation for a band breaking up, we had 'musical differences' and stopped writing to each other as result.

Despite having nothing more to show for their nation's musical ability than a three-times Eurovision failure, Denmark can hold its head high when it comes to its influence on eighties music. It's an influence that comes, bizarrely enough, via another Danish export: bacon. Danish bacon became big in Britain in the late nineteenth century, with 90 per cent of Denmark's pig exports ending up in the UK: it's not surprising that the country spent money advertising their wares. And here's where we come to Denmark's musical contribution to the decade. Because hanging up on the office wall of an executive at Virgin Records was one such Danish advertising poster from the 1920s.

This particular poster depicts a singing chicken stood on top of an upturned plant pot, and a pig leaning over a wall, listening. The owner of this particular poster was part of the team working on a new series of compilation albums, which were in need of a name. (To give you an example of what they were up against, one of the biggest-selling compilations of the year was the Indiana Jones-themed *Raiders of the Pop Charts.*) And, as he glanced around the room for inspiration, said executive noticed the strap line across the top of the poster. This – presumably referring to the match made in heaven that is (Danish) bacon and eggs – read simply: 'Now, that's what I call music'.

Before the launch of the *Now That's What I Call Music* series, compilation albums had always enjoyed a reputation for being a bit naff and low rent. That was primarily due to the long-running *Top of the Pops* series – a collection that was related to the TV show only in that the BBC had forgotten to trademark the name and thus had to allow Pickwick Records to release their compilations under the same banner. The songs bore little resemblance to the actual songs pinging up and down the Top 40. What the unsuspecting listener got instead was an approximation of the original record by a group of session musicians (these included a pre-famous Elton John back in the 1960s). The quality of the compilations was topped off by a record sleeve that boasted the de rigueur seventies 'dolly bird', posing in something appropriately inappropriate like a leopard-skin swimsuit, or yellow leotard and multi-coloured hold-ups.

The *Top of the Pops* albums weren't the only compilations out there before the *Now . . .* albums: K-Tel and Ronco also offered listeners their own low-cost alternatives. As well as 'read the small print' cover versions to be wary of, another pitfall for the unsuspecting record buyer was the reduced length of the tracks included: in order to cram as many hits as possible on to a single disc, you could find your favourite songs fading out after a couple of minutes.

The *Now* . . . albums were a product of the major record labels getting together, rather than that of a small independent. The initial idea came from Virgin Records, who in 1983 had enjoyed a bumper year in terms of hits and were working out ways of making more money out of them. Someone had the brainwave to get together with other record companies to create a double album of songs. Virgin's partner in crime was EMI, who would go on to offer up the bulk of the compilation's tracks, with a smattering of songs brought in from other companies.

The double-album idea was *Now* . . .'s other masterstroke. Rather than having all the hits squeezed on to a low-quality single disc or cassette, the *Now* . . . series played out over two records, offering the listener a value-for-money thirty or so songs. The tape version came in a chunky back-to-back double-cassette pack, with Cassette One behind the front-cover image and Cassette Two nestled in the track listing on the back. The box might not have been a design classic but it felt reassuringly solid and slotted in happily next to the rest of your cassette collection.

Open up the sleeve and inside would be dotted with thumbnail pictures of the artists and the sort of chart-fact titbits to keep the likes of me quiet: Tracey Ullman's 'They Don't Know', for example, 'charted at no.69 on 21st

September 1983 and reached no.2 on 12th October 1983 and was no.2 for 2 weeks'. As the series went on, the information became a little wider ('Mai Tai come from Dutch Guyana and take their name from a cocktail of rum and fruit juice') and was even injected with a little humour (Sister Sledge's risible 'Frankie' was 'not about Paul, Holly, Ped, Mark and Nasher'). For a short while, the sleeves memorably featured the infamous cartoon pig on the front cover (specifically *Now* . . . 3, 4 and 5), exactly the same as the one on the original Danish drawing but sporting a pair of sunglasses. With Brian Glover providing the voiceover on the TV adverts, there followed a pork bellyful of pig-related puns: 'The compilation series that makes the others sound like pork scratchings!' 'thirty-two original chart-hoggin' hits on one piggin' great double album!'

I can only guess that the record companies ran out of bacon jokes, because the pig was dropped for *Now* . . . 6: the series was now defined by the logo of a white lettered N, O and W in red, blue and green circles, 'That's What I Call *Music*' underneath in a zigzag of yellow lightning, and the number of the compilation in a final, usually pink circle. The logo would then be slotted into a pig-free, slightly more upmarket backdrop: for *Now* . . . 6, it was the black inside lining of a jacket, *Now* . . . 7 was dressed up to look like a shopping bag.

The original *Now* . . . album was slightly different in feel: the title, to start with, still featured the comma from the original poster ('Now, That's What I Call Music'). And instead of the pig or later logo, the sleeve was emblazoned by a single huge 'NOW', with the letters filled in by pictures of the artists included. It's fair to say that the original *Now . . .* album had an impressive line-up: eleven of the thirty songs featured were Number 1s, and this in the days when getting to Number 1 meant something (rather cheekily, the sleeve listed the remaining five Number 1s from 1983 that weren't featured). The honour of Cassette One, Side One, Track One went to Phil Collins's 'You Can't Hurry Love', which feels an odd choice even now – it was neither the year's biggest hit nor quite appealing to the album's potential target audience. The topsy-turvy *Top of the Pops* feel continues with Duran Duran's 'Is There Something I Should Know' (which really should have a question mark) and UB40's 'Red Red Wine'. Other noteworthy numbers include Heaven 17's 'Temptation', Men at Work's 'Down Under' and the Rock Steady Crew's '(Hey You) the Rock Steady Crew'.

A number of the artists get more than one song: UB40 return on Cassette Two, Side Three; Culture Club are present with both 'Karma Chameleon' and 'Victims'; Phil Collins returns with Genesis on Cassette Two, Side Four (he even gets two photos on the album sleeve, which is two more than the Cure ('The Love Cats'), Simple Minds ('Waterfront') or New Edition ('Candy Girl'). But no one gets more airtime than one particular band whose members feature on each of the first three sides of the double cassette; a band who, one solo single on *Now . . . 4* aside, would never feature on a *Now . . .* album again. They were, briefly, one of the biggest bands in the UK – and a band with haircuts about as silly as their name.

TOO SHY

Good-looking, talented singer/ songwriter/ frontman, looking for musicians to form what should be a successful band. Influences: Japan, Yazoo, Soft Cell [. . .] no Des O'Connor fans.

It is fair to say that the advert placed by Chris Hamill in *Melody Maker* was not imbued with a sense of modesty. One band who read *Melody Maker* and didn't like Des O'Connor was a group called Art Nouveau. Art Nouveau were a slightly worthy New Romantic outfit from Leighton Buzzard with a slap-bass-driven sound. As it happened, Art Nouveau had put an ad for a lead singer in *Melody Maker* a few weeks earlier, but Chris Hamill hadn't seen it. They needed a lead singer . . . and Chris needed a band: in early-eighties small-ad terms, it was a match waiting to happen.

Upon getting together, both band and singer changed their names: Chris Hamill decided to turn his surname into an anagram, and rearranged the letters to become Limahl. Art Nouveau, meanwhile, rebranded themselves as Kajagoogoo – a name that, it has been suggested, originated from a phonetic spelling of baby-speak (gaga-goo-goo). 'You can't blame me for that one,' Limahl later admitted. 'It was the bass player's idea.' Wherever the name came from, there's no doubt that Kajagoogoo is up there with one of the worst monikers of the decade. There's a theory with band names that what a group decides to call itself is only an issue until they get their first hit. If that's true, Kajagoogoo is perhaps the exception that proves the rule – a fact that even the group later acknowledged by shaving off the 'googoo' to become Kaja.

Kajagoogoo's big break came thanks to Limahl's evening job as a waiter at the Embassy Club on London's Old Bond Street. On one particular night, Limahl found himself serving champagne to Duran Duran's Nick Rhodes and his manager. As he poured Nick his champagne, he managed to smooth-talk the Duran keyboardist into taking home the band's demo tape. Rhodes not only listened to the tape but also liked it and passed it on to his record company. And not only that: he offered his services as a producer for the band too.

The result was Kajagoogoo's debut single, 'Too Shy', which went to Number 1 – something that at that point Nick Rhodes's own band had not managed themselves. It was also by far the group's most successful record (it reached Number 5 in the US) with an accompanying video featuring the band going back in time and playing at a dance to celebrate the end of the Second World War (the bit where the returning soldiers told the band to pull themselves together and get some bloody haircuts was presumably left on the cutting-room floor). The song is the band in microcosm: there's that long slow Brit-funk beginning, all built around Nick Beggs's bass-playing. Then in comes Limahl, all teenage-girl-teasing, telling the female listener to come nearer and not be so shy about things. As it turned out, there were plenty of teenage girls who would have liked nothing more than to go 'eye to eye' with Limahl. Limahl, as his *Melody Maker* advert put it, was good-looking – prime *Just Seventeen*-poster material. This despite having the sort of haircut that suggested the barber had run out of dye halfway through, leaving it look-ing as though a seagull had crapped on top of his mullet.

The problem was that the band had loftier ideas, both musically and lyrically. Their debut album's title track, 'White Feathers', refers to First World War pacifists (who were handed feathers as a sign of their cowardice in not fight-ing): 'Frayo', meanwhile, tackled the imposition of martial law in Poland. It wasn't all politics: how many other bands of the era wrote a song called (and about) 'Ergonomics'? Musically the group had similar pretensions. In some ways bass guitarist Nick Beggs was simply too good at playing his instrument. This led to the band's default mode of a Leighton Buzzard funk workout, with Beggs giving it some serious low-note virtuosity.

You can hear the discrepancy on the concert Kajagoogoo recorded for the BBC at the Hammersmith Apollo in May 1983. There are the teenage girls screaming en masse (and occasionally fainting) at the sight of Limahl in his trade-mark yellow singlet. And there are the band, struggling to make themselves heard with their set opener 'Kajagoogoo', a muso-level instrumental number with Limahl doing little more than occasionally spelling out the band's name into the microphone. Despite the fact that the hits kept coming ('Ooh to be Ah', 'Hang On Now'), the band decided that the way to shed their poppy image was to jettison their good-looking lead singer. I don't want to talk about white feathers, but . . . Rather than telling Limahl in person, the group instead got their manager to ring him up and tell him. 'It was like a knife in the heart,' Limahl told VH1 many years later, 'because I felt so instrumental in the success of the group [. . .] It was me who met Nick Rhodes; I was part of the songwriting, was so integral.'

There was, however, room for only one strange eighties haircut in the band. Nick Beggs, whose blond bird's nest was finished off with a curtain rail of beads at the back, took over singing duties. Removing Limahl certainly worked in shedding the band's teenage fans. Unfortunately, it also served to shed the rest of the band's following. Subsequent Kajagoogoo and Kaja albums failed to sell and the group split up. Beggs went on to form Ellis, Beggs and Howard; he ditched the haircut and the music sounded half decent, but by this point no one was listening. The same was true for Limahl, who had one bona fide hit with 'Never Ending Story' but whose musical career was quite the opposite.

It's not often than one finds a touch of poignancy on the cover of *Now That's What I Call Music* album, but in this particular case there is. In the middle of the letter 'N', beneath Paul Young and Howard Jones and above UB40, stand a Limahl-less Kajagoogoo. As far away as it is possible to be, at the top right of the letter 'W', sits Limahl. While Kajagoogoo are looking out at the record buyer, coolly confident and assured, Limahl's expression is a pout that is probably meant to be sexy but comes across as more than a little cheesed off with being dumped. Musical differences within a single album cover, then, with the letter 'O' foursome of Genesis, Madness, Rod Stewart and Tracey Ullman between them to keep the peace.

*　　*　　*

If, as been suggested, the eighties was a great decade for singles as opposed to albums, then the success of the *Now That's What I Call Music* series is proof of that. The series is still more than going strong: appropriately enough, it's heading into the eighties. *Now . . . 81* is the most recent UK release at the time of writing; worldwide, sales of *Now* albums are now over the 200 million mark. That's a track record comparable with the likes of Pink Floyd and the Rolling Stones. Indeed, so successful did these singles compilations become that when *Now . . . 10* stopped Madonna reaching Number 1 in 1987 it was decided that the albums should be given their own chart. Before the shift, *Now . . . 1* to *10* had spent fifty-one weeks at Number 1 in the album chart – basically a whole year at the top during a four-year period. And they would certainly have gone on to dominate in a similar way: the series' biggest seller to date wasn't until 1999, when *Now . . . 44* shifted 2.3 million copies (just as the actual charts reached their nadir, too – go figure).

Not that the *Now . . .* albums had it all their own way. When the other major record companies saw the success of the compilations, it didn't take them long to get together to produce their own alternatives. The result was CBS and WEA's *Hits* albums, which went head to head with *Now . . .* until the end of the eighties. Unlike *Now . . .*'s chunky double-cassette box, the *Hits* series (Volume One of which was called, a little confusingly, *The Hits Album* and *The Hits Tape*) oscillated between having two separate cassette boxes and a larger, thinner single box in which the cassettes sat side by side (and which unhelpfully stuck out on the shelf). This inconsistency continued with a car crash of different designs for each collection, with no defining logo let alone a funky pig wearing sunglasses. They did at least look better than Chrysalis, MCA and Polygram's short-lived *Out Now!* Series, though. This went for the worst of both the rival boxes by having a *Hits*-style double box that spilt in two and opened like a pair of double doors.

If the *Hits* series didn't have the snappy style, branding and title of the *Now . . .* series, it could for a while make up for this by offering a strong rival selection of artists. At the height of their battle, the strengths of the compilations depended on how well the respective record companies had done over the previous six months or so: Virgin and EMI had enjoyed a great 1983, so had a bumper selection of hits to choose from. CBS and WEA, meanwhile, could bring, among others, Madonna, Prince, Bruce Springsteen, Michael Jackson and George Michael to the table. They were a bit better at sequencing, too, in shoving all the ballads (out of the way?) on to one side, whereas the *Now . . .* habit was to dole them out at the end of each side. In the long run, however, the better branding of the *Now . . .* albums won out, and 1989's *Hits 10* (Pat and Mick, the Funky Worm) was the last of the series.

The *Now . . .* albums and their rivals were part of growing up in the eighties: like most people, I bought them for a specific time period and then stopped (for me it was *Now . . .*s 3 to 7, and *Hits 1* to 5). I think what happened at that point, as I got a bit older, was that my musical tastes started to diverge from what was on the compilations, and I started buying albums by bands I liked rather than compilations of music that had me fast-forwarding past every third song. That and the fact that I got a tape-to-tape player and started making my own compilations instead.

Track Eight

Thriller

If you thought choosing Showaddywaddy as my first single was embarrassing enough, you should probably look away as I tell you about my time in the Cub Scouts. I was, in my formative years, an enthusiastic member of this strange, Rudyard Kipling-themed organization for young boys. Each Tuesday night I would don my uniform – green top, grey shorts, neckerchief held in place by that all-important woggle – and promise to dib dib dob and do my duty to God and to the Queen. The leader of the pack was not the one that the Shangri-Las had sung about but instead was Akela, a grown man pretending to be some sort of wolf.

The highlight of being a Cub was 'camp', where one would go and sleep out under the stars and fail to make a fire out of bracken and damp twigs. For us this invariably meant a trip to the 'Snowball Plantation', a Scout-owned bit of woodland about five miles out of York. Here we'd set up tents in sites called Warren or Glen, and be invited to make our own fun to entertain the pack around the campfire: to use the technical term, a 'gang show'.

My memory of who my three partners in crime were on one particular night is lost in the mists of time. But, as the previous act stood down to muted applause, the four of us stood up, ready for our turn. Earlier that afternoon, as we'd debated what our offering should be, someone suggested that we recreate the dance of a famous eighties Number 1. Which was how I came to be stood there, in front of the campfire, holding a twig that was meant to be a microphone and wearing a towel as a skirt . . .

One of my formative musical memories, and there's no way round admitting this, was of Bucks Fizz winning the Eurovision Song Contest in May 1981. The Eurovision Song Contest, as you might imagine, was something that appealed to my inner musical Motty; another chance to jot down numbers and get excited about collecting statistics. Not only that, but this had an international element too: it was like the winners of *It's a Knockout* going on to compete in *Jeux Sans Frontières*, or Brian Clough's Nottingham Forest competing in the European Cup.

It was also a musical event that united the whole family. For my parents, there were the reassuring witticisms of Terry Wogan to guide them through the evening. There was the chance for them to wax lyrical about past Eurovisions as well: Sandie Shaw winning with 'Puppet on a String'; Cliff Richard being robbed with 'Congratulations' (they were right about the robbing, by the way: years later it was alleged that the Spanish winner, Massiel's 'La, La, La', had been helped to victory by some extracurricular arm twisting from her slightly-right-of-centre president, Francisco Franco).

By the start of the 1980s, the prerequisite for winning the competition had moved away from entering the safer end of the swinging-sixties singing pool and instead preferring the double-couple foursome of two boys and two girls. ABBA, of course, were the starting point of this, thanks to their 1972 victory with 'Waterloo' – still by some distance the finest song written about a mainline British railway station. ABBA were so good that they would no doubt have become a global success even without entering the competition – hey, even *my* sixties-obsessed parents had their greatest-hits collection. It wasn't long before the bestowing of credibility switched sides: the Eurovision win had initially given ABBA credibility; now ABBA's success bestowed credibility on Eurovision.

Following up on the boy-girl-foursome formula were the Brotherhood of Man, a perhaps overly masculine name considering that 50 per cent of the group were female. The Brotherhood had been Britain's last success in the competition, in 1976, with their 'Save Your Kisses for Me', a winking, thumbs-aloft number with a sickly sucker-punch in the final line for those bothering to pay attention to the lyrics: it wasn't a love song after all! He was singing to his three-year-old child! How they must have rolled their eyes in Reykjavik and gone 'Aww' in Oslo. But there was to be precious little 'Money Money Money' for the Brotherhood of Man, whose musical career was quickly given the kiss-off. Perhaps their lack of success was why the British turned away from what was clearly the winning formula. The following year, we sent in Lynsey de Paul singing the aptly named 'Rock Bottom'.

In 1981, however, it was time to try the two-by-two formula again. Bucks Fizz were put together by husband-and-wife team Nichola Martin and Andy Hill. The Bucks were Bobby G and Mike Nolan, two cheerful, smiling chappies topped with the sort of mop of blond hair that makes you think, 'That reminds me, I really must clean the kitchen floor.' The Fizz, meanwhile, were Cheryl Baker and Jay Aston. Cheryl was the sort of fresh-faced, clean-living girl-next-door type who could have been a children's TV presenter (she later became co-host of Roy Castle's *Record Breakers*). She also had Eurovision experience, having been part of Co-Co, Britain's entry in 1978. Aston, meanwhile, fulfilled that important role of being the fanciable, slightly dirty one – a baton later passed on to Geri Halliwell in the Spice Girls and Sarah Harding in Girls Aloud. Such a chord did Aston's looks strike with the young boys of Britain that even in 1984, long after the Fizz had gone decidedly flat, she was still being voted fourth most fanciable female in the *Smash Hits* Readers' Poll.

The fact that Bucks Fizz were chosen as Britain's entry was something of a surprise at the time. Sure, there was some absolute crap they were up against in the Song for Europe competition. The nadir of which was probably a band called Headache. Headache's song – and I'm using the word 'song' in the loosest possible sense – was called 'Don't Forget Your Ticket', a lyric whose sole message seemed to be to emphasize just how imperative it was not to attempt to travel without the right documentation.

'Making Your Mind Up', by contrast, was a tuneful, if more throwaway number. Even its writer, Andy Hill, considered it more of a commercial than a proper song. The song had a flavour of rockabilly to it, chiming with the 'blink and you'll miss it' rock-and-roll revival of the time: artists like the Stray Cats and Shakin' Stevens, the supposed 'Welsh Elvis' who scored wobbly-kneed Number 1s with 'Green Door' and 'This Ole House'. Although Hill dismissed the song, it was (a) commercial twice over: unashamedly populist and easy on the ear, it was also instantly catchy – handy in a competition where the judges are going to hear the record only once.

The reason that Bucks Fizz beat Headache, then went on to beat Germany by a whisker and every other entrant at that year's competition in Dublin was not that they had the best song. It wasn't because they did the best performance, either – at the Eurovision Song Contest itself, some of the singing was about as wobbly as a set from *Neighbours*. Instead, it was because of the moment that everyone remembers when they hear the name Bucks Fizz: it was this moment that scored itself on retinas across the continent and resulted in competition success.

Halfway through the final verse, after all that endless talk about speeding up and slowing down, the unintentional innuendos about being taken from behind by your 'indecision', whatever that was meant to mean, Bobby and Mike reached down for Cheryl and Jay's red and green ra-ra skirts; and, at the end of the line about seeing some *more*, off came the skirts with a theatrical swish, revealing a matching set of miniskirts and two pairs of what TV presenters could still get away with calling a 'lovely set of pins' without having to raise an accompanying eyebrow in irony.

As dance moves go, it's not exactly Fred and Ginger. It lacks the wow factor of a moonwalk, or the neck-breaking potential of a top-class breakdance. And yet, at the same time, in its low-key British way, it is spectacularly, memorably good. So memorable, in fact, that credit for the move has been claimed by a number of different sources (take your pick from choreographer Chrissie Whickham, Cheryl Baker, Jay Aston and band manager Nichola Martin). So memorable that it became part of British culture, and I found myself recreating the dance routine at Cub camp a couple of years later, having my towel 'skirt' ripped off to a round of applause.

The British might have contributed much to music in the early eighties in terms of sound and style. However, the fact that the Bucks Fizz skirt routine was an early-eighties highlight says much about the quality of our dance routines. For most of the time we got away with our inherent lack of rhythm: the New Romantics and synthpop movement allowed many of the new generation of pop stars the opt-out option of standing behind their keyboard and looking intently serious instead. When the British did step out, the results were often shambolic: a professionally amateurish, amateurishly professional choice of routines.

The stock-in-trade dance style was that employed by Bananarama and Susan Ann Sulley and Joanne Catherall from the Human League: the shuffling, side-by-side sway of the provincial nightclub. Phil Oakey was not over-complimentary about his fellow Human Leaguers – 'Susan Ann flails about like an octopus and Joanne's completely out of time,' he supportively told *Smash Hits* – but that, in a way, was their charm. Bananarama, too, offered that same sort of grumpy, strumpet-y side-to-side shuffle, the girl in the club who was dancing with her mates and could tell the man in the waistcoat to bugger off out of it at forty paces.

Not, of course, that I was frequenting nightclubs at my age. The sticky-floor delights that York had to offer – Ziggys and Toffs – would have to wait. Instead, there was either the dreaded school disco or the sort of birthday party for which an overambitious parent hired out a church hall, decorated it with a couple of token balloons and brought in a local DJ who thought he was Bruno Brookes in waiting. My resounding memory of these events was the sheer emptiness of the hall as Modern Romance's 'Ay Ay Ay Ay Moosey' boomed around us and a fug of adolescent awkwardness pinned everyone's backs against the walls.

Such a deadlock would be broken by one of two things. Firstly, by one of the boys initiating a sliding competition, where he would run the full diagonal of the hall before sliding to an impressive or more likely burn-inducing pose into the corner. The other was when the DJ gave up trying to convince the partygoers that they really should be listening to Shalamar and dusted down one of the several novelty dance records that was guaranteed to get everyone up and joining in.

The British loved a novelty dance routine in the eighties. We couldn't help ourselves. Take the Gap Band, for example. A perfectly reasonable, fairly inoffensive funk band, whose nine-minute workout 'I Don't Believe You Want to Get Up and Dance' had been edited down into the international hit 'Oops Upside Your Head'. All around the world, people were happy to shuffle along to its gentle Parliament-meets-Shalamar groove. But not in Britain, oh no. In a routine whose origins are unclear (it has been suggested it began at a holiday camp on the Isle of Wight), British listeners would respond to the song by rushing to sit down in lines and proceeding to row along in time to the music. Apparently (and again this is unconfirmed, but I'm leaving it in as it is such a lovely image), when the Gap Band toured the UK, they watched in utter bemusement as they struck up the song and the audience started sitting down in rows. After all, it's not as if the song has anything whatsoever to do with rowing, boats or water.

Having got his audience warmed up, our local DJ would keep them going by pulling out 'The Birdie Song' by the Tweets: a memorably irritating number that spent thirty years incubating on the continent as 'Vogerltanz' before being exported to the UK in 1981. In fact, it was imported several times over as, in something akin to a novelty-record gold rush, several groups released versions to capitalize on that summer's dance craze among peeling Brits on holiday in Torremolinos. Somewhere along the line someone added lyrics to the song, which aren't on the record but which everyone knows: 'With a little bit of that / A little bit of this / And shake your bum . . .' (the latter guaranteeing a giggle at the pre-teenage parties I went to).

One of the acts who attempted to capitalize on 'The Birdie Song' was Busby, a group named after the *Rhubarb and Custard*-style cartoon bird that British Telecom used in its adverts at the time. Busby, it turns out, was a pseudonym for the local DJ's star turn: the triple-record medley of dance naffness that are the three Top 10 hits of Black Lace. I'm rather embarrassed to admit that this most heavyweight of musical outfits hail from Yorkshire and were, at the height of punk, voted Yorkshire band of the year by BBC Radio Leeds. Yorkshire's embarrassment quickly became a national one, as the group were chosen to represent Britain in the 1979 Eurovision Song Contest.

The 'Lace' might have been pipped in their attempts to cash in on 'Vogerltanz', but continued to cast their net around the continent for more dances they could bring back to Britain. In 1983, the band (now twosome Colin Routh and Alan Barton, who looked like a painter-decorator version of Limahl) hit pay dirt with their Top 10 version of 'Gioca Jouer', a 1981 hit for Italian DJ Claudio Cecchetto. Rechristened 'Superman', the song boasts less of dance routine as a dance rout, with participants carrying out a somewhat random selection of actions such as pretending to ski, spraying on deodorant and ringing the doorbell – all accompanied by Black Lace telling you, without any trace of irony, how good you were looking.

The following year, Black Lace found further continental inspiration with their version of Michel Delancray and Mya Simille's 1971 song 'Agadou'. A bit like 'Vogerltanz', the song had been pushing its 'L'ananas' around Europe for years: Black Lace discovered it in, of all places, the Pink Coconut nightclub in Derby (these days the naughtily named Destiny and Elite) where the bar staff had come up with their own dance routine to the song. The band's manager, John Wagstaff, noticed the audience participation to the record, and got his group in the studio pronto to record it.

'Agadoo' became the ubiquitous sound of the summer in 1984, with only George Michael's 'Careless Whisper' volunteering to stop it from reaching Number 1 (the song did go on to grace the top spot, sort of, thanks to Spitting Image's parody, 'The Chicken Song'). It is a mark of the time, and its popularity, that the band turned up on ITV's show *TV-AM*, where fitness instructor Mad Lizzie, adapted the actions into her early-morning keep-fit routine. These days, everyone can't fall over themselves quick enough to say how much they hate the song, regularly voting it at the top of those 'worst songs of all time' lists that clog up E4 and BBC3 on Bank Holiday weekends. I can't quite bring myself to say 'to be fair to Black Lace', but it's worth pointing out that the song sold seven million records worldwide, so *someone* went out and bought it. As much as we might laugh at Black Lace, Black Lace have laughed all the way the bank for years.

For what it's worth, the original French lyric of the song has a slightly different feel. It tells of a holiday to Tahiti, where the singer comes across a ukulele-playing girl selling a selection of beautiful fruits. Whether these fruits are actual fruits or 'fruits', the singer can't help himself from sampling her 'apples'. Whereupon he is thrown in jail, and has to pay the girl's father for all his 'pears' and 'pineapples' in order to be let out. If you go to Tahiti, the singer ruefully concludes, beware of ukulele girls offering beautiful fruit – only a fool would go there. Somewhere along the line, something got lost in the translation. What was once a playful take on holiday romances has now morphed into the slightly-less-subtle sight of people running about the stage in giant pineapple and banana costumes.

A few months after 'Agadoo' had dominated the summer-holiday season, Black Lace returned with their final Top 10 hit in time for the Christmas-party season. 'Do the Conga' did exactly what it says on the record sleeve, exhorting everyone on the dance floor to form some sort of human train, flicking out legs left and right. The conga was a bit like the Mexican Wave of early-eighties school discos: the pressure to join in was all but irresistible, for fear of looking like you'd had a fun bypass if you didn't. There would come a tipping point when simply *everyone* would join in, swinging round the dance floor, and out through the kitchen into the car park and down the street, leaving the local DJ standing alone on the stage, as at the beginning of the evening, playing his Shalamar records to no one but himself.

* * *

In New York, rather than old York, the dance scene was in somewhat different shape. Rather than broken-English dance routines, the in-thing was instead the upcoming culture of breakdancing. The term comes from the instrumental breaks in the music, looped over and over by the DJ, during which a dancer could strut their stuff. It began in the Bronx in the late 1970s with 'B-Boying', with dancers creating moves to accompany the nascent hip-hop scene. As the scene became bigger, the media began lumping B-Boying with other similar styles of dancing, such as popping, locking and electric boogaloo, which originated elsewhere (California) and to different types of music (funk) and just called the lot by the single generic term.

For someone such as myself, who thought he had this dancing thing licked with his pineapple-pushing moves and dreams of one day ripping off Jay Aston's skirt, breakdancing was something of a shock to the system. Suddenly there was a whole array of 'power moves' to get my head round, called things like jackhammers, windmills and turtles. There seemed quite a preponderance of flinging oneself against the floor and spinning round at breakneck or possibly neck-break speed. Popping and locking, meanwhile, seemed more to be built around looking as though you'd just dislocated a joint and then popped it back in again – or just dislocating a joint, if someone like myself tried it. On the whole, it seemed safer all round to watch the films on the big screen – *Breakin'* and *Breakin' 2: Electric Boogaloo* – and let the experts get on with it.

The other early-eighties dance craze, often imitated and never got close to, was the moonwalk. Although the step has existed in various guises over the years – Cab Calloway and Marcel Marceau both danced something similar – for most people its association starts and ends with Michael Jackson, who, to screams and cheers, employed it during his performance of 'Billie Jean' at the 1983 concert to celebrate twenty-five years of Motown. Quite why the step is called the moonwalk is a little unclear: if it was replicating an actual moonwalk, then Michael Jackson would have been jumping about in slow motion around the stage. Which, let's face it, would not have looked quite so cool as the illusion of walking forwards and sliding backwards at the same time.

When it came to dance in the eighties, Michael Jackson was the man by quite some distance. The impact of his album *Thriller*, and the accompanying videos for 'Billie Jean', 'Beat It' and the title track, is difficult to quantify. 'The album is the eventual sequel to what Epic Records rightly describe as his landmark LP *Off the Wall*,' *Smash Hits* told its readers, 'which was released in 1979 and went on to sell a staggering total of seven million copies worldwide. A hard act to follow.' The follow up to this 'hard act to follow' has since sold in the region of 110 million copies.

Numbers though, should never be seen as the story itself (unless you're the chap in finance with the calculator): far better, I think, to take those colossal sales as a reflection of Jackson's talent, and the effect he had on everyone who saw and heard him. It is the combination of his voice and his dance moves that is crucial to understanding Michael

Jackson's success. For whereas the original 'British Invasion' videos that dominated MTV were all about fashion and haircuts, advertising clichés and breaking glass, Jackson upped the ante by bringing in a bit of Broadway: in came the choreography, the banks of dancers and the routines. After the *Thriller* videos, singing your song and looking good was not enough.

It seems remarkable now – and so remarkable that the station have disputed it – but when MTV were shown the video for 'Billie Jean' they initially turned it down, in an echo of seventies AOR-radio thinking, on the grounds that it wasn't for their demographic. 'I screamed blue murder,' Walter Yetnikoff, Jackson's label boss, wrote in his auto-biography, *Howling at the Moon*. 'They argued that their format, white rock, excluded Michael's music. I argued they were racist assholes – and I'd trumpet it to the world if they didn't relent. I've never been more forceful [. . .] threatening to pull *all* our videos. With added pressure from [Jackson's producer] Quincy Jones, they caved in.'

Whatever the truth of that, the result was that 'Billie Jean' was one of the biggest (and one of the best) videos MTV have ever shown. The video was directed by Steve Barron, whose film for the Human League's 'Don't You Want Me' had impressed Jackson. It was Barron's idea for the Yellow Brick Road-style pavement, with every stone lighting up as Jackson stepped on it, and everything he touched glowing in Midas fashion. The song itself had its origins in Jackson's experiences with one of his early crazed fans, who claimed that Jackson was not only her lover but also the father of one of her twins. According to Daryl Hall, it also has its origins in Hall and Oates's 'I Can't Go for That' – in 2009, he told *Rolling Stone* that during the making of 'We Are the World' Jackson admitted to borrowing the song's bass line. Maybe Quincy Jones wasn't a big Hall and Oates fan, because Jackson's erstwhile producer was initially not a huge fan of 'Billie Jean', especially the thirty seconds at the beginning before the vocals come: he felt the start was 'so long you could shave to it'. Jackson's instinct, though, won out. 'That's the jelly,' he said of the introduction. 'That's what makes me want to dance.'

The fact that Michael Jackson dances alone in 'Billie Jean', the fact that everything he touches lights up, feels symbolic. This is a man, the video says, who is special and unique: this man is a star. Having established that, the subsequent videos, 'Beat It' and 'Thriller' went for the big-budget, crowd-scene approach. 'Beat It' was a song written in response to Quincy Jones's desire for a 'My Sharona'-type song on the album: with Eddie Van Halen called in to set off some guitar pyrotechnics, the song was the sort of rock-crossover number that must have pleased MTV no end, and likewise widened Jackson's appeal still further. The video is often taken as a nod to *West Side Story*, but the inspiration in fact comes from a story told to the promo's director, Bob Giraldi, when he was working in a factory as a teenager – 'of a fight [. . .] in the Bronx between two gang leaders, who ended up tying their wrists together and killing each other.'[1]

Just as Eddie Van Halen brings an edge to the song with his guitar solo, so the video also sparkles with a frisson of danger. Jackson insisted on using real members of the LA street gangs, the Crips and the Bloods, who by the end of the first day of shooting were so close to kicking off that the second day's dance sequence had to be done there and then. When Jackson had his wrist bound with the rival gang leader, Vincent Paterson, the pair found on the director's call of 'Action' that the fake knives they thought they were using had in fact been swapped for real ones.

So successful were 'Billie Jean' and 'Beat It' that MTV stumped up hundreds of thousands of dollars for the budget of 'Thriller' – the only time they have paid for a video (the money was nominally for the accompanying *The Making of Thriller* film, to stop other record companies coming cap in hand). If some of the early music videos had copied from advertising techniques, 'Thriller' was the genre heading for Hollywood, with an A-grade director on board (John Landis, whose previous work included *The Blues Brothers*, *Trading Places* and *An American Werewolf in London*) and a fourteen-minute length that was more mini-movie than pop promo.

Its showing on TV was every bit an event. For someone my age, it had everything – a great song, a great video and a helping of what these days the censors would call 'mild peril' – enough to make a ten-year-old from York jump, at any rate. In a way, the Michael Jackson in the video is similar to the one in 'Billie Jean': once again, the motif is that he's different to normal people, except this time in a zombie rather than Midas manner. That final shot of the video, where he tells his girlfriend (played by former *Playboy* model Ola Ray) everything is OK before turning to the camera with yellow eyes, is a both wonderful and spooky image to close on.

There are 'what if' stories that accompany any success and *Thriller* is no exception. To start with, the title track of the album was originally called 'Starlight'. You can find a version without too much trouble on the Internet, if you want a listen: it was written by Rod Temperton, a songwriter who grew up in, of all places, Cleethorpes; Quincy Jones wasn't quite happy with the title, and told him to come up with something else. Another factor is the timing of the album along with the existence of a fledgling TV music station: Jackson made MTV, and MTV made Jackson. If that hadn't been around, and people hadn't seen him dance, then *Thriller* may well have had an impact closer to that of *Off the Wall*. Indeed, strip away the videos and, although the production might have been bigger, and the contributors more A-list, I'm not convinced that *Thriller* is actually a better album than its predecessor: both have four or five killer songs accompanied by an equal amount of guff. And at least *Off the Wall* doesn't include 'The Girl is Mine', another of Paul McCartney's toe-curling eighties duets.

By 1983, though, it wasn't just about the music: it was about the complete package – and that's what Michael Jackson had. No pop star was naturally more talented as a dancer, and no one else could take full advantage of the visual medium in quite the same way. Re-watching the videos now, I'm struck by how technically brilliant the dances are but also by how curiously sexless they are at the same time. Steve Barron describes how Jackson came up with the routines by dancing in front the mirror, and there is an element of that throughout his moves. The stars that came in his wake, notably Prince and Madonna, danced for the viewer: they looked out at who was watching, and danced for them rather than for themselves. There might be an element here of looking back from a culture that has become more sexualized and judging Jackson's routines accordingly. But even within the beauty of Jackson's genius lies the genus of a confused and troubled soul.

There is a well-known philosophical conundrum that comes in various forms, but is most commonly known as the Ship of Theseus. In this problem, posited by the thinker Plutarch, the ship sailed by the legendary Minotaur-slaying character has got a couple of decaying planks. These are replaced, perhaps not unreasonably (no one likes a boat with a hole in it) with a couple of shiny new ones. But what happens when a couple more planks are replaced, and then some more? Is the mixture of new and old planks still Theseus's ship? What if all the planks are replaced by new ones? Or what if all the planks are replaced by new ones, and then – as suggested centuries later by Thomas Hobbes – all the old discarded planks are nailed together to create another boat? Which, at this point, is the real Ship of Theseus?

Many years after they last graced the chart (1986's 'New Beginning' turning out to be something of a false dawn) Bucks Fizz have transformed themselves from Eurovision-winning pop act into a modern day Ship of Theseus. The planks in this case are the various members – fifteen in all – who over the past three decades have come and gone through this particular revolving door. By the late noughties there were not one but two Bucks Fizzes out there. One version, the equivalent of Theseus's original boat with some new planks added, contained the founder member Bobby G. Then there was another version, a sort-of-new boat but containing some founding planks: this group were calling themselves the Original Bucks Fizz and featured the other three members of the Eurovision winning line-up – Mike Nolan, Cheryl Baker and Jay Aston.

At one point in the 1990s, the line-up briefly featured David Van Day, formerly the male half of the far better Dollar. Van Day left and, with the man he'd originally replaced, formed a rival Bucks Fizz outfit: 'Bucks Fizz starring Mike Nolan and co-starring David Van Day'. The reason I mention this particular version is because Van Day's outfit came up with the idea of reinventing the band's famous skirt-ripping routine. Instead of just taking the female members' skirts off with a knowing Eurovision wink, why not rip off their tops, too? The reason why not is that the resulting routine is somewhat tawdry and only a wardrobe malfunction away from something even more unpleasant.

Anything this offshoot of Bucks Fizz could do, however, Black Lace could sully still further. Here there was a similar revolving door of band line-ups, one of which decided to rewrite and rerecord ruder versions of the group's greatest hits. The result was the Black Lace *Blue Album*, which I can only hope no Joni Mitchell fan has had the misfortune to pick up by mistake. For however much you might have groaned when 'Agadoo' came on the radio, and found the song still going round your head at three in the morning, at least it was preferable to its rewritten cousin, 'Have a Screw'. For all your gnashing of teeth when the DJ at the party put on 'Do the Conga', be grateful he never played 'Do the Condom' instead. And, for sheer awfulness, I sincerely hope that your ears never come across the explicit version of 'Superman', with no sense of irony now rechristened 'Supercock', which comes complete with the sort of hand actions best carried out in the privacy of your own bedroom.

An explicit version of a cheesy dance hit is probably about as sad as you can get, in one sense of the word. The other type of sadness – true, proper sadness – is reserved for real stars, and for moments like the death of Michael Jackson in 2010. It might seem incongruous to switch from someone like Black Lace to the man who wrote, sang and danced 'Thriller', but the juxtaposition is everything: the Grand Canyon of a contrast between a rubbishy routine that even someone as two-footed as I can manage and the effortless, liquid steps of a born dancer.

Yes, Michael Jackson might have ended up as 'wacko' as Black Lace were 'wacky'. And yes, had he made his comeback in 2010 it would probably have been the solo equivalent of having several members of the original line-up missing. But no one can take away his moment of early eighties magic, a Fred Astaire for the MTV generation, his footsteps forever lighting up the pavement in luminescent gold.

Track Nine

Club Tropicana

In *The Wizard of Oz* the adventure begins when Kansas farm girl Dorothy gets knocked unconscious by a window frame blown in by a tornado, her house gets picked up by the storm and lands down in the land of Oz, killing the Wicked Witch of the East in the process. What also happens is that when Dorothy and Toto open their front door the film changes from its original sepia-tinted black and white to sparkly, shiny, glorious Technicolor. It sort of has to: 'Follow the shade-of-grey-brick road' just doesn't have the same ring to it, does it?

A similar sort of journey took place with the music press. Before the eighties, music journalism was also predominantly carried out in black and white. This was the era of the 'inkies' – the music weeklies of the *New Musical Express*, *Sounds*, *Melody Maker* and *Record Mirror*. In the mid-1970s, the *NME* and *Melody Maker* were the market leaders, each selling about 170,000–180,000 issues a week. The *NME* figures, though, were on the rise after having been much lower earlier in the decade, and having brought in new writers such as Nick Kent and Ian MacDonald. These are (or, sadly, in the case of Ian MacDonald, were) great music writers: MacDonald would go on to write *Revolution in the Head*, the Beatles book that makes most music writing read like the Rutles; Nick Kent, whose finest pieces are collected in the equally wonderful *My Dark Stuff*, would write huge and erudite essay-length discussions on everything from hanging out with Keith Richards to the disappointment of meeting his hero, Brian Wilson. This was serious rock journalism, befitting an audience that regularly voted Led Zeppelin as best band in the end-of-year polls. Then came the 'tornado' in the shape of punk rock. The *NME* wrote an advert asking for 'hip young gunslingers' – who duly arrived in the shape of Julie Burchill and Tony Parsons. A mixture of these new writers and 'getting' punk (eventually) led to the magazine increasing its readership: by the end of the 1970s, the *NME* was selling 200,000 copies to the *Melody Maker*'s 140,000.

But, for all the gusto that the *NME* was showing in the late 1970s, the Technicolor music press was coming. In 1978, former *NME* man Nick Logan set up a new, full-colour music monthly. The first edition of the magazine featured a now obscure pop star on the front called Plastic Bertrand. It also offered readers a poster of John Travolta and the lyrics of various chart hits by the likes of Clout and

A Taste of Honey. The publishers of the magazine debated between two different names for their new product: one was *Disco Fever*; the other, as I'm sure you guessed, was *Smash Hits*.

Nick Logan wasn't the editor of *Smash Hits* for long (heading off to set up another glossy, full-colour, and equally influential monthly magazine, the *Face*). But the magazine he left behind went from strength to strength. The switch was made from monthly release to a regular fortnightly edition, out each other Wednesday, and by 1983 each issue was selling 400,000 copies: more than the *NME*, *Melody Maker*, *Sounds* and *Record Mirror* combined. At its peak, *Smash Hits* would sell just under 800,000 copies a fortnight, and would be as part of cultural furniture of the eighties as, say, *Heat* magazine was in the noughties.

So what was this success about? The colour certainly had something to do with it: the eighties was very much a visual decade in terms of music – the fashion, the good-looking bands, the videos. *Smash Hits* as a magazine was able to make the most of this. For a teenage music fan, it offered a complete kit to support your favourite band: posters to put on the wall, the lyrics to their latest songs, reviews of their albums and interviews with the group. But what the magazine also offered was a different style to the other music papers: rather than the seriousness of an *NME* or *Melody Maker*, *Smash Hits* offered a less critical, more irreverent approach to music. Pop, it decided, was both fun and inherently a little bit ridiculous, and should be treated accordingly.

CLUB TROPICANA

This was a magazine unafraid to ask the questions no one else was asking. Questions like: 'What colour is January?' (Red, according to Wayne Hussey of the Mission); 'Are you any good at marbles?' (Fish from Marillion wasn't, but he wasn't bad at basketball); 'Does your mother play golf?' (The Pet Shop Boys' Neil Tennant's mum did, and was ladies' captain of her club); and 'Have you ever considered posing in the nude?' (Nick Heyward from Haircut One Hundred would do so for £39.50 a session).

This was a magazine with its own language. Bands whose career was on the skids were 'down the dumper'. Groups returning after a long lay-off were 'Back! Back!! BACK!!!' Attractive female singers were 'foxtresses' while slightly-past-their-date male stars were 'Uncle Disgusting's. Good things were either 'swingorilliant' or 'ber-illiant', while a bad idea was greeted with a 'pur-lease'. A few fortunate pop stars received the ultimate accolade of a *Smash Hits* nickname: Billy Idol was knighted as Sir Billiam of Idol; David Bowie became a dame; Paul McCartney was 'Fab Macca Wacky Thumbs Aloft'; and the lead singer of a-ha was affectionately known as Morten 'Snorten Forten' Harket. And anyone who went on too long was treated to the editorial . . . (*sniiiiiiiiip!!!*)

This was a magazine that put such searing questions on its front cover as 'Billy Idol – Is He Bonkers?' and 'Sigue Sigue Sputnik: the Future of Rock and Roll or a Load of Codswallop?' Readers who were lucky enough to get a letter in the magazine had their words taken apart by the mysterious Black Type and were sent a tea-towel in the post for their troubles. If you wanted to enter a competition to win, say, the new Matt Bianco picture disc, you were told to send your answers in on, I don't know, a 'lazy bed'. In response to which, readers would actually try to make a lazy bed in true *Blue Peter* fashion out of a Fairy Liquid bottle and a couple of pipe cleaners.

Quite where all this came from, I'm not too sure. Presumably the addled minds of the staff had something to do with it: quality music writers like Mark Ellen, David Hepworth and Chris Heath, future Pet Shop Boy Neil Tennant, who was assistant editor before leaving to become a bona fide pop star, and especially the late, great Tom Hibbert, who got the accolade of interviewing Margaret Thatcher ('Cliff Richard has done *wonders*') and would go on to lacerate the rich and ridiculous in Q magazine's 'Who the Hell' feature for many years. Tom Hibbert died in 2011 after a long struggle against illness: one of those news stories that felt sad and shocking and surprising all in one go. I was surprised how much his death affected me: I'd only ever known him through the articles that he'd written. But it made me realize just how important *Smash Hits* was when I was growing up.

Smash Hits didn't always get it right: on the week of Band Aid it opted to put Strawberry Switchblade on the front cover. Duran Duran, who would grace the cover more than any other band (fifteen times to Wham!'s ten), had their debut single, 'Planet Earth', taken apart: 'Why don't they send the synthesizers back to the shop, trash the *Play in a Day Guide to Funky Bass* book and leave the sounds to bands like Sparks, who did this kind of thing years ago with considerably more style and grace and didn't make half the fuss about it.' But more often than not it did get it right. The reason that it was so successful was that in the mid-eighties it chimed with the musical times: when pop music was in its prime, *Smash Hits* was the place to read about it. Buying the magazine felt like paying the entrance fee to a club – a club that by 1984, with the jet-setting antics of Wham!, Duran Duran and Spandau Ballet, went under the name of Tropicana.

Three years earlier, things had been very different. As *Top of the Pops* celebrated its 900th edition, the Number 1 song was 'Ghost Town' by the Specials. 'Oh dear,' commented presenter DJ David Jacobs, 'that wasn't very cheery, was it?' Yet both in its wonderful, eerie, almost Middle Eastern melodies, and in its powerful, quietly angry lyrics, 'Ghost Town' was the sound of the extraordinary summer of 1981, when half the country watched a fairy-tale wedding that turned out to be nothing of the sort, and the other half lived through a different type of Grimm storyline: unemployment, poverty and rioting.

The Specials had seen the human cost of the economic policies that Margaret Thatcher's Conservative government were pushing through: unemployment might have felt 'a price worth paying' in Whitehall offices, but out of the million people who lost their jobs in less than a year, the cuts fell disproportionately on the young and the ethnic communities (the latter out of work rose by 82 per cent).

The Specials, whose home town of Coventry was not exactly having the best of the recession, were seeing the same scene again and again as they toured up and down the country: 'You travelled from town to town and what was happening was terrible,' recalled band leader Jerry Dammers. 'In Liverpool, all the shops were shuttered up, everything was closing down [. . .] In Glasgow, there were these little old ladies on the streets selling all their household goods, their cups and saucers. It was unbelievable. It was clear that something was very, very wrong.'[1]

This dark political mood was combined with an equally toxic atmosphere within the band: the 'us-against-the-world' togetherness that had been part of the Specials' earlier success, and had defined the two-tone scene with hits like 'Gangsters' and 'Too Much Too Young', had dissipated into inter-band tensions, inflamed by drink and drugs. Making the song in the spring of 1981 had been a tense affair, with not everyone sharing Dammers's vision, or the song's feel; at one point Dammers walked out of a rehearsal when other band members refused to try his ideas out; even when the song was being recorded there were members 'rushing into the control room [. . .] going, "No, no, no, it sounds wrong! Wrong! Wrong!" '[2] By the time of the *Top of the Pops* performance the Specials were barely speaking to each other – and three of its members used the occasion to announce they were leaving.

All of which added to the brooding sense of menace that envelops the song. Power oozes out from this: the song 'bites' because it doesn't 'bark'; this is the low growl of a dog you really don't want to mess with. It also had power because it topped the charts just as the main riots of summer 1981 were in full flow. These riots weren't the first of the eighties – those happened in Bristol the previous year. They weren't even the first of 1981 – those had occurred in Brixton a few months earlier, just as the 'Ghost Town' sessions were coming to an end. The riots in July 1981 were significant for the way that they spread across the country like wildfire: like a macabre echo of a Specials tour, they began in Toxteth in Liverpool before moving on to 'dates' in Southall, Manchester, Birmingham, Leeds, Brixton and dozens of other cities from Newcastle down to Southampton. The timing of the song and its warning of a population 'getting angry' felt eerily prescient. It might not have been 'very cheery', but for many people *life* wasn't. 'Ghost Town', to borrow from a lager commercial, reached out to parts of the country that its politicians seemed simply incapable of reaching.

The starkness of the political situation, and the sense of alienation that came with it, created both the conditions for civil disobedience and also a politicization of popular music (quite why riots spread remains as unclear in 2011 as they did in 1981: though a similar 'voiceless-ness' of the young may have had something to do with it). While you might have expected political lyrics from the likes of Paul Weller ('Town Called Malice') and Elvis Costello ('Shipbuilding'), you could find similar engagement from the Human League ('The Lebanon') and even Bananarama ('Rough Justice').

Perhaps the best example of how far politics had filtered down came in the arrival of George Michael and Andrew

Ridgeley on the music scene and what became known as the 'protest pop' of their early singles. Wham! had had its origins in the same musical roots as the Specials: George and Andrew's music career began as part of the Executive, a similarly two-tone sort of band with self-written songs called things like 'Rude Boy' and ska versions of everything from 'Can't Get Used to Losing You' (à la the Beat) and, er, Beethoven's *Für Elise*.

The Executive fizzled out, and George and Andrew found themselves finishing school at the worst time for a half a century: Andrew went on the dole while George did a succession of casual jobs, including being a cinema usher and DJ-ing at a local restaurant. It was a scraping-by existence, but what the duo did have was a selection of more than half-decent tunes. In the kitchen of Andrew's flat in Peckham, a conversation about life on the dole turned into what would become 'Wham! Rap' (the song that also gave the band their name). Taking a bus to do his restaurant DJ-ing, George was handing over his money when a melody for a saxophone line popped into his head; this was the beginnings of 'Careless Whisper'. As chance would have it, living literally a few doors down the road from Andrew Ridgeley's parents were the Dean family, whose son Mark was one of the hottest properties in the record business. Dean was the man who had discovered both Soft Cell and ABC, and such was his reputation that, despite still only being in his early twenties, CBS had agreed to bankroll his own label, Innervision.

Dean had been hassled by Andrew Ridgeley when he was in the Executive. Dean dismissed the tape of the band as 'dreadful', and not only passed up the opportunity to see them live but was also similarly disinterested initially when Ridgeley returned with the Wham! tape. He wasn't the only one: while the tape included versions of 'Wham! Rap', 'Careless Whisper' and 'Club Tropicana', no A&R man could get beyond the rough quality of the recording: rather than containing full songs, the demo tape consisted of twenty-second fragments of each number as recorded in Andrew's front room. However, a mixture of Mark's mother bending his ear about the boy from down the road, and the boy from down the road accosting him at the local pub, wore Dean down and he agreed to listen. Unlike everyone else in London, he spotted their potential. In this instance, the phrase 'signing them up on the spot' is apposite: Dean turned up at a rehearsal in Holloway with a contract and wanted the duo to sign the deal there and then – which they duly did, in a greasy-spoon café round the corner.

This contract would later become notorious for the punitive clauses it imposed on Wham!. It offered a £500 advance for each offset against future earnings: the duo were to deliver an album a year for the next five years, with the record company allowed to ask for a further album each year (in other words, up to a maximum of ten albums; one every six months). Should the band split before the end of the contract, a new contract would be triggered – with both George and Andrew owing the record company a further ten albums each. Among the maze of miserly royalty rates the contract offered, my particular favourite is how much the duo would earn from twelve-inch singles – a generous

0 per cent. In Mark Dean's defence, the terms he'd signed with CBS to set up his label weren't much better: as Tony Parsons says in *Bare*, 'CBS were tough on him (though they were granting his deepest wish), he was tough on Wham! (though he was making their dreams come true). It was a tough deal all round.'[3] The result was eventually much litigation as Wham! attempted to renegotiate their way out of the contract.

All of which was for later, and the lawyers. For now, the band set about recording the debut album and doing a string of club PAs at glamorous night spots like Level One in Neasden. 'Wham! Rap' was the Tony Manero of *Saturday Night Fever* transported into the suburban Britain of the early eighties: rather than a dead-end job, this was a life lived down the dole office; rather the disco delights of a weekend, this was a manifesto for fun all week round, a full time job in having a good time. Wham!'s take on the economic situation is different to that of the Specials: rather than anger at young people being left on the shelf, here the mood is accepting – we're not going to change what it's like, so let's screw them and have a good time at their expense.

The first time 'Wham! Rap' was released, however, it flopped. To begin with, its follow-up, 'Young Guns (Go for It!)' didn't do much better: it entered the charts at Number 72, climbed to 48 . . . and then dropped, back down to 52. Had it gone down again, that might well have been it for Wham! Instead, what followed was a pull-out-the-stops attitude from both record company and publisher. Wham!'s appearance on Saturday-morning children's TV programme

Saturday Superstore, which was due to be cancelled because of the fall, was saved after much arm-twisting. An independent record-plugger was hired to push the single: record stores were convinced to play the record. All of which was enough for the record to jump to Number 42. Even though the record was still outside the charts proper, the saved *Saturday Superstore* appearance was enough to convince *Top of the Pops* to have the band on.

'A load of firsts tonight,' DJ Mike Smith introduced that week's show, 'the first chart of November, it's my first *Top of the Pops* and it's their first *Top of the Pops* . . . Wham!' This was the shop window the duo needed: backed by Shirlie Holliman and Dee C. Lee (Helen 'Pepsi' DeMacque would replace her the following year), Wham! delivered a tightly choreographed routine around the song's ministory: George discovering that his fellow soul boy Andrew was getting married; George telling Andrew he should stay single and have a good time; Andrew's fiancée (Shirlie) telling him she didn't like George; Andrew telling his 'chick' that no one talks to his mates like that. All the while, George cavorted around, bare-chested under a sleeveless brown leather jacket. This was the performance that made the band: the single reached Number 3 and was quickly followed into the Top 10 by a re-released 'Wham! Rap'.

In the summer of 1983, Margaret Thatcher was re-elected with a thumping majority. This was partly because of the 'feel-good factor' from victory in the Falklands War. It was also partly because of the state of the Opposition: Michael

Foot, donkey jacket and all, led a Labour party whose manifesto was famously described as 'the longest suicide note
in history'. They only just avoided finishing third behind
the SDP-Liberal Alliance. Throughout the country, but
particularly in the south, perceptions began to change. It
depended where you lived, but for many not only was the
worst of the recession over but actually things were beginning to pick up. Unemployment remained stubbornly high,
but it wasn't continuing to rise. While it mattered hugely
to those it affected, for others it became yesterday's news.
London, if not swinging, was beginning to shuffle again,
from side to side around its metaphorical handbag.

Wham!, meanwhile, were beginning the shift to the
second, slicker half of their brief career. The band's fourth
single, 'Club Tropicana', I had originally been one of their
earliest compositions. Like 'Wham! Rap' it was centred on
what they knew – this time a similarly softly satirical take
on the nightclub culture that they were part of: the 'Club
Tropicana' of the song was a spoof of the sort of tacky themed
nights designed to draw punters in. By the summer of 1983,
however, the original inspiration of the song had disappeared and the expensively shot video put a different spin
on things. Now the boys were partying by the pool in Ibiza,
with George Michael wearing a pair of budgie-smuggling
speedos as white as his smile – a smile so dazzling in fact that
he had to wear shades at night so as not to be blinded. After
some eyeing-up fun and frolics with Shirlie and Dee, the
video's final twist was that Andrew and George were pilots
for one airline and Dee and Shirlie air hostesses for another.

In the years before a succession of reality-TV programmes revealed serving warmed-up Spanish omelettes to half-asleep, half-starving passengers to be the grim, exhausting profession it actually is, air hostessing was exactly the sort of glamorous, see-the-world profession to aspire to.

The properly glamorous, see-the-world profession in the early eighties was that of pop star. Anything that Wham! could do, the likes of Duran Duran and Spandau Ballet could more than match. With the pull of MTV to justify opening up the video budgets, Duran Duran found themselves sent to Sri Lanka with Russell Mulcahy to film promos for 'Hungry Like the Wolf' and 'Save a Prayer'. The videos referenced *Raiders of the Lost Ark* and *Heart of Darkness*, with Simon Le Bon being chased around by a succession of exotic women. After Sri Lanka, the next stop was the Caribbean for the filming of 'Rio': I don't know, maybe Russell got his directions wrong again or something. 'Rio' wasn't Duran's biggest hit, but it remains arguably the best of their singles and its video their most memorable: that iconic shot of the band speeding through the water on an expensive yacht, Simon Le Bon sitting on the front in a pastel Anthony Price-type suit with the sleeves rolled up. If you ever wanted a single image that captured music in the eighties, this would surely be on the shortlist.

Duran Duran were huge in Britain and all around the world. Their good looks and flashy videos felt tailor-made for the MTV age, and they managed to 'break' America without really breaking sweat: *Rolling Stone* even christened them the 'Fab Five'. Back at home, they achieved what was then a rare accolade of having a single go straight in at Number 1 ('Is There Something I Should Know'). Simon Le Bon's lyric writing might have left a little to be desired by this point – 'Is There Something I Should Know' contained the very eighties comparison between how difficult it was to get along with someone and a nuclear war – but that was just a warm up for 'The Reflex'. This song, the band's biggest hit, was actually the last single to be taken from their third album, *Seven and the Ragged Tiger*; and if you listen to the album version you can understand why. The song lacked a certain something, which led to the record company bringing in Nile Rodgers (he of Chic, one of the band's original inspirations) to remix the song. It was he who added the 'ta na na' introduction and stuttering 'fl-fl-fl-flexes', though there was little he could do with the words themselves. The chorus of the song was a Ted Rodgers 3-2-1 of a riddle, incorporating treasure, lonely boys, shores, clover and unanswered questions.

With all this success came the riches: Duran larged it, living the rock-and-roll dream that most bands can only aspire to. John Taylor, who by now was pretty much the most fanciable male on the planet, went out with a succession of not-very-ugly women, including Playboy models and Bond girls. (In one interview, Taylor described his keep-fit regime as 'two hours on stage a day, having an active sex life and eating well'; in another, he described his ideal woman as 'someone who could tie me up and whip me and make me bacon sandwiches'). His garage groaned with expensive cars, including the iconic DeLorean (made famous by *Back to the Future*). He had three Aston Martins, one of which he never even got round to driving and sold a couple of years later at a loss. Simon Le Bon, meanwhile, chanced upon his future wife, Yasmin, by flicking through the pages of a modelling agency's catalogue. The band were even exposed for taking cocaine by the tabloid press, but all the 'Duran Shame' headlines didn't really even dent their reputation (and probably not their appetite): their next single, 'Wild Boys', pretty much seemed to sum up their lifestyle.

Duran's original New Romantic rivals had been Spandau Ballet, and they, too, found themselves packing their bags to exotic climes: the video for 'Only When You Leave' saw them swishing about in Hong Kong; 'I'll Fly for You' took them to New Orleans. The original rivalry between the two bands had smoothed down into a more jocular, laddish affair: 1984 saw the bands take on each other in a special edition of Mike Read's TV show *Pop Quiz*. Duran Duran won – which felt appropriate somehow, as the rivalry between the two groups had looked increasingly one-sided. Whether it was the number of *Smash Hits* front covers the two bands gleaned (15:3 was the final score) or the number of hits in the US (a solitary Top 10 hit for Spandau compared with several Duran Number 1s), there was little doubt who were the bigger deal.

While Duran Duran had stuck to their New Romantic combination of synthesizers and guitars, Spandau Ballet had pretty much ditched their keyboard sound after 'To Cut a Long Story Short'. While Duran's career went from strength to strength, Spandau struggled with their second album, in terms both of defining what their 'sound' was and of what singles like 'She Loved Like Diamond' were about. It had taken a helping hand from Trevor Horn to arrest what could have a terminal decline – and it was a good job he did, because Gary Kemp found his voice, coming up with two albums of a slick, more soulful sound. The catalyst for much of this was, oddly, Clare Grogan, lead singer of Scottish band Altered Images and star of the film *Gregory's Girl*. Kemp wasn't the only male in the country to find her attractive, but most of us stopped at watching her sing on *Top of the Pops*. Kemp put pen to paper, writing a number of songs that would end up on the *True* album, including the title track. The soulful sound suited not just Kemp's romantic yearnings but also Tony Hadley's voice. 'True' became the band's first (and only) Number 1, beating Duran Duran to the punch in the process.

George Michael, meanwhile, hit 1984 with the claim that he would have four Number 1s before the year was out. As it turned out he was almost right. 'Wake Me Up Before You Go-Go', a record that even *Melody Maker* made single of the week, was the first to go to Number 1. Its origins were in a 'Wake Me Up Before You Go-Go' note that Andrew had left for his parents and George had spotted. 'Careless Whisper' and 'Freedom' also hit the top spot, and 'Last Christmas/ Everything She Wants' was only stopped from completing the set by 'Do They Know It's Christmas?' (which George Michael was singing on anyway). Having got themselves a new manager in Simon Napier Bell, the band had set about extracting themselves from their original record contract and then set about the charts with the same sense of determination.

'Careless Whisper' was a solo George Michael single. Although it was one of the first songs that the group had come up with, George Michael was savvy enough to hold it back until he felt the time was right. It would be his calling card for a more mature, post-Wham! career, to prove to the world that he was about more than just shoving a shuttlecock down his shorts and hitting it into the audience (as the group had done on their Club Fantastic tour). Whereas the Wham! look was large Katherine Hammett T-shirt with 'CHOOSE LIFE' in big letters (later replaced with a triumphant 'NUMBER ONE' when 'Wake Me Up' hit the top spot), the solo George Michael was all designer stubble, Diana-type coiffured hair and cream-coloured jacket. For 'Careless Whisper' George Michael was determined to get everything right. A session was set up with legendary American producer Jerry Wexler and one of the best saxophonists from LA was flown in to record the song's solo. George Michael, however, was convinced it wasn't quite there yet, despite the calibre of people he was working with, and insisted it was scrapped.

He was right, too: this version ended up on the B-side of the song's Japanese release and, to borrow from *Catchphrase*'s Roy Walker, it's good, but it's not right. George Michael had come a long way from being the young man needing Andrew Ridgeley for confidence and support. The question has often been asked what Andrew Ridgeley did in Wham! and that, pretty much, is your answer: he was the fledgling superstar's crutch. Once George Michael came to the conclusion he didn't need a crutch, the logical extension was that he didn't need his school friend any more either.

The contrast between the two men was starting to widen, and not just in terms of their respective talents. 'Careless Whisper', with its five weeks at Number 1, had another glamorous video shoot and George Michael singing classy lines about how people feeling bad about things have difficulties in dancing properly. Andrew Ridgeley, meanwhile, was the man the press were dubbing the 'vomit fountain' and following up on his nights out was a sure-fire way for a tabloid journalist to get themselves a front-page story. One particular nadir saw a page-three 'lovely' describing her 'tug of war' over Andrew – though this was a model whom Andrew had no recollection of meeting. Upon closer inspection, the newspaper's photo actually featured the girl with her arm draped round not Andrew himself but a cardboard cut-out of him.

By 1985 Wham! had more than fulfilled the *Make It Big* title of their second album. They became the first Western band to tour Communist China, a half-iconic, half-awkward event that was most famous for the band's trumpeter having some sort of emotional breakdown and getting a knife out (or 'Wham Man in Hari Kiri Horror' as the *Sun* tactfully described it). From here it was a stadium tour of the US, where Wham! had enjoyed three Number 1 singles and played to 300,000 people over eight shows, supported by the likes of Sister Sledge and Chaka Khan. One of these Number 1s was 'Everything She Wants'; with all this success, George Michael had everything he wanted, and yet at the same time it wasn't quite enough.

The international success of Duran, Wham!, Culture Club, and Spandau Ballet led to criticism of their lifestyle. All the swanning about on boats and so forth resulted in suggestions that the contemporaneous success of British pop and Thatcherism was no coincidence. This was music by, and for, the new nouveau riche of British society, went this line of argument: instead of the politicized songs of the early eighties, the lack of message in this pop music spoke of groups out only to earn and enjoy themselves.

Rather than an intense rivalry between these bands, what developed was a shared camaraderie of back-slapping and one-upmanship. At Italy's San Remo Festival in early 1985, top of the bill were Duran Duran, Spandau Ballet and Frankie Goes to Hollywood. In *Like Punk Never Happened*, Dave Rimmer describes the like-punk-never-happened scene of the groups drinking and arsing about in a club together: Nick Rhodes taking photos of everyone, while Spandau's drummer tells him they'll be 'crap, just like your book'; Martin Kemp pulling pearls from a necklace and chucking them about; Frankie's Mark O'Toole trying to score, while band-mate Nash shouts, 'If you don't have her fuckin' kit off in thirty seconds . . . then you are a pouf!'; Andy Taylor wandering around telling people they are 'wankers' and that Nash is not well-endowed; Nash taking umbrage at Andy Taylor's remarks, and the pair pulling down their trousers to compare sizes.[4]

This isn't anything as sophisticated as approaching a political statement: this is just straightforward, unthinking rock-and-roll excess. In his book on Duran Duran, Steve Malins uses the term 'Ferryism' to describe the attitude of Duran, and I think that is a better description of this elite band of pop stars: they weren't downing champagne because they were happy Margaret Thatcher was in power with a stonking majority (though they didn't mind her cutting taxes for high-earners); they were downing champagne and everything else because they were emulating the glamorous lifestyle of the original lounge lizard, Bryan Ferry.

The politics of the earlier eighties hadn't disappeared completely, and some stars led a contradictory double life. Gary Kemp, for example, was a pop star who would join the rest of Spandau Ballet for a year's tax exile to save money, yet at the same time would take part in Red Wedge, a Labour-supporting youth movement that also included Paul Weller and Billy Bragg. George Michael might have been unhappy enough with his hair during the filming of the 'Careless Whisper' video to halt filming and fly over his hairdresser sister to sort it out at a supposed cost of £17,000, but Wham! also played at a benefit gig for the families of striking miners a couple of months later (for which they got booed for their efforts). For all these stars, there was Band Aid and Live Aid to negotiate, which would bring such contradictions into full public glare.

Track Ten

Relax

It might be quicker to tell you the records I *did* understand in the eighties, rather than the ones I didn't. It's one of the pitfalls of growing up, not understanding every nuance and reference to sex and drugs in rock and roll.

Like the lead singer of Scritti Politti, I was something of a green child. One of the on-going features of my school career was being told jokes I didn't understand, and laughing along as though I did. It saved face in the short term, but left me none the wiser as to what anyone was talking about – and I found myself at an age that confessing to such ignorance was a thought beyond embarrassment.

If I could have been so clueless with school-ground jokes, you can only begin to imagine the sort of mollycoddled musical world my brain inhabited. It probably started with Musical Youth's 'Pass the Dutchie', an irritatingly catchy, rubbishy reggae Number 1 from 1983. Because the band were young and black, they were quickly picked up by worthy TV shows like *John Craven's Newsround* and *Blue Peter* as a heart-warming good news story. On the latter, presenter Simon Groom (I say presenter, but he was so dull as to be barely present at all) asked the band what a 'dutchie' was. To which the band replied, with a smirk, that it was a West Indian type of saucepan. The smirk, of course, was there because everyone knew that a dutchie was really slang for joint. Everyone, that is, except for me, who swallowed the saucepan story, Dr Hook, line and sinker.

'Pass the Dutchie', though, was only the musical youth of my eighties misunderstandings. Grandmaster Flash and Melle Mel's 'White Lines (Don't Do It)' was another song whose meaning I struggled with. In my own, oddly innocent world, the white lines were the road markings in the middle of the road, and the song was about the dangers of overtaking. The shouts of 'freebase!', meanwhile, were the cue for the band's John Taylor to start improvising. Depeche Mode's 'Master and Servant' was in my head all about historical re-enactment societies, with people dressing up in an attempt to understand the feudal relationship between a Lord of the Manor and his attendant.

So when Frankie Goes to Hollywood released their debut single, 'Relax', I never really stood a chance. *Don't do what?* was my innocent response? What did the band have against relaxing anyway? I *liked* relaxing. What could be better than kicking back in your A-Team slippers, cracking open a packet of Monster Munch and watching Debbie Greenwood flirt with the sixth formers on *First Class*? What's more, why did the lead singer keep going on about socks? It was only when the song was banned that it confirmed my suspicions that something rude might have been going on. Though what that was, I had precious little idea.

The first time that Frankie Goes to Hollywood appeared on the public radar was when they performed on *The Tube* in early 1983. At the time the band were still unsigned: in fact, they only got this career-changing gig because the band *The Tube* really wanted, Dead or Alive, were unavailable. Rather than being filmed at *The Tube*'s usual North East studio, Jools Holland was sent out to watch and interview them at the State Ballroom in Liverpool – a grand, decaying building of Grade II-listed glamour that in 1982 had reopened as the UK's first laser disco.

As singlet-wearing drummer Peter 'Ped' Gill bashed out a simple, monotonous beat, the viewer was ushered into the ballroom by the Leather Pets, a somewhat scrawny double act of scantily clad dancers, complete with whips. The cameraman was led to the raised stage, which looked like nothing more than a boxing ring, where the main contenders were all waiting for the bell in a hybrid of bondage and boxing gear: guitarist Brian 'Nasher' Nash, bass player Mark O'Toole, dancer Paul Rutherford, and gun-toting lead singer Holly Johnson.

As the Leather Pets proceeded to writhe around the corner poles of the stage, Frankie performed what now seems like a pared-down, disco-driven version of the song:

with its time changes and relentless, banging beat, it is curiously reminiscent of 'Take Me Out' by Franz Ferdinand. Following the performance, there was a somewhat awkward interview with Jools Holland, who, being fully clothed and coated, seemed somewhat overdressed for the occasion. Holland asked the band about their response to people who'd consider their image sexist. 'Good', was the band's response, in true Spiñal Tap style, wondering what was wrong with being sexy.

One person watching *The Tube* that night was Trevor Horn. Horn, who'd launched MTV with his 'Video Killed the Radio Star', had swapped the microphone for the mixing desk, to become the pop producer of choice for the early eighties. It was Horn who'd been behind the controls for ABC's *Lexicon of Love* – the fantastically classy debut album by the Sheffield band that remains one of the era's standout records. With hits such as 'Poison Arrow' and 'The Look of Love', lead singer Martin Fry and his gold lamé suit brought a touch – and a touché – of Bryan Ferry-style glamour to the charts. The album soars thanks to the freshness of the sound – Horn was just about getting the hang of his then new-fangled Fairlight computer – and the rawness of the source material. Fry's lyrics are all about getting dumped by his girlfriend. A perhaps not overly sensitive Horn insisted on getting the dumper into the studio: she's the one who says 'Goodbye' on 'The Look of Love'.

ABC were by far from being the only act on which Horn sprinkled his magic mixing dust. There was Dollar, in the days before David Van Day was sexing up Bucks Fizz dance routines. There was Yes, Horn's earlier band, whose 'Owner of a Lonely Heart' hit Number 1 in the US. Then there was Horn's career-saving hand in Spandau Ballet. After two flop singles in a row ('Paint Me Down' and 'She Loved Like Diamond') the band were in desperate need of a hit. In stepped Horn to throw what is technically known as the kitchen sink at 'Instinction', which in return did the decent thing and returned the band to the Top 10 ('Instinction', as my spell check is correct to tell me, is not actually a word). The Spandau–Horn collaboration would have continued with the band's third album – imagine what pyrotechnics might have been added to 'True' had this idea reached fruition – but, not for the last time, Horn was unconvinced about the musical ability of those he was recording. The eye of his ire was focused on the Spandau drummer John Keeble: Horn told the band he'd have to be removed if he was to continue producing; the Ballet decided to stick up for their mate.

All this production success led to Trevor thinking bigger: what if he set up his own record label where he could keep pegs on all parts of the pop process? Together with his wife Jill Sinclair, who ran the business side of things, and Paul Morley, then a razor-sharp *NME* scribe, who brought in a McLaren-meets-Mandelson eye for image and publicity, he set up Zang Tuum Tumb, or ZTT, a phrase taken from a 1913 Futurist poem called 'The Art of Noises'. The poem also came in handy in naming the label's house band, who, as well as helping out with the ZTT acts, had hits of their own with songs likes 'Close (To the Edit)'. Other acts the label would go on to produce were the German band Propaganda, whose sparkling single 'Duel' remains for my money one of the hidden gems of the decade.

Back on *The Tube*, Trevor Horn was watching Frankie Goes to Hollywood and liking what he called their 'Donna Summer meets heavy metal' sound. According to which version you believe, he then either rang the TV company immediately to get their details or, according to Holly Johnson's autobiography, *A Bone in My Flute*, waited until he heard the band's subsequent Radio One session for DJ Kid Jensen before pouncing (as well as 'Relax', the band recorded a sparse and spiky version of 'Two Tribes'). Whichever was true, the ZTT deal was not perhaps the most generous record contract ever offered: £250 advance for the band's first two singles (which respectively would go on to become the fourth and eleventh bestselling singles of all time), and a £5000 offer for the band's publishing rights. The latter was well below what the band might have expected had they shopped around on the back of getting a record deal, but it was an all-or-nothing deal and, desperate for success, the band signed. So small was the advance that the band continued to sign on to make ends meet while the recording took place: it was only once they'd appeared on *Top of the Pops* and realized they'd be recognized that they went back to the label to ask for more money.

These early versions of 'Relax' and 'Two Tribes' are available on the Internet: one of the myths that Frankie endured upon being successful was that they were nothing but a load of Trevor Horn puppets, with their parts played by session musicians. What the pre-ZTT versions of their songs showed, however, is how strong the songs were even at this early stage. Horn worked wonders, there's no doubt about that, but it's worth remembering he had the makings of a silk purse to start with, rather than having to attempt to remix the equivalent of a sow's ear.

Trevor Horn was, in a way, the Brian Wilson of the eighties. Just as the Beach Boy had the genius to wring every last drop out of the recording equipment of his day, so Horn was the master of his. Just as Brian Wilson reduced the rest of the band to bystanders, coming in to record the vocals and leaving the rest to him, so Horn used Holly Johnson's vocals and reduced the rest of the band to walk-on parts. And, just as Wilson spent six months in getting 'Good Vibrations' just right, so Horn spent a similar amount of time and a huge amount of money (almost £100,000) getting 'Relax' exactly the way he wanted it to sound.

The musicians in Frankie – drummer Gill, guitarist Nash and bass player O'Toole – were collectively known as 'the lads'. This was partly because of their beery antics, but also because of their age. They were young – sixteen to eighteen – and relatively inexperienced musicians: they were good, but Horn wanted better. Horn, who hadn't been afraid to give the Spandau Ballet drummer short shrift, showed similar compunction here and jettisoned their early recordings: indeed, the only contribution the lads really made to 'Relax' was the sampled sound of them falling into a swimming pool. Horn tried again, this time by bringing in the Blockheads (as in 'Ian Dury and the') to re-record the music. Their version is a bit more funky, but still lacked the elusive something that Horn was looking for. What that was, it turned out, was something more mechanical: together with studio stalwarts like the Art of Noise's J. J. Jeczalik, and using his Fairlight computer and Linn drum machine, Horn was able to lock the bass and beat tightly together. That's what gives the song its recognizable *thump thump thump*, a bang-on relentlessness that none of the recorded musicians were quite able to achieve on their own. So who actually played on 'Relax' is thus one of those musical misnomers – lots of people and no one is the unhelpful answer.

When 'Relax' was eventually released, in late autumn 1983, the initial response of the public was not to do it. The band did a PA tour of nightclubs with some of the dancers from the video and a blow-up sex doll. Having charted towards the bottom of the Top 75, 'Relax' then faced the ignominy of going *down*, rather than up. Once again, the band found themselves with *The Tube* to thank: after they performed live on the show (or at least as 'live' as it was possible to perform the song), the song finally made its way up to Number 35. Then, having squeaked into the Top 40, the band got lucky again and were picked for *Top of the Pops*. With Holly Johnson wearing a yellow handkerchief in his back pocket (club code for being into water sports), their performance saw the song rise again, this time up to Number 6. It's important to remember that before all the hullabaloo the song was already a hit and hurtling up the charts: such was its trajectory and quality, it would probably have got to Number 1 on its own accord anyway – without the helping hand it got from Mike Read and Radio One.

Radio One by the mid-1980s was in its Smashy-and-Nicey, pump-up-the-volume prime. From its beginnings back in 1967, when Tony Blackburn had spun 'Flowers in the Rain' by the Move, the station had grown gargantuan-like, gathering in huge audiences and making celebrities out of the DJs. The station's disc jockeys were household names who could pull in big money for personal appearances: if you wanted to hire a Radio One DJ in 1984 it would set you back £900 per hour for a Simon Bates or a Gary Davies, £1000 for Peter Powell or DLT and £2000 plus VAT for sixty minutes of Mike Read's time. Each summer the Radio One Roadshow would tour the beaches of Great Britain, where tens of thousands of fans would turn out to watch a hungover DJ spin a few records, play 'Bits and Pieces' and tell some hilarious anecdote about what he and Smiley Miley had got up to the night before involving a young lady and a fire extinguisher.

If Radio One's daytime style could be summed up in three words, they would probably be *quack*, *quack* and *oops* (the sound effect contestants were given when they got a question wrong on DLT's 'snooker on the radio' quiz, Give Us a Break). The evenings were a slightly different kettle of fish, with John Peel and Janice Long given the latitude to do their own thing: I remember once hearing John Peel reading out a listener's request for him to play some Whitney Houston, to which he responded by playing Megadeath.

Occasionally these two worlds would collide, as when Peel was cajoled into presenting *Top of the Pops* or being forced to take part in a 'fun' day. One such incident from the seventies involved the Bay City Rollers playing on an island in the middle of a lake while frogmen attempted to stop screaming fans from drowning as they waded into the water to reach their idols. All the while, Peel dryly noted, Tony Blackburn was zooming around the lake in a speedboat that was being driven by a Womble. It was that sort of set-up.

I always think that one's opinion of Radio One depends where you grew up in the country. If you lived in London, for example, and had alternatives such as Capital to listen to, then you probably didn't quite feel the same sense of attachment. For much of the country, and certainly for us in York, the option on the dial for someone growing up was Radio One and nothing else. As a result, the station loomed large in any teenage consciousness – it was an integral part of my youth. And, yes, it was rightly ridiculed for being full of itself and ridiculous and over the top and all the rest of it, but at the same time it is very easy to forget the many hours of pleasure it gave to many millions of people, myself included. This was, as the jingles had it, the 'nation's favourite', the 'rhythm of Britain', the 'big one' where 'you'll always hear a better song', non-stop 'action radio' (or 'wadio' as it was oddly pronounced). It was the 'happy happy sound' of Mike Read, Mike Smith and Simon Mayo that I listened to in the morning, getting ready for school. Following the weekday *Breakfast Show* would be Simon Bates. Lunchtime, or the 'bit in the middle' was the preserve of 'Ooh' Gary Davies.

RELAX

After Steve Wright in the afternoon, the teatime show was the preserve of radio chipmunks like Bruno Brookes and Peter Powell: two DJs who also took it in turns to go out with Anthea Turner.

Actually, Peter Powell is not the only person to have a bone to pick with Bruno Brookes. During Brookes's teatime stint, I was once lucky enough to have a letter read out on his show. It was for a feature where listeners sent in puzzles for people to solve. These consisted of tales like the man trapped in a room with no doors and windows: how did he escape? (The answer was: through the roof – at no point, Brookes a little smugly told his audience, did he ever mention that the room had a ceiling.) Obviously I was impressed by all of this, and somewhat in awe of such powers of lateral thinking. So you can imagine my sheer delight when Bruno chose to read out my contribution for the slot – the conundrum I chose is, sadly, lost in the hiss of medium wave, but I think I'd nicked the one about a chicken and a fox going across a river in a boat without the latter eating the former. I can still recall, however, with a sort of FM clarity, Bruno reading out my letter. 'This puzzle comes all the way from Chestnut Avenue, York, North Yorkshire,' said the Brookster, possibly filling time by reading my address out in full. It was the weirdest experience, hearing it come out of the speaker: my brain was whirring at $33^{1}/_{3}$ to begin with. Oh, that sounds a bit like my address. Oh, that *is* my address. *Bloody hell, Bruno Brookes is reading my letter out*, I finally realized, just as he was finishing it.

It perhaps says much about my sheltered early years and the power of Radio One that Bruno Brookes reading my letter out was one of the highlights if not *the* highlight of my life at that stage. Bruno Brookes was talking to me! He called me 'mate'! I was Bruno Brookes's friend! My letter, he told me, was a 'great one' and as a reward, 'I'll send you a pen in the post, mate.' That latter promise not only added to my excitement – my very own Radio One pen! – but also served as useful ammunition at school the next day. For, rather than turning up and receiving the expected adulation in the schoolyard, the anticipated standing ovation and girls throwing themselves at me failed to materialize. No one, it transpired, had heard my letter read out on the radio. In playground parlance, that meant that no one believed me. In fact, accusations of lying and making stories up began to be bandied about; my reputation, rather than being raised on a pedestal, was being shoved in the gutter. All, though, was not quite lost. What had my new best friend Bruno promised me on the radio?

'I'll prove it,' I said. 'I'll bring in my Radio One pen and then you'll *know* I've been telling the truth.'

Except that you never did send me the pen, did you, Bruno? It's not like you didn't have my address: you read the damn thing out on air. But rather than slip it in a Jiffy bag, perhaps with a signed black-and-white photo ('Great letter, mate! Your pal, Bruno'), you went off for a night out in London's latest hot spots while some of us were sat at home waiting patiently for the post to arrive and watching our reputation in the playground be slowly ripped to shreds. So yeah, thanks, Bruno, 'mate'. Thanks a bunch.

The host of the Radio One *Breakfast Show* in 1984 was Cliff Richard-alike Mike Read. Read had begun his radio career back in 1976 at Thames Valley Radio, where he co-hosted a show with his subsequent Radio One colleague Steve Wright: the programme was called, with no little inevitability, *The Read and Wright Show*. From here, Read followed the career path of Peter Powell, taking his slot on Radio Luxembourg and then on to the 'big one'. In 1981, he took over the *Breakfast Show* from the 'hairy cornflake', Dave Lee Travis, who was off to play his 'snooker on the radio' at the weekend instead. Read quickly established himself in the role, winning the *Smash Hits* readers' poll for best radio show in 1982, 1983 and 1984.

Read, as we saw earlier with his strumming of 'Lucy in the Sky with Diamonds' in the BBC canteen, fancied himself as a bit of a musician. He also knew his pop knowledge, being part of the team that set up the *Guinness Book of Hit Singles* in 1976, and host of music's answer to *A Question of Sport*, *Pop Quiz*. When Read wasn't threatening to get his guitar out or wowing you with pop trivia, he'd be playing tennis with his friend Cliff or working on his poetry: in 1989, he published *Elizabethan Dragonflies*, a collection dedicated 'to all the dreamers and romantics of this world'. Even at his literary book launch, though, he still couldn't quite shake off his wacky 'wadio' past: 'He autographed a copy for an Australian,' chuckled his publisher, 'and he signed it *upside down*. He's quite the prankster.'[1]

On 11 January 1984, Mike Read was playing 'Relax' on his *Breakfast Show*. This was by no means the first time the song had been heard on Radio One: as well as having been previously recorded in Radio One sessions for both John Peel and Kid Jensen, it had been played in the region of seventy times on the station. What was different this time was that Read was taking a moment to read the words on the back of the twelve-inch record sleeve. On this, Paul Morley had in no way provocatively penned a different sort of graphic novel: 'Get down there and lick that shit off my shoes!' Frankie demanded in 'chapter two'; 'Frankie was a monster. No one could imagine what he demanded of his nephew,' read 'chapter six'. Morley's novel ended by saying 'we hope you won't believe a word of what we have not said'. Read, though, thought differently, lifted the needle off the record and (without smashing it in two, as is often falsely remembered) declared he was no longer going to play the single as it was 'obscene'.

Although it seems prudish now, Read's reaction to 'Relax' is not wholly out of keeping with the social mores of the time. I remember scouring the pages of *Smash Hits* to read what the controversial lyric was, only to discover it wasn't there: 'We decided weeks ago not to print it because we thought it was a bit rude,' the magazine told us. Similarly, Holly Johnson recalls bumping into musicologist and DJ Paul Gambaccini on the morning of filming *Top of the Pops*: 'Gambaccini [. . .] said that he was amazed that the record was being played. He said no one had got away with such obvious sexual innuendo since Lou Reed's "Walk on the Wild Side".'

RELAX

The reactions of *Smash Hits*, Gambaccini and Mike Read to 'Relax' are, on one level, not dissimilar. The difference, though, was the timing. *Smash Hits* and Gambaccini were both smart enough and attuned enough to recognize what the song was about right from the beginning. Radio One in general, and its *Breakfast Show* host in particular, were somewhat slower off the mark. So, by the time they worked out what the record was really about, it felt like an excruciating handbrake U-turn and alerted much of the country to a rudeness they also hadn't realized was there. Compounding the embarrassment further, the BBC went on to wetly declare that the record wasn't banned, it just wasn't being played. When the now notorious record inevitably hit Number 1, 'Relax' was played on neither *Top of the Pops* nor the Top 40 countdown: 'Because of the nature of the lyric we don't think [it is] suitable for broadcasting' was presenter Simon Bates's line on the latter.

In the same way that a ministerial resignation is seldom about the misdemeanour itself but usually about the cover-up, so the Frankie ban was less about the song and more about the record cover: the latter spelled it out in a way that the music didn't. Rock and roll, after all, might not always be about sex but it quite often is – and its history is littered with acts getting away with whatever euphemism they could: the Rolling Stones managed it with '(I Can't Get No) Satisfaction', for example, but had to change 'Let's Spend the Night Together' to 'Let's Spend Some Time Together' to get played on American TV. That was the fine line that

'Relax' carefully, and in the tradition of pop music, tried to tread.

Sometimes, of course, an act *does* want to get banned. Take Duran Duran's video for 'Girls on Film'. Godley and Creme were the directors and 'were told by Duran's management simply to make a very provocative, sexy video that had some sort of tenuous connection to the band and would be seen in clubs'.[2] With all the sophistication of an X-rated Athena poster, the band played in the background while lingerie-clad models took turns to have pillow fights, pour champagne over each other and rub their nipples with ice cubes. Soft-porn clichés they might have been, but having a 'banned' video gave Duran credibility and helpfully reasserted their heterosexual credentials for the American audience, just in case anyone misunderstood their frilly shirted New Romanticism.

Similarly, when George Michael split up Wham! the first single off his solo album was 'I Want Your Sex'. As with Duran, this felt like deliberate positioning: the teen idol was now an adult star; the shuttlecock down the shorts had very much left the shuttle behind. As it happened, the song itself was essentially quite conservative: with fears about AIDS looming large in the background, the lyrics espoused the virtues of monogamy.

The notoriety gained from getting yourself banned does an act no harm at all. For Duran and George Michael, the bans were all about image; for 'Relax', it delivered the sort of exposure that is worth its weight in Spandau Ballet gold. By falling for Paul Morley's provocative liner notes, Radio

One didn't just give the band a huge boost of publicity: it also placed the station on the wrong side of the line. As the record sold by the bucketful, and stayed at Number 1 for five weeks, Radio One looked every inch the establishment and out of touch with the kids (the following year, the song won the award for best single at the Brits, as voted for by listeners of, er, Radio One). The *Sun*, which might have been expected to support the ban, labelled Read as 'prissy'. It accused the DJ of double standards, claiming he had 'been keeping quiet about his own saucy past. Mike posed for a sexy soft-porn photo session with topless former page-three girl Tessa Hewitt long before Frankie Goes to Hollywood recorded their million-selling hit.'[3] By the end of the year, the ban ('ban') was quietly dropped, Mike Read was doing voiceovers for the TV ads for Frankie's debut album, and the band were being invited to perform the song on the end-of-year *Top of the Pops* Christmas special.

The success of 'Relax' and the publicity that went with it was not a one-off: the summer of 1984 belonged to Frankie. This was partly due to the follow-up single, 'Two Tribes', which went straight in at Number 1, stayed there for nine weeks, and found itself re-joined by 'Relax', which climbed back up to Number 2. It was also because of the ubiquitous 'FRANKIE SAY' T-shirts. These were Paul Morley's adaptation of Katherine Hamnett's then trendy oversize T-shirts with slogans on the front ('CHOOSE LIFE', for example). The Frankie T-shirt range included 'RELAX DON'T DO IT', 'WAR! HIDE YOURSELF',

'ARM THE UNEMPLOYED' and 'BOMB IS A FOUR LETTER WORD'. The design was incredibly easy to imitate, and soon every rip-off T-shirt manufacturer in the country was making them: one estimate suggested the band lost in excess of £1 million in royalties through pirated shirts. The rival manufacturers came up with slogans of their own: two girls in Swansea were arrested for wearing 'FRANKIE SAY . . . FUCK ME' T-shirts: the judge was just about the only person left in the country who didn't know who Frankie were, and had to be told that they were a band 'in the Hit Parade, m'lud'.

'Two Tribes' hadn't been the first choice for Frankie's follow-up single. Originally chosen was 'Slave to the Rhythm' – and one can only imagine what Paul Morley might have done with that – but the Frankie version wasn't working so instead, 'Two Tribes' – a song that Holly Johnson had originally come up with after watching *Mad Max 2* – got the nod. The mid-eighties were the height of the Cold War stand-off between the United States and the Soviet Union (height in terms of tension, if not historically, for the imminent arrival of Mikhail Gorbachev was to transform the conflict). Certainly, the threat of nuclear war felt very real: I vividly remember reading Raymond Briggs's *When the Wind Blows* and feeling terrified enough to hold my duvet tighter that night (because that would really have helped).

For Frankie and ZTT, however, nuclear war came across not so much as something to be feared as an event to get yourself a ringside seat for. Adverts for 'Two Tribes' in *Smash*

Hits included scientific data on the result of nuclear fallout: 'The table shows the biological effects of a 5000 megaton nuclear war, using one third of the superpower's arsenal. A moderate exchange of warheads by the superpowers would lead to a "nuclear winter" and the possible extinction of the human species.' Which is an interesting way to sell a single, I'm sure you'll agree. The accompanying video featured lookalikes of US President Ronald Reagan and then Soviet Leader Konstantin Chernenko punching each other in a cock-fighting ring. The song, or at least one of its many mixes, with cheery names like 'Annihilation' and 'Carnage', started with a spoken introduction by Patrick Allen, the actor who had voiced the government's 'Protect and Survive' films about what to do in the event of a nuclear attack.

For all the hype, the song manages to pull off its trumpeted going-out-with-a-bang-not-a-whimper ballast. I'd go as far as to say that 'Two Tribes' is my favourite single of the entire decade: the 'air-attack warning' beginning, complete with siren and piano lament; the incoming F-16 of a bass line; Anne Dudley's orchestral stabs; the switchback structure; the nuclear levels of NRG; Johnson's soaring vocals, complete with the pay-off line tweaked from the cult fifties British film *Cover Girl Killer*: 'Surely sex and horror are the new Gods in this world of so-called entertainment.'

You can't really beat five million sales for your first single and three million for your second. In terms of impact, numbers – pretty much everything – Frankie were sweeping the board and ruffling feathers at the same time. The pecking order of the pop elite – Duran, Wham!, Culture Club and Spandau Ballet – were finding themselves being overtaken, and not always gracefully so: Frankie ads claimed that the band made Wham! look like 'Pinky and Perky' and Spandau Ballet 'completely soft'; Gary Kemp responded by saying it'd be Frankie Goes to Hospital if they weren't careful. Boy George was dismissed as a 'Widow Twankey' figure and Culture Club the subject of obscene phone calls from 'the lads' while in the studio.

One of the longest-standing chart records was that achieved by Gerry and the Pacemakers back in 1963, when the Liverpool group reached Number 1 with their first three releases. Frankie cemented their reputation as singles royalty when 'The Power of Love', a luscious ballad with another sweeping Anne Dudley score, got to Number 1 in December. To make the leap from singles band to album act, however, proved to be a taller order. There was no lack of ambition in *Welcome to the Pleasuredome*, but its double-LP length was pushing their luck (and talent?) that bit too far: 'a single LP stretched over four sides [. . .] a pretty thin package at times' was the *Smash Hits* verdict. The album had huge pre-orders – a then record of over £1 million – but failed to deliver.

Welcome to the Pleasuredome had the smell of the Beach Boys' *Smile* to it. That was meant to be Brian Wilson's magnum opus, but the effort and time taken in producing two corking singles ('Good Vibrations' and 'Heroes and Villains') took it out of him, and the rest of the album failed to match up. Similarly here, Trevor Horn had lavished so much time and energy getting 'Relax' and 'Two Tribes' just right that to polish the rest of the album to the same standard would have taken years: the result would no doubt have been brilliant, but for a pop band the timing would have been unsustainable. Aside from the three Number 1s and the title track – an utterly glorious fourteen-minute epic that took up virtually all of Side One on its own – the cupboard was sadly bare.

What Trevor Horn and ZTT should have done with Frankie was to do what they ended up doing with their reject song 'Slave to the Rhythm'. This was re-recorded by Grace Jones, and a whole album was put together around the single tune, a variety of versions like 'variations on a theme'. These days, we'd call such a release a 'remix album'; given the material Frankie had, this would have suited them far better. They'd probably have been hailed as both avant-garde and a 'rip off' at the same time: something that would have pleased their record label down to the ground.

As for Radio One, they learnt their lesson and tried a bit harder to be in with the kids. A couple of years later, Mike Read's successor as *Breakfast Show* host, Mike Smith, followed in his predecessor's footsteps when he took the Jesus and Mary Chain's 'Some Candy Talking' off air half-way through on the grounds that he thought it was about drugs (candy being cocaine). This time round, the Radio One controller decided to ask John Peel what he thought: Peel said he thought it was fine, and the station continued to play the record.

Track Eleven

Do They Know It's Christmas?

It's autumn 1984 and I'm stood on Stockton Lane, at the point where the lollipop lady used to help pupils across the road on the way to Hempland Primary. Except I'm not waiting for the lollipop lady to cross the road any more, I'm waiting for the bus to take me to secondary school instead. I've got a place at Huntington Comprehensive.

Huntington Comprehensive was comprehensive in both its admissions policy and its size. From being at a school of a few hundred, I was now joining one that boasted one and a half thousand: there were more people in my year than there had been in my entire primary school. Its intake mopped up most of the outer fringes on the northeast side of York, and a good swathe of countryside and villages, too, whose children were all bussed in and out again. The bus driver on my bus, rather than tuning the coach stereo into Radio One, instead subjected us twice a day to his collection of tapes. Or, to be more specific, his tape. Either our coach driver had come to the conclusion that Status Quo's *12 Gold Bars* was the only album worth owning, or he'd got it stuck in the machine and couldn't get it out. Either way, I must have heard that album more times than any other I have listened to – morning and afternoon for five days a week, forty-odd weeks a year. That, let me tell you, is a lot of 'Whatever You Want'.

Each day as we drove up Huntington Road, we passed a building site on our left, where we'd watch as a Lego set of identikit houses was put together, brick by brick. As the development progressed and eventually neared completion, the time came to name this particular road. Ways to name a street include mentioning where it's going (London Road, say) or paying homage to a high-profile historical figure. Some of these stand the test of time: hence the fact that there are sixty or so sturdy-sounding Churchill Avenues dotted around the country, for example. Others haven't fared so well: one has to have a working knowledge of British athletics in the eighties to understand what London's Tessa Sanderson Way is all about.

It was somewhere in the middle of the Tessa-Churchill axis that this newly built street off Huntington Road was called. I presume that whoever it was at the council or the developer's office who came up with the idea must have thought they were being pretty damn cool. Which is why we drove past one day (appropriately enough with 'Rockin' All Over the World' on the coach stereo) to discover that the new street had been christened after the sainted Irishman himself: Geldof Road.

By 1984 Bob Geldof was not exactly at the elite end of the pop scene. It was five years since 'I Don't Like Mondays' had hit Number 1 and the releases from the Boomtown Rats' latest album had reached Number 73 and Number 50 respectively. He wasn't even the most famous person in the Geldof household: that honour went to his girlfriend, Paula Yates, the coquettish interviewer of rock stars bigger than Bob on *The Tube*. The Boomtown Rats' album that Geldof had tried and failed to promote was *In the Long Grass*, and it was only a matter of time before that was where the band were booted. In *Smash Hits* parlance, Geldof was 'down the dumper'.

Then, in November that year, Geldof sat down in front of *The Six O'Clock News* and found his career problems put acutely into perspective. The report in question was by Michael Buerk, and was an unflinching account of the famine in Ethiopia. 'Dawn,' Buerk began, 'and as the sun breaks the piercing chill of night [. . .] it lights up a biblical famine, now in the twentieth century. This place, say workers here, is the closest thing to hell on earth.' The pictures of starving people were horrific, and for Geldof impossible to ignore: 'the camera wandered amidst them like a mesmerized observer, occasionally dwelling on one person so that he looked directly at me, sitting in my comfortable living room.'[1] Geldof was also moved by an interview Buerk did with a young Red Cross nurse, Claire Bertschinger, who was given the unenviable task of choosing a few hundred to feed out of the thousands who were at the camp: the ones she didn't were almost certain to die.

It was an astonishing report and Buerk's usual dispassion-ate delivery was pierced with emotion: 'it was the voice of a man who was registering despair, grief and absolute disgust at what he was seeing.'[2] These were feelings that soon trans-ferred to Bob. Talking about the report later, he picked out the word 'biblical', which Buerk had chosen to sum up the enormity of what he had seen but perhaps struck Geldof in a different way. Was there something about that and the guilt of sitting there that struck a chord with the Catholicism of his early childhood? Reading his autobiography, one is struck, too, by Geldof's comment about how his remark-able project pulled together: 'I am not a great believer in notions of coincidence, serendipity, synchronicity and all the other rag, tag and bobtail of karmic law, but some things seemed too easy.'[3] He's almost going out of his way to use every word to describe what happens next except perhaps the obvious one: I might not be a religious man myself, but suspect that faith has been founded on less.

Geldof was by no means the only person to react strongly to Michael Buerk's report. Donations from the public were pouring in to the associated charities to the tune of £100,000 a day. Geldof wasn't even the first person in his household to react. He got up the next day to find a note from Paula stuck to the kitchen fridge: 'Ethiopia. Everyone who visits this house from today onwards will be asked to give £5 until we have raised £200 for famine relief.' Paula had left to go up to Newcastle to film *The Tube*, leaving Bob alone in London with his thoughts about whether there was something he could do. As chance would have it, the band on *The Tube* that week was Ultravox, and when Bob rang Paula that afternoon in her dressing room with his thoughts about making a charity record, she was sat next to Midge Ure. Paula put him on the phone and he became the first of many pop stars to be corralled by Bob into taking part over the following months.

Midge agreed to meet Bob for lunch at Langan's Brasserie in Mayfair for lunch the following Monday to discuss his idea. Bob went back to Ireland to see family and friends for the weekend, and he was in a taxi to visit one of them (a sculptor called Kuka) when the lyrics came to him – to the tune of a scrap of a song called 'It's My World' he'd been thinking about developing with the Boomtown Rats. 'I wrote fluently, with little crossing out,' Geldof remembers, 'the words poured out'.[4] At Kuka's house, Geldof's friend found him an old Spanish guitar and a tape player to record what he'd written (the bare bones of the first half of the song).

Midge, meanwhile, came up with his contribution to the song after his lunch with Bob on the Monday. Geldof didn't show him what he'd written – 'I might have a bit of a thing,' he told Ure – but was keener to know if Midge had anything. For all his bluster, the lack of hits had got to Bob: his confidence as a writer was shot (not that he'd say as much). 'Artists don't confess weakness and self-doubt to other artists, even if they are mates,' Midge recalls.[5]

Midge went home and started playing around with a Casio keyboard on the kitchen table, trying to think 'Christmas'. What he came up with (essentially the second half of the song) he thought sounded like 'Jingle Bells mixed with the *Dambusters* theme.'[6]

Geldof's reaction was slightly different: 'It sounds like fucking *Z Cars*,' was his response, though he was no less complimentary about his own contribution. 'It's a bit fucking corny,' he warned as he played Midge what he'd written on his twelve-string guitar – which had only seven strings, all of them out of tune. 'The song was in his head but he couldn't play it,' Midge remembers, trying in vain to get Bob to let him tune the guitar. 'Every time he sang it, it was different,' Midge wrote in his autobiography, *If I Was . . .* 'The lines, even the melody was changing constantly [. . .] the choruses were different lengths, the verses seemed to change, part of it he seemed to make up on the spot.'[7]

Eventually, Midge felt he had enough to work with (or had had enough of Geldof's out-of-tune strumming) and suggested that he was left to sort the music and the arrangement, while Geldof got on with rustling up the band. It's no surprise that the first producer the pair thought of to get in touch with was Trevor Horn. It's perhaps no surprise, either, that Horn said he would need a minimum of six weeks to record and mix the song. They settled instead for Midge taking the producer's role, and Horn supplying a day's use of his studio, SARM West, just off the Portobello Road. Midge, meanwhile, began pulling the song together. He used a drum sample from Tears for Fears' 'The Hurting' for the song's beginning, then stapled his '*Z Cars* theme' to Bob's 'corny' bit via a middle-eight section about raising a toast.

Bob, meanwhile, was going into overdrive to get people to sing on the record. The luck was undoubtedly with him: he rang up Sting, who just happened to be at home and said yes immediately. He bumped into Simon Le Bon in the street. He was walking past the Pushkin Gallery in Chelsea when he saw Gary Kemp through the window. He rang up a gallery at random from the *Yellow Pages* to find out how he might get hold of Peter Blake, the artist famous for, among other things, the cover for the Beatles' *Sgt. Pepper's Lonely Hearts Club Band*. The random gallery happened to be Blake's agent: Blake was on board within half an hour.

The more stars that Bob got on board, the more everyone wanted to be on board: pretty soon, he had the cream of the current pop crop signed up, together with Kool and the Gang and Status Quo. The line-up ended up being quite male – Sade, the Thompson Twins and the Eurythmics were all asked but couldn't make it, so Bananarama and Jody Watley were the only women there (unless you count Marilyn, who wasn't actually invited but turned up anyway). The other noticeable absentees were David Bowie, who Geldof had wanted to sing the opening lines, and Frankie Goes to Hollywood, who were in the middle of an American tour: both recorded messages that went on the B-side of the record.

At the same time as pulling the line-up together, Geldof was cajoling every part of the production chain to give up their section of the £1.30 single price they were due. The publishing rights were his and Ure's, the artists were singing for free and Horn had given them the studio time. Then the record company, Phonogram, waived their profit too, leaving just two to tackle: the retailers, and the government (who would take a chunk through VAT). Geldof got on the phone to the likes of Woolworths and Our Price and in his words 'systematically lied' to them: 'I read out to them not only the list of those who had agreed, but the list of all those I intended to approach.'[8] He went on to say that all the other chains had already signed up (they hadn't) and that they were the last retailer he was ringing up (they weren't – apart from the last one of course). In the end, only Margaret Thatcher's government wasn't for turning: so, with the exception of the VAT, every penny spent on the single went to famine relief. (After heavy criticism, the government eventually announced they would increase overseas aid to Africa by an equivalent amount.) Even with the VAT deduction, Geldof's original calculation that the record might raise something in the region of £70,000 was looking very modest indeed.

The person perhaps more worried than anyone during the approach to recording day – Sunday 25 November 1984 – was Midge Ure. It wasn't that the backing tracks weren't all in place, because these had already been recorded during the week: John Taylor and Sting had slipped in on the Saturday to put down some bass guitar and harmonies; Paul Weller had also turned up to add some guitar, which everyone agreed sounded great but didn't fit with the rest of Ure's keyboard-heavy arrangement and was quietly dropped. (Later, on the Sunday, despite Ure protesting that he was quite happy with the electronic drums he'd come up with, Phil Collins turned up with his kit and insisted on adding his. He set up, waited six hours, then did his part in ten minutes – he wasn't quite happy with the first take, so did it again – and went home.)

The reason for Midge Ure's nerves was an interview that he'd given to *Smash Hits* earlier in the month, to promote Ultravox's greatest hits, *The Collection*. Midge had been not exactly complimentary about some of his contemporaries. George Michael and Andrew Ridgeley, he declared, were 'prats'. *The Unforgettable Fire*, meanwhile, hadn't found a place in his record collection: 'I was going to buy the new U2 album but then I decided I didn't like them. They're a bit boring and the vocals are always far too loud.' And as for Duran Duran's 'Wild Boys' and Simon Le Bon's singing? 'Their new single's pathetic. I cannot believe they put it out with his vocal on like that. His vocal is terrible. It's awful.'[9]

Midge, though, was in luck. This was a day when pop stars left their egos, bygones and trappings at home. The only flashes of rock-star behaviour came from Spandau Ballet and Boy George. Spandau Ballet and Duran Duran had both been in Germany the night before, recording *Tommy's Pop Show*, which was a huge annual TV event. There followed a night of drunkenness where the bands attempted to drink each other under the table, so much so that everyone's recollection of events is slightly different.

Tony Hadley remembers their manager passing out in a toilet and having to climb over the top of a cubicle to get him out. Gary Kemp remembers drummer John Keeble going 'bonkers on Jack Daniel's'. Andy Taylor's memory of the evening, meanwhile, is of waiting for the hotel staff to go to bed before creeping downstairs and raiding the kitchens with Billy Idol.

The following morning the extremely hungover bands flew in their private jets to Heathrow, where Nick Rhodes had arranged for a make-up artist to meet them to sort them out before they headed for the studio. And while other artists captured the low-key mood of the day – Sting turning up on foot, for example, with a Sunday newspaper under his arm like he was off out for breakfast – Spandau Ballet were driven to the front door in black Daimler Princesses. When asked by a television crew if he had a message for the people of Ethiopia, saxophonist Steve Norman replied, 'Yeah, I'd just like to say sorry we couldn't tour down there this year but we'll try and fit it in next year.'[10]

Anything Spandau Ballet could do, Boy George could do better. While the rest of the pop world were awkwardly saying hello to each other in the studio, he was still asleep. In New York. 'Where the fuck are you?' was his gentle early morning call from Geldof. (Which was one of those stupid questions to ask: having called him in his hotel room, Geldof knew exactly where he was – which wasn't in a West London studio.) George made it on to the early morning Concorde, eventually breezing into the studio properly rock-and-roll late towards the end of the afternoon. 'Can someone get me some brandy?' he asked on arrival. 'Get on with it, you fucking old queen,' was Geldof's response.

What marked the day out, though, was how much everyone got on. Tony Hadley, who got the poisoned chalice of singing his solo lines first, received a round of applause from everyone for his troubles. An awkward and out-of-place Bono, who likened the day to a 'blow-drying convention' found himself being put at ease by Simon Le Bon. 'Do you want a drink? Are you OK? [. . .] I thought he had some grace and a sense of humour.'[11] On the sofa, in front of the telly, sat Paul Weller, Marilyn and Bananarama. In the toilets, Status Quo were busy making friends: 'Rick and I might have felt a little incongruous at first, milling about with all these eighties haircuts, but you know what they say: you're never alone with a bag of coke.'[12]

Boy George might have turned up late, but when he did arrive he sang with that clear-blue soul voice only he could pull off. In fact, with the exception of Status Quo, who spent an hour trying and failing to hit their middle-eight harmonies, all the singers pulled off their respective parts. Bono got the line nobody wanted, or more specifically he didn't want: 'it's the most biting line, and actually reveals how selfish a mindset we all have underneath'.[13] My guess is that Geldof gave it to him because he was the one singer there who would really 'get' the line, partly from the sort of songs U2 wrote, and partly from his religious beliefs. (Put it this way, it wouldn't have had the same impact if Kool and the Gang had sung it.) 'I can't sing that, Bob,' Bono told Geldof. 'This is not about what you want, OK?' Geldof replied. 'This is about what these people need.'[14] So Bono sang it, doing what he described as 'an impersonation of Bruce Springsteen'. 'I jumped,' remembers Midge Ure, who was standing next to him. 'It felt as if I was standing next to an opera singer, he had the same massive power.'[15]

Band Aid was a moniker suggested by someone working in the record company's press office. With its clever pun, suggesting that the efforts were a sticking plaster when a bigger response was needed, the name was a vast improvement on the other ideas floating about: Food for Thought, or The Bloody Do-Gooders. With all the contributions in the can, it was left to Midge Ure to work through the night to mix the song – or least try to while Bob had a shouting match on the phone with Robert Maxwell over photo permissions.

'Do They Know It's Christmas?' might not be the greatest song ever written, but as mega-selling singles go it's the best of the bunch. It's certainly more listenable than the song it overtook to become the biggest selling UK single of all time ('Mull of Kintyre') or the one that eventually overtook it (the England's Rose version of 'Candle in the Wind'). It sold four million copies in the UK and a further eight million around the world. In the US it shifted a million copies, outselling the Number 1 single by four to one, but – thanks to the byzantine Billboard ranking of sales and radio play – only got to Number 13. That, though, was academic: instead of raising the anticipated seventy grand the record actually brought in £8 million.

It also slotted seamlessly into the tradition of great Christmas songs. I've always held to the theory that a truly great Christmas single has to have a shard of darkness in there somewhere, almost as if it's not just about the birth of Christ but the chill of winter, too: think Jona Lewie's 'Stop the Cavalry', Gary Jules's cover of 'Mad World' or Simon and Garfunkel's '7 O'Clock News/ Silent Night'. Geldof's lyrics have been criticized for being overblown and portentous – 'clanging', to borrow a phrase. But they're in keeping with the language used in the Michael Buerk report that inspired Geldof, and there's undoubtedly a power through their directness.

It wasn't the intention, but Band Aid served to bring together all the big British pop acts from the first half of the eighties. This was the high watermark for this era of bands. But rather than defining the times through confrontation, in a decade that was often seen as synonymous with greed, here was a moment of collaboration, of good. It's easy to be cynical, now, regarding everyone's intentions: to assume that the 'good cause' being promoted was their own careers. But I think that's putting a more modern, self-aware mindset on earlier times. Band Aid was different because it was new. In a way, it was a bit like the first series of the reality-TV show *Big Brother* compared with all the others. In later series, because everyone had already seen the show, contestants behaved differently and more knowingly: they went in on the assumption they could become famous, and hammed it up accordingly. In the first series that awareness simply wasn't there. The same is true, I think, with Band Aid. After the success of that single, everyone knew the effect these things could have:

the 'charidee' element that crept into future projects was a result of that.

While the first half of the eighties was something of a charity-single desert, the second half found the charts stuffed with them, blocking up the Number 1 spot in the same way that the *Now . . .* compilations were dominating the album charts. The first of these was 'We Are the World' from the American answer to Band Aid, Harry Belafonte's USA for Africa. Co-written by Michael Jackson and Lionel Richie, the song actually combined the pair's mushy side, resulting in a composition so saccharine that if you listened to it more than twice in a row you were in danger of having your teeth fall out.

Everything about the USA for Africa recording was done on a grand scale: there were the big-name participants, from Diana Ross to Stevie Wonder, Paul Simon to Tina Turner; there was the Quincy Jones production and the hiring of Charlie Chaplin's old studio, A&M, for the recordings; there was the long line of limos waiting for their celebrities, and fights between the chauffeurs as to who should take priority; then there was the £50,000 of food laid on for the stars, the centrepiece being a giant fish carved out of ice spouting caviar and champagne. Bob Geldof, who had been invited over to watch proceedings, was not impressed.

It wasn't just the biggest names who responded to the Ethiopian famine. Perhaps the most credible of this batch of charity singles was 'Starvation' – a sort of two-tone All Stars, featuring the Specials, Madness, UB40 and the Pioneers.

The single was a double-A side, with the reverse featuring 'Tam Tam Pour L'Ethiopie' by a collaboration of African artists, including Youssou N'Dour, King Sunny Adé and Salif Keïta. Then there was the coming together of the hard-rock fraternity in the shape of the hilariously named Hear 'n Aid: their single 'Stars' was written by Dio and featured the members of Judas Priest, Iron Maiden, Mötley Crüe and even Spinal Tap.

Pretty quickly it became the de rigueur reaction to a disaster for someone to pull together a charity record in response, though not everyone had Harry Belafonte's contacts book or Bob Geldof's way of twisting arms. When fifty-six people died after a fire at a Bradford City football game, Gerry 'and the Pacemakers' Marsden put together the Crowd to record 'You'll Never Walk Alone' to raise money. His terrace of singers was a slightly mixed line-up that included Motörhead, Black Lace, Keith Chegwin, Phil Lynott, Rick Wakeman and the Barron Knights.

Two years later it was the victims of the Zeebrugge ferry disaster who got the charity-record treatment. This time the driving force was the *Sun*, as a number of the 193 passengers who died had bought cheap tickets through a promotion with the paper. Being associated with the *Sun* was undoubtedly a sticking point for some pop stars, hence the Ferry Aid recording of 'Let It Be' featured an eclectic line-up that included Paul McCartney, Boy George, Mark King, Ben Volpeliere-Pierrot and Kate Bush, with Su Pollard, Mandy Smith and Bucks Fizz in the crowd scenes. Two years later, Gerry Marsden and Paul McCartney completed a sort of charity-record trilogy when they joined forces with the Christians and Holly Johnson to sing 'Ferry Cross the Mersey' following the Hillsborough tragedy.

In the wake of Band Aid came Sport Aid and Comic Relief, both with tie-in singles. For Sport Aid someone had the brilliant idea of inserting the word 'run' into a popular song: so Tears for Fears' 'Everybody Wants to Rule the World' became 'Everybody Wants to Run the World' – identical in every way to the original single bar that one word; similarly, Status Quo's 'Rocking All Over the World' became, well, I'm sure you can work it out. Comic Relief, meanwhile, introduced the idea of a comedy charity single, where pop stars would team up with comedians and produce vaguely humorous results. Cliff Richard and the Young Ones' 'Living Doll' sort of worked – there was at least some sort of connection between the singer and the characters. The link between Mel Smith and Kim Wilde was that their names became Mel and Kim; by the time French and Saunders and Kathy Burke were La Na Nee Nee Noo Noo, their choice of duet with Bananarama ('Help!') seemed somewhat appropriate.

Most of these songs, you'll note, tended to be the classic cover-version option rather than something new. This could create problems in that the music publishers were due a chunk of royalties and, as happened in the case of the Crowd's 'You'll Never Walk Alone', could decide to pocket their share. But why cover a classic song when you could cover a whole album? In 1988, the *NME* organized a re-recording of the Beatles' *Sgt. Pepper's Lonely Hearts Club*

Band in aid of ChildLine. The resulting album, *Sgt. Pepper Knew My Father*, saw a strange selection of bands each given a different song to massacre: rare was the music fan indeed who must have thought, 'The Fall playing "A Day in the Life"? Wet Wet Wet singing "With a Little Help from My Friends"? The Courtney Pine Quartet doing "When I'm Sixty-Four"? This is the record I've been waiting for!' The Wet Wet Wet song, backed with Billy Bragg's 'She's Leaving Home', produced another charity Number 1 and one of the most excruciating *Top of the Pops* performances of the decade: Bragg had taped the lyrics to the studio floor only to find them being swallowed up in a sea of dry ice; also lost in the musical mist was the tune.

For all the cynicism attached to some of the participants on the later records, there was no mistaking the sincerity of Geldof's original motives, nor his extraordinary drive and determination in pushing things through. I think it's a little trite to say that he gave music a conscience: the truth is that his actions probably checked the eighties excess a bit. But for that, and for all the money he raised, he was what Bonnie Tyler had been holding out for. Bob Geldof is a hero.

Side Two

(1985–1989)

Track One

A View to a Kill

Bob Geldof is a bastard.

Oh yes, you can give him all the 'he's what Bonnie Tyler had been holding out for' adulation, the pats on the back and knighthoods and deifications and all the rest of it. And yes, he might have had a hand in helping the starving children of Ethiopia escape an otherwise certain death and setting in motion a charitable impulse among pop stars that went on to raise money for numerable good causes. But, at the same time, he is the man responsible for single-handedly ruining the second half of the eighties for teenage music fans in the city of York.

In the early months of 1985, in the aftermath of Band Aid's extraordinary success, Bob Geldof briefly went back to the day job, with a tour to promote the Boomtown Rats album no one was interested in. On the plus side, all the publicity generated by Band Aid had filled out the auditoriums that would otherwise have been half-empty, even if the extra punters were generally people who just wanted to see Bob, or shake his hand. As much as the band might have wanted to, they couldn't get away from Band Aid: the buckets put out for people to put money into were overflowing, and the 'action' on the tour bus after the show was reduced to counting this out.

As part of the tour, the Boomtown Rats came to play the Central Hall at York University. I think it is fair to say that York was not a city overburdened with great music venues in the mid-1980s. For local bands, there were two backroom-of-the-pub venues in which wannabe rock stars could strut their stuff: the Winning Post and the Spotted Cow. By the end of the decade, there'd be Fazers, a pub/club venue that seemed to shut and open with a new name every six months – one constant being the stick of the carpet and the damp sweat on the walls.

The only place in York to see a proper band was the university's Central Hall. Over the years, it had played host to the likes of Genesis, Dire Straits and Emerson, Lake and Palmer. The hall itself was a slightly strange design, sort of a cross between a multistorey car park and something from *Blake's 7*. It also had a stringent 'sit down' policy: like an extension of that town where Kevin Bacon lived in *Footloose*, dancing was forbidden. The justification given for this was that the hall was next to the university lake, and too much adverse movement might damage the foundations and potentially sink everything. It wasn't very rock and roll, a sit-down venue, but that was the deal: we Yorkies did as we were told, and the half-decent bands added York to their tour dates in return.

After the experience of Band Aid, however, Bob was not a man to be told what he could or couldn't do. Such was the force of his persuasiveness that *Spitting Image* lampooned 'We Are the World' as 'We're Scared of Bob', with the American stars cowed into doing whatever he said, just as long as he didn't shout at them again. So when the man from York University politely tried to explain to him that dancing wasn't allowed, Geldof wasn't having any of it.

Instead, the lead singer of the Boomtown Rats allegedly encouraged the audience to ignore the stewards, come down to the front and boogie away to the band's latest Top 75 smash. Local legend has it that he said something along the lines of, 'It's not going to sink; this isn't fucking Venice you know.' Legend also has it that as fans clashed with stewards the concert descended into a 'near riot', though I suspect that (this being a university hall) 'near riot' is a way of saying not actually a riot at all. There was an orchestra pit in front of the stage, which was covered over, and that got a bit damaged. And I believe a couple of chairs got broken too. Certainly, it wasn't on the scale of when Frankie Goes to Hollywood played Chicago's oddly named Bismarck Theater a couple months earlier: here the auditorium floor gave way completely and it was only the carpet being nailed down tightly on top of it that stopped people falling through.

Even so, in the aftermath of the gig, as Bob wandered away to count his buckets of Band Aid money, the damage to the hall was estimated to run into thousands of pounds. The Students' Union were liable (the gig was part of rag week) and were all for suing, but decided that, given how the rest of the world thought Bob walked on water, it was probably not the best PR move to try to push things too much. The university authorities, meanwhile, decided to ensure that such an incident never happened again. And from that point on, groups were – if you'll pardon the pun – banned.

One of the epiphanies of the teenage years is that first-gig experience. I was thirteen by 1985, music mad, and ready for those life-changing first memories. In a sea of music, York was suddenly cast adrift. The only option was to go down to a local travel agent who offered gig-and-coach packages to what then seemed exotic-sounding places like Nottingham Rock City or Manchester Apollo. These, though, tended to leave York before the end of school and arrived back at three in the morning. It was one thing to try to persuade my parents to let me see a concert at the university a couple of miles away; it was quite another to get them to let me go on such a package.

So yes, Bob, you might have fed the world, but you also starved my teenage years of gigs at the same time. So thanks. Thanks a lot, Bob.

Just to rub in the fact that I wasn't going to see any gigs in the near future, Bob proceeded to go on and put together the biggest concert of all time. I can't quite say for definite where Bob got the whole Live Aid idea from, but put it this way: the week before he came to play in York, our local paper, the *Yorkshire Evening Press*, ran a front-page story about a possible York Rock Festival to be held at the racecourse in the middle of July. Among the big names apparently being lined up to play were Queen, U2, Duran Duran and someone called the Curse (who I can only assume were actually the Cure but the subeditor had never heard of them). As it turned out, the festival never happened: in proper provincial style, it was discovered that the proposed date clashed with the summer fete at nearby St Chad's Church and the vicar was worried the Curse might drown out his own prior booking: the Railway Institute Band. As the Railway Institute Band booking took precedence, Queen, U2 and Duran Duran suddenly found themselves with a free weekend in the middle of July. Handy, that, if you happened to be organizing an international rock concert.

The idea for Live Aid actually came about in the aftermath of Band Aid and Bob Geldof's subsequent trip to Ethiopia. Upon seeing the situation for himself, Geldof was aware just how much the £8 million the single had raised was a single drop in the desert. What made him particularly determined to raise more money was his desire to break the trucking cartel that distributed the aid. If the Band Aid Trust had more money, it could use its own transport and get the aid directly (and more cheaply) to those who needed it.

The notion of a charity concert was not, of course, a new one. That particular idea can be traced back to George Harrison and Ravi Shankar and their 1971 Concert for Bangladesh, held in response to another horrific tragedy:

in this instance Bhola Cyclone, which killed an estimated 500,000 people. Harrison's address book included the likes of Eric Clapton, Bob Dylan and Ringo Starr, and the line-up played to 40,000 people at Madison Square Garden (twice, in fact: once in the afternoon and again in the evening). It is estimated that the concert, together with the subsequent album and film, raised $12million.

The Concert for Bangladesh took place in an earlier technological era. The mid-eighties was the MTV era, and advances in television and transmission offered a new wealth of possibilities. Even five years previously the thought of running a show on both sides of the Atlantic, with each concert beamed to screens at the latter, together with feeds from other countries around the world, would have been met with a 'can't be done' shake of the head. Before Live Aid, the most complicated piece of international television had been the 1984 Los Angeles Olympics, where for the first time at the Games countries could mix the home footage with coverage they'd filmed themselves. Here, though, all the footage was all going in the same direction, and required the use of a couple of satellites. Live Aid had its two main concerts, and additional feeds as it brought in an INXS from Australia or an Autograph from the Soviet Union: its complexity required sixteen satellites to work. However, work the system did: the only idea dropped on technical grounds was a suggested duet between Mick Jagger and David Bowie, each singing their parts on opposite sides of the Atlantic.

As much of a challenge as the satellites was the line-up itself. Band Aid was relatively straightforward in this respect as Geldof got the main players on board from the beginning and everyone else followed suit. Here, though, logistics, money and nerves were a factor: one estimate of flying in a band and equipment was something in the region of £20,000[1]: for that you got fifteen minutes of fame (or five if you were Adam Ant), no sound-check and the risk of looking awful in front of two billion people (at two a.m. on the night before the concert, the U2 camp rang Geldof about precisely this: 'Fuck 'em,' was Bob's exhausted reply).

Geldof brought in promoter Harvey Goldsmith to help put the line-up together. He continued the trick he'd used with the record shops for Band Aid, claiming that people were playing before they'd actually committed. So at the press launch Queen were a little surprised to find themselves announced – though perhaps not half as surprised as the Who, whom Geldof had just unilaterally reformed for the concert. It was the American end where things were particularly difficult, with the politics of promoters not helped by a slightly rubbish choice of venue: the 'back of the parking lot' vibe of Philadelphia's JFK Stadium. In the press adverts for tickets (a very reasonable £25, billed as £5 for the ticket and a £20 donation), no fewer than eight members of the supposed US line-up failed to come good (including Billy Joel, Huey Lewis and the News and Paul Simon). Many of the main USA for Africa stars – Michael Jackson, Diana Ross, Stevie Wonder – also declined in what was described as being like a 'block vote'. This led to some criticisms of an overly white line-up – the *Voice* newspaper talked of a 'Band

Aid Blacklist', and in London Sade was the only major non-white artist to perform. Geldof's response was: 'I don't care if they are orange, luminous pink or green, the object is to stop people dying.' He pushed for the biggest stars he could get, as these would generate the biggest audience and hopefully raise the most money: he wanted the likes of Michael Jackson and Stevie Wonder there; they just turned him down, and they weren't the only ones.

Prince had failed to turn up to record 'We Are the World', so his no show wasn't a huge surprise; his contribution (a token video aside) was helping out with the choreography for Madonna, who'd visited him in Minneapolis the week before. Bruce Springsteen, meanwhile, was such a potential pull that at one stage in proceedings Geldof offered to move the date of the concert to accommodate him. Springsteen, though, had just got married, and was exhausted from finishing a huge European tour – in fact, he'd only just played Wembley himself. It was on his stage that the London leg of the concert was performed.

The comments of the *Voice* and other criticisms of the line-up came about because of the astonishing power that the pulling together of the line-up created. Live Aid was acclaimed 'the day the music changed the world', 'the biggest rock event in history', and 'the greatest live concert in all time'. It was one of those moments that would be seen to define a generation: that was what people sensed, and why it mattered who was on the line-up. After all, ask anyone about music in the eighties and many will tell you that the first things to pop into their head are their memories of 13 July 1985.

What I remember about the concert, in a strange kind of way, are the colours. While some recollections fade into sepia, Live Aid's palate remains resolutely rich. There's that clear, desert-blue sky over both London and Philadelphia, fittingly cloudless, perhaps, or maybe a flicker of African heat for a few hours. There's the audience, people as far as the camera can stretch, so many they're reduced to pink and white flecks. And on stage there are the stars in their full eighties regalia: an assortment of pastel shirts, white trousers and technicolour dreamcoats with the sleeves rolled up.

In fact, the only faded thing all day was the denim worn by the opening act, Status Quo. With the exception of Rick Parfitt's fluorescent-pink shirt, Quo's performance could have been straight out of any year of their career. Their choice of opener – 'Rocking All Over the World' – reduced Wembley Stadium to the back room of a pub. Even though I was somewhat over acquainted with it, there's no doubt it was a brilliant song to begin the show with: cheesy and cheery, feel-good and familiar. It is a harsh person indeed who cannot watch that performance without some sort of smile on their face.

As Bob Geldof wrote in *Is That It?*, 'Quo were the cartoon encapsulation of everything rock and roll is meant to be – ordinary blokes with long hair in denims playing a twelve bar loud.'[2] Band Aid had been a pop single but Live Aid was a rock concert. While the former had pulled together a specific generation of music stars, the latter spread its reach wider and further: here weren't just the eighties bands, but also the best of the sixties (Paul McCartney, Mick Jagger, Bob Dylan, the Who) and the seventies (Led Zeppelin, David Bowie, Queen); here was classic soul (the Temptations), heavy metal (Judas Priest, Black Sabbath), even AOR bands like REO Speedwagon that MTV pop had been meant to kill off.

Looking again at the line-up, what feels striking now is not that Live Aid defined a generation but how it put one in a wider context – this was the moment when the musical stars of the eighties shared the stage with the stars of the sixties and seventies and found out, in front of the world, whether they were good enough to cut the mustard. Here, for example, were not just Duran Duran and Spandau Ballet, but also the two men who inspired them in the first place: David Bowie and Bryan Ferry; here was not just George Michael, but also his own particular idols: Queen and Elton John.

Bob Geldof's description of Status Quo as 'everything rock and roll is meant to be' is strikingly different to what music in the early eighties had been about: this had been pop, not rock and roll; this was blow-dried hair with highlights, not lanky and tied back in a ponytail; this was Antony Price suits, not faded denim jackets. Above all, this wasn't 'twelve bar' with its guitar-based lineage back to the blues, back to its American roots: eighties pop had been more European, more about synthesizers than six strings, less about learning your craft and more about listening to Kraftwerk.

Live Aid was the self-styled 'day the music changed the world', but it was also 'the day the music changed'. The people given the job of hosting the BBC coverage weren't the *Top of the Pops* stable of Radio One DJs, but were the presenters of BBC2's *The Old Grey Whistle Test* (Andy Kershaw, Mark Ellen, David Hepworth and Richard Skinner). That decision fitted with what was happening on Bruce Springsteen's stage: the big moments that everyone remembers from the concert are all the rock ones – Status Quo kicking things off, U2 with Bono plucking a girl out of the crowd and Queen's remarkable six-song tour de force. These were all about playing live, about performance, about switching off the synthesizers and strapping on the guitars: Live Aid, in essence, was the birth, the opening riff, of stadium rock.

It was also the beginning of the end of early eighties pop. A week might be a long time in politics, but six months in the short attention span of fickle pop fans is an eternity. In 1984, everything had come good for the 'big five' – Duran, Spandau, Wham!, Culture Club and Frankie. But by the summer of 1985 each of these of these were facing their own individual struggles, and would never reach the same *Smash Hits* heights of stardom again. Live Aid might have been the making of U2, but it was also the last performance by the original line-up of Duran Duran until their reunion tour two decades later. This was the second time in half a decade that British music had gone pop, but this time it was in a different way.

*   *   *

How Frankie Goes to Hollywood and Culture Club would have fared at Live Aid is one of those 'what if?' questions favoured by historians with too much time on their hands. Such was their status that had either had said yes to Bob, the likes of Nik Kershaw or Howard Jones might have found themselves squeezed out. The bands had different reasons for turning the offer down: for Frankie, it was Holly Johnson who wanted to do it and the rest of the band who didn't; for Culture Club, it was the rest of band who were keen and Boy George who was saying no. For the Frankie refuseniks, the issue was the tens of thousands it would cost to get the band and their gear there; for Boy George it was 'a mixture of fear and loathing. I didn't think we could cut it in front of two billion people and disliked the pomposity of it all.'[3]

In spring 1985, billposters advertising Frankie's new single declared 'Welcome to the Pleasuredome' as the band's 'fourth Number 1'. It wasn't, making it only to Number 2 behind Phil Collins and Philip Bailey's 'Easy Lover'. In fact, Frankie's fourth Number 1 would never materialize – every single they released sold less than the one before: 'Two Tribes' couldn't match the amazing numbers of 'Relax'; 'The Power of Love' spent one week rather than the nine weeks of 'Two Tribes' at Number 1; 'Pleasuredome' didn't even get to Number 1; the singles off the second album, meanwhile, got to Numbers 4, 19 and 28 (lack of) respectively.

Frankie were an eighties pop band who fell at the same hurdle so many other British bands have done: America. It's a less media-savvy audience and less centralized music press was not wowed by the Paul Morley pyrotechnics that had propelled Frankie to notoriety in the UK: a tour that coincided with the 1984 presidential election saw the T-shirts tweaked to 'FRANKIE SAY . . . SHIT THE POLITICIAN'. It saw the band's cover of Bruce Springsteen's 'Born to Run' treated as something approaching sacrilege. It found Frankie as a live act failing to replicate the sonic thump that had made their name: 'extremely tame' was *Smash Hits'* disappointed verdict – 'there's little of the punch of their records'.[4]

Perhaps most importantly it found Frankie as a band splitting in two, with Johnson on one side and the 'lads' on the other – and Paul Rutherford increasingly falling in with the latter. The wedge was Wolfgang, Holly's new boyfriend, who he took on tour with him. The lads, by now enjoying the high jinks of a seventies rock band, objected to the breaking of rock's cardinal 'no partners' rule; Johnson, by contrast, objected to the group's boozy behaviour and their attitude towards Wolfgang. This was to come to a climax on the group's final tour, where 'eye-holes were burned into pillowcases to create Ku Klux Klan-like masks' and the lads banged on Johnson's door, shouting 'Come out you fucking Nazi bastards!'[5] By this point, Johnson was travelling separately to gigs by plane and train, while the rest of band were larging it together on the bus.

None of which provided an exactly harmonious atmosphere in which to record the band's second album, *Liverpool*. On top of this, the sprinkling of Trevor Horn's magic production dust was also largely absent: second time round he was executive producer only. The result was that, in a harbinger of the Stone Roses' subsequent musical journey, the group's second album ditched the dance elements in favour of a straighter (and less interesting) rock sound. The result was, more than anything, a rather sad album, with an unmistakable whiff of decay: the first single, 'Rage Hard', took its inspiration from Dylan Thomas's 'Do Not Go Gentle Into That Good Night', and its lumpish backing was every bit the sound of a band struggling 'against the dying of the light'. Gone were the joys of Coleridge's 'Pleasuredome': the second single pitched the band as 'warriors' of T. S. Eliot's 'Wasteland'. The group's final single, 'Watching the Wildlife', had a more prosaic inspiration – Johnson observing the rest of the band's behaviour on tour. It was the best song on the album, but served only to sum up the end of a band who, however briefly, had looked like world-beaters.

A month after Band Aid, Boy George took ecstasy for the first time: 'the next morning I woke feeling liberated, like I'd opened Pandora's pillbox and found the meaning of life.'[6] George had always been resolutely anti-drugs ('sipping English breakfast tea' when he could have been out 'whoring and scoring') but pretty soon was making up for lost time. Cocaine came next – first by means of snorting it, then the 'orgasmic and desperate' rush of freebasing it – and then finally heroin. In his autobiography, Boy George describes his 'skinny, sweated and addicted' self flying back to Britain on Concorde next to Dave Stewart, 'who entertained me with tales of acid and mushroom tripping while I vomited the five-star cuisine into a sick bag'.[7] As George's drugs use became an open secret in the industry, the tabloids offered a £50,000 reward for anyone willing to spill the beans. It wasn't long before the stories came and he was re-christened 'Junkie George' for his troubles.

The drugs ultimately did for the band – it was 'quietly accepted' it was over, remembers George – but the fault lines were starting to show before that first ecstasy pill. A *Smash Hits* interview with Culture Club during the filming of the video for 1984's 'The War Song' found a group already at odds, and not just the traditional tension between George and Jon Moss. 'Everybody's egos seem to be catching up with them,' claimed Mikey glumly. 'All our personalities have changed.' A couple of weeks later Paul Young joined in, comparing his fame to that of Boy George: 'I'd rather become a millionaire in ten years than two – a rise like Boy George's would be just too fast. I couldn't cope with that. Boy George isn't coping so well himself, by all accounts.'[8]

Musically, Culture Club's stock was already falling away before Boy George had an irate Irishman down the end of the phone asking where the hell he was. *Waking Up with the House on Fire*, released at the end of 1984, had nothing on it to compare to the likes of 'Church of the Poison Mind' or the catchiness of 'Karma Chameleon'. The only proper hit off the album was the aforementioned 'The War Song', whose six-figure Russell Mulcahy video couldn't hide the fact that the single was based around the supposition that war was, for want of a better word, stupid. As trite messages went, this was right up there with Depeche Mode's 'People are People', which had famously argued that we shouldn't behave so 'awfully' to each other. *Smash Hits* slated the Culture Club album as 'a disaster of mediocrity', describing one song as something 'Shakin' Stevens would be deeply ashamed of' and another as 'remarkably awful'. The following autumn a patched-up Culture Club were headlining a tour of Japan, supported by the Style Council and Go West. The sell-out crowds of previous tours, though, had disappeared: at the 30,000-capacity Yokohama Stadium, just 5000 turned up to watch.

The two bands of the 'big five' who did turn up to play at Live Aid were the original New Romantic rivals, Spandau Ballet and Duran Duran. This time, though, there was to be no back-slapping backstage or sharing make-up artists, for Duran were performing in Philadelphia (twice in the case of the Taylors John and Andy) while Spandau were back in Britain.

If Frankie and Culture Club were beset by classic rock problems of partners on tour and drug use, Spandau were enjoying that other rock-star cliché: the tax break. Essentially, this involved spending most of the year outside of the UK (you are allowed back in for a small set number of days) and getting a not inconsiderable amount of tax written off as a result. If you've ever wondered why bands go out on ridiculously long world tours, and then moan to all and sundry that they're missing home, that's your answer.

The problem for Spandau was that on the third night of the American leg of the tour saxophonist Steve Norman slid across the stage and did in his anterior cruciate ligament in the process. His Band Aid 'hopes' of making it to Ethiopia, or indeed anywhere else, were over. The world tour was cancelled, but because of the tax situation the band couldn't come back to Britain. Instead, they holed up in Ireland to write a new album. Except that not only did the band not have a world tour, but they also didn't have a record label: cross at their lack of success in America and the perceived lack of promotional support they'd received, the group were in the middle of extricating themselves from their current deal. All of which meant that to pop fans like me it was as though the band had disappeared off the face of the earth: it wasn't to be until summer 1986 that everything was resolved and they finally released a new single.

Live Aid, then, was something of a fillip for Spandau Ballet, and a welcome return to the UK, even if their lack of American success found themselves playing in the early afternoon sunshine before the US concert had even begun. Despite the heat, Tony Hadley insisted on wearing an enormous full-length leather coat. Being given three songs, the band decided to premier one of the new songs they'd been working on: 'Virgin', which would go on to be an album track on their next release, went down like a lead balloon on a day when everyone else was playing their biggest hits. To compound a bad day at the office, Gary Kemp took the opportunity to say hello to his childhood hero, David Bowie: '"David? Hi. It's Gary Kemp." His eyes flicked round at me. "Hi." And then returned to the guy he was with.'[9] Kemp added, a little forlornly: 'from Spandau Ballet', to which Bowie merely nodded, as if to say 'I know'.

Unlike Frankie and Culture Club, when Spandau did finally break their hiatus they came back with perhaps their best song, 'Through the Barricades' – a 'Romeo and Juliet'-style number about the Troubles in Northern Ireland. It had the reach and sweep to match Tony Hadley's vocals, and was perhaps the most heartfelt song they recorded: every songwriter needs a subject, and it sounded as though Gary Kemp had found one that properly inspired him for the first time since Clare Grogan. But, as strong as the song was (it was their last Top 10 hit), and hard as they were trying, it wasn't quite enough to save them. Nowhere was this more summed up than when, during the album's recording, the band had returned to Britain for a party hosted by Charles and Diana for the Prince's Trust. Having leapt out of their limos, the band waved to the crowd and photographers and bounded up the steps . . . and into the closed door of the shoe shop next to the venue.

The unravelling of Duran Duran, meanwhile, took a little longer to reveal itself. It was masked by the fact they were still having huge hits, but in fact their big singles were a succession of one-offs: so Number 1 single 'The Reflex' had been a remix by Nile Rodgers; the 'Wild Boys' was for a Russell Mulcahy film based on a William Burroughs story that never materialized; 'A View to a Kill' was a James Bond theme. So, while their presence in the singles charts was being kept up, the only 'new' album in the same period was

Arena, a recording of the band in concert. The first three Duran albums had been released in three years: the fourth would take the same time again to appear.

Physically, and musically, the members of Duran Duran were in different places. The fault line here was probably between Nick Rhodes and guitarist Andy Taylor – 'Nick is very much the Andy Warhol kind of elitist artist, whereas Andy is a rock'n'roller who wants to get down and dirty.'[10] Where Duran worked was when they combined these two contrasting instincts, the cool keyboard chords and the rough rock riffs. But for the making of *Seven and the Ragged Tiger* the rock side of the band felt the keyboards had dominated. The response of Andy and John Taylor was to fall for yet another rock cliché: the side project. The self-titled *The Power Station* boasted Robert Palmer on vocals and Chic's Tony Thompson on drums, and was named after the New York studio where it was recorded. It was indulgent rock folly of the highest order: half a million pounds in recording costs, a residency at the exclusive Carlyle Hotel ($50,000 a week at today's prices), and an album that included covers of childhood favourites like 'Get it On'. Anything John and Andy could do, however, the rest of the band could do better. On the other side of the Atlantic, Nick Rhodes's desire was to make a 'delicate' record. At the equally exclusive Hôtel Plaza Athénée in Paris, the rest of Duran took an entire floor for months. Their offshoot project, Arcadia, resulted in the equally forgettable album, *So Red the Rose*, which cost a million pounds to make.

Still the spending and the indulgence continued. This time it was Simon Le Bon's turn, and his chance to fulfil his lifelong sailing dreams. Le Bon bought into *Drum*, a million-dollar, seventy-seven feet 'maxi yacht' that was named after the sound it made while whizzing through the water. The *Drum* dream was to sail it in the Whitbread round-the-world race – and Le Bon was to achieve exactly that in early 1986, joining the crew for the New Zealand to Uruguay section and again for the closing leg (*Drum* finished third). But the real drama took place in the ship's warm-up event, the Fastnet Race around Britain. On 11 August 1985, a few miles off the coast of Cornwall, *Drum* found itself in a force-eight gale and capsized. At the time, Le Bon was between shifts on deck and asleep downstairs. He and the others trapped inside found an air pocket and waited. By this point, the air below was thick with petrol fumes and hydrogen chloride: the estimate of the diver who rescued them was that they could have survived for an hour at most; fortunately, an automatic signal was set off when the boat went over and a Royal Navy helicopter was at the scene in twenty minutes.

By the time Simon's boating adventures were over, and the side-projects were out of everyone's system, the band the press had once dubbed the 'fab five' were now a somewhat lighter-walleted threesome: Rhodes, Le Bon and John Taylor. In a way, the new look Duran Duran was actually just another offshoot, this time a funk-friendly version that was partly fuelled by the choice of producer, Chic's Nile Rodgers, and partly via copious amounts of partying: 'I was so smashed out of my mind, I can't remember all those songs,' Rodgers remembers (if you can remember something you can't remember); 'I had a lot of good times with Nile,' John Taylor says, 'it got to the stage with cocaine where I didn't even have to ask, it was always just there.'[11] Along with those other 1986 comeback albums, *Liverpool*, *From Luxury to Heartache* and *Through the Barricades*, *Notorious* had its flashes of former glory, a solitary Top 10 single, and – like Simon Le Bon thinking wistfully back to his round-the-world adventures – the sound of a band missing the boat.

Live Aid, it turned out, was the final performance of the original Duran Duran line-up, though no one knew that at the time. It probably wasn't the way they'd have wanted to be remembered: 'a pretty reluctant and unconvincing showing' was *Smash Hits'* verdict. On the plus side, the band performed at quarter to two in the morning UK time, by which point most Duran fans were tucked up in bed. The other plus point was that the band were somehow higher up the bill than Led Zeppelin, whose set was so rotten they refused to allow it on the DVD twenty-five years later. Coming on after them, Duran looked comparatively slick – though in truth they seemed distracted and unrehearsed: on 'A View to a Kill' (another song left off the DVD), Simon Le Bon reached for and missed a high note by quite some distance; on 'Save a Prayer', Nick Rhodes's keyboard was wonky (I think because of the weather) and everything was similarly out of tune. Meanwhile, John and Andy Taylor, fresh from playing as the Power Station a couple of hours earlier, are throwing rock shapes left right and centre. The whole band had gone brunette for the occasion and, with the exception of Simon Le Bon's sleeves-rolled-up red jacket, were all dressed in black and white. In look as well as sound this was an off-colour final performance.

The last man standing of this generation of pop stars was George Michael. Here was a sharp pop brain at work; even at the height of Wham!'s success in 1984 Michael was laying down a marker with his single 'Careless Whisper'. And here and there among the Wham! concerts and publicity there started to be solo appearances: at Band Aid, Andrew Ridgeley was, like Boy George, still in bed, though no one felt the need to wake him up; at a Motown anniversary concert in May 1985, George Michael's singing partners were the slightly more illustrious Smokey Robinson and Stevie Wonder. At Live Aid, he was introduced to huge cheers by Elton John, who quickly added 'and Andrew Ridgeley!' as the other half of Wham! appeared by his side. Ridgeley, though, knew his place, which was in the line of backing singers at the rear of the stage, sharing a microphone with Kiki Dee. Every inch the eighties pop star in shades, leather jacket and white T-shirt, George Michael sang Elton's 'Don't Let the Sun Go Down on Me': 'very average' was Michael's own verdict; 'really quite moving' was *Smash Hits*'. The truth was that he had been welcomed to – and deserved his place at – music's top table.

Wham! had worked in the first place because Andrew Ridgeley supplied the confidence that George Michael lacked. Once Michael had got that, and realized how good he actually was as a singer and songwriter, he didn't need his partner any more. The crunch point came on the band's

American tour in the summer of 1985, when the band's management presented them with a huge offer to do a Pepsi commercial: $3.3 million. Signing the contract would mean extending the life of Wham! by at least another year (the duration of the proposed campaign); at this point George Michael decided enough was enough.

Wham! did in late 1985 and 1986 what Duran Duran had done in 1984 and early 1985: carry on by releasing a couple of stand-alone singles ('I'm Your Man' and 'The Edge of Heaven'). Unlike Duran Duran and their unintended and ramshackle last performance, Wham! ended by claiming the Live Aid venue for themselves with 'The Final', a carefully choreographed farewell concert at Wembley Stadium. A million people applied for the 72,000 £13.50 tickets, and those who got lucky sat patiently through a somewhat bizarre bill of Gary Glitter and Nick Heyward before Wham! appeared for the very last time. The group's final song, 'I'm Your Man', saw the duo joined by Elton John and Simon Le Bon.

Like Duran Duran, Frankie, Spandau Ballet and Culture Club, Wham! released an album in 1986. Theirs, though, was different: a greatest-hits collection, also called *The Final*, which swept up the singles in chronological order and was by far the bestselling of this somewhat rum bunch. Wham! made their exit at the right time: whether that was well-judged on the band's behalf, or fortuitous timing in terms of George Michael's development, the result was that the group (unlike Simon Le Bon) went out hitting all the right notes. Andrew Ridgeley retired to Monaco to crash cars, while George Michael's musical adventure was just beginning.

Track Two

Alive and Kicking

With irrepressible timing, my mother called me for tea just as Jack Nicholson in Philadelphia was announcing the arrival of a band from Dublin on the Live Aid stage at Wembley. I have to confess, I was not making my only wrong rock-and-roll choice as I pressed 'record' and 'play' on the cassette recorder and settled down to eat. Nine years later I found myself at Glastonbury for the first time when a friend attempted to persuade me to see some new Mancunian band down the bill on what was then called the NME Stage. I can hardly believe I am admitting this, but I eschewed watching Oasis and went to the circus field to watch some juggling. A year later, also at Glastonbury, I was so disappointed when Saturday headliners the Stone Roses failed to show that I didn't stick around for Pulp's career-making stand-in performance, but came back to catch its brilliance only at the end.

ALIVE AND KICKING

Putting the Live Aid line-up together might have been hard work for Bob Geldof but, let me tell you, a boy needed sustenance after sitting through several early afternoon hours of Howard Jones, Nik Kershaw and Ultravox, all interspersed with being sworn at by Bob for not donating enough money. Then there was that tricky task of recording proceedings on the block of blank cassettes I'd stacked up by the stereo. U2 were a band who fell into my 'keep' category, which meant they got a new cassette all to themselves.

It was only later – the next day, in fact – that I got round to listening to U2's performance. By then I'd heard comments that it was one of the highlights of the entire show, but as I listened I couldn't help feeling a slight sense of disappointment. Where, in the name of love, was their big hit, 'Pride'? All they'd got through was 'Sunday Bloody Sunday' (fair enough) and an extended version of an album track called 'Bad' that just seemed to go on forever. Indeed, about half-way through the song, Bono just stopped singing: there was an audible thud, as though the microphone had broken down, and then nothing, for minute after minute, while the band played on behind. Then, after an absolute age, Bono was finally back again, this time running through a litany of Lou Reed and Rolling Stones lyrics. And with that, to a final cheer, they were off. I was confused. Had I missed something?

As it turned out, I wasn't the only one who was disappointed with U2's performance. 'I really thought we were crap,' was the Edge's recollection. 'I thought [Bono] had completely fucked it up [. . .] completely blown it,' thought

237

Paul McGuinness, the band's manager. 'The band were very, very upset,' recalled Bono, who was in 'a very dark mood, depressed' for days.[1]

Back in 1985, what didn't come across to those listening on radio, or people like Paul McGuinness watching in the wings, or the Edge, Adam Clayton and Larry Mullen Jr standing on stage and wondering just what was going on, was the astonishing power of the television images that Bono's mid-song walkabout had created. It was only days later that I discovered what had really happened, when I watched the performance proudly recorded on a VHS cassette by a friend. On television, everything looked and felt different. Here was Bono, charged up and bouncing on the balls of his feet like a championship boxer. Here was the crowd, who out of nowhere had produced Irish tricolours and U2 flags.

What Bono did was to single-handedly bridge the gaps between artist and audience and between Live Aid stage and television screens at home. His was the first performance that day to be aware of the TV cameras: halfway through, he was guiding a cameraman by the arm, pointing to the ramp beneath the stage where the roadies and photographers were crouching. Bono wasn't just going to jump down there for the stadium's benefit – he was savvy enough to ensure the TV cameras were following him for the audience at home as well.

Equally, the decision to pluck a girl out of the crowd during 'Bad' was not a spontaneous, spur-of-the moment decision. In fact, throughout the band's Unforgettable Fire tour, Bono had been doing exactly that during this particular song: the difference was that the girl was usually hugged on stage; here, because the gap was so big (and the crew wasn't theirs and didn't know the deal) Bono had to go down, disappear out of the band's sight, and find someone himself. The fact that the moment was at least partly premeditated doesn't, I think, stop it from being electrifying: there's an irresistibility to the scene, that overriding sense of jeopardy, the sheer drama of Bono jumping down from ramp to ramp like a rock-and-roll version of Donkey Kong, the women in the audience reaching out, trying to crawl their way over the top of the security guards. In the confusion, three girls got out, two making their way to the stage, standing awkwardly – like everyone else, not quite sure what they were doing. The third, a young Wham! fan called Kal Khalique, Bono embraced, and, with the world's media all around them, artist and audience danced a few steps.

The inspiration behind the song 'Bad' is heroin addiction, specifically on the streets of U2's hometown: 'We're from Dublin,' Bono had introduced the song. 'Like all cities it has its good and its bad. This is a song called "Bad".' As Eamon Dunphy notes in his book *Unforgettable Fire*, 'heroin isn't mentioned in the lyric. "Bad" is about pain.'[2] The result is what rock music is meant to be all about: starting from a specific experience, the song evokes a universal sentiment that anyone can relate to, can infuse with their own feelings. What Bono did by dancing with Kal Khalique wasn't just to break down the barrier between the act and the fans, it was also as if to say, 'We understand your pain, and we're there for you.' Bono had picked out a young Wham! fan, but he could have been dancing with anyone, European or Ethiopian.

'Bad' also goes to the core of what stadium rock is all about. To communicate with large crowds, the eighty or ninety thousand people it takes to fill up a football stadium, you have to sing and play in the broadest of brushstrokes. To mean something to that many people, the songs have to touch on the most universal of sentiments. To take flight in such a large venue, the tunes and the music have to be melodically straightforward. It's why people who don't like such music often criticize it for being empty, but why those who love it hear not emptiness but space.

Having inspired the New Romantics, the twin influences of David Bowie and Roxy Music now belonged to U2. While David Bowie had snubbed Gary Kemp backstage at Live Aid, by contrast he made a beeline for Bono: 'David Bowie came over to me. And I was like, "David Bowie just came to talk to me!" [. . .] this is the man who, more than any other, set fire to my vivid imagination.'[3] It was Roxy Music, however, who were to have the bigger influence of the two: at the beginning of 1984, U2 were looking around for a producer for their new album. They wanted a different sound to the ones they'd created before and, as Adam Clayton remembers, 'Roxy Music was a name that kept coming up, with a sense that this was the sonic territory of European pop music as opposed to American rock.'[4] So they tried Rhett Davies, who'd produced the band, and when that didn't pan out they went to Brian Eno.

At the time, U2 were just one of a crop of young rock bands, all jockeying for position and trying to find a way to break clear of the pack. The leaders were probably just about Liverpool's Echo & the Bunnymen, led by another teenage David Bowie fan, Ian McCulloch. McCulloch was not short of confidence: the band's first album was called *Heaven Up Here* on the grounds that they were better than everyone else. He also quickly got the nickname 'Mac the Mouth' for his ability to offer up caustic comments on his rivals: Paul Weller was 'as thick as two short planks'; Boy George was 'an old sodding queen mincing [. . .] I don't mind a good mincer but he's not even that'.[5] His main ire, meanwhile was reserved for U2, whom he dismissed as 'spud-peelers' and 'cunts who no one likes' and whose biggest hit, 'Pride', he called 'a horrible little totally vacuous song'. Beneath the boorishness and the baiting, there was a great, even sensitive songwriter in there ('The Killing Moon', 'The Cutter', 'Nothing Lasts Forever'), but McCulloch couldn't quite bring himself to make the leap U2 were about to make: the follow-up to 1984's *Ocean Rain* took three years to arrive, and included a number of unused songs from that album's sessions.

From north of the border, meanwhile, came Big Country and Simple Minds. The former with hits such as 'Fields of Fire'. 'In a Big Country', wore their Scottishness on their checked-shirtsleeves, with a distinctive twin six-string sound that became christened 'Gaelic guitars'. 'If anyone else asks me how I make my guitar sound like bagpipes, I'll flatten them,' said guitarist Bruce Watson.[6] In Wales there was the Alarm, who were originally inspired by the Clash but supported U2 and would go on to follow a similar sonic journey with songs like 'Rain in the Summertime' (which they liked, which was just as well considering where they were from).

Simple Minds were perhaps musically the most interesting of all these bands in the early eighties: their album *New Gold Dream 81/82/83/84*, for example, had an electronic edge that their rivals lacked. The sense of place was still there too: 'Waterfront', up to that point their biggest hit, was inspired by the docks of their hometown, Glasgow. 'Glasgow was packed with empty ships, like ghost ships,' Jim Kerr remembers. 'Even from the factories you could hear from the echoes and the acoustics that they were all empty, just shells.'[7] A sense of space could be found in the song itself, its starting note, a single repeat note on the bass, giving way to the crash and thud of keyboards and guitars. The song, from 1984's *Sparkle in the Rain*, hinted at what was to come, but, like all their other previous singles, still failed to break the Top 10.

What U2 and all these bands had in common was their location, and their sense of identity in where they came from. That's an important and often overlooked element in a group's sound, as evident in the factory landscapes of Düsseldorf and Sheffield that infused Kraftwerk and the Human League. The New Romantics had been very much a London scene that fed into (and off) the fashions and the fads of the capital. These fledgling stadium-rock bands, by contrast, hailed from Wales, Scotland and Ireland, Liverpool, Glasgow and Dublin. This was a sound where, Ian McCulloch aside, the centre of gravity was what is sometimes disparagingly referred to as the 'Celtic fringe', by which I don't mean the half-badger, half-mullet then sitting on top of Bono's head.

It was a centre of gravity that was equally disparagingly referred to as 'the north': Victoria Wood's spoof TV announcer once famously said, 'I'd like to apologize to our viewers in the north. It must be awful for them.' By the mid-eighties, the effects of Thatcherism were becoming clear. Britain was feeling increasingly like a two-tier country, with the brunt of job losses falling away from London and the Home Counties and a north–south divide (with its border notionally drawn at Watford Gap services on the M1) opening up. The miners had failed to do to Margaret Thatcher what they'd done to Ted Heath in the seventies, and the Labour party, now under the leadership of Neil Kinnock, were a long way from looking like an alternative government.

These bands tapped into a different sense of musical identity, one not defined by being London but very much by *not* being London. Theirs was a sound that drew on their surroundings – a combination of the deprivation in the cities and the rugged beauty of the countryside around. Theirs was a voice that was political in its most basic, moral sense: being about right and wrong, about causes like Northern Ireland and South Africa. There was a passion and a seriousness here, too: war wasn't a laughing matter, as Frankie had suggested, or 'stupid' as Boy George had frivolously offered; it was something to take a stand against. One can criticize their sentiments on all sorts of grounds – and someone like Ian McCulloch was not slow in doing so – for being naïve, or pompous, self-righteous and all the rest of it. But, in a country where the Conservatives were clearly going to be in government for years to come, these bands offered the north an alternative voice, a sense of belief and a moral authority that the government (and its opposition) lacked.

By 1983, U2 had sort of plateaued, if that is the right word for a performance on the top of a mountain. The performance in question was at Red Rocks, Colorado. Ten miles out of Denver, 8,000 feet up, is a bizarre collection of sandstone boulders that make up a sort of natural amphitheatre. It was at this stunning setting in June 1983 that U2 recorded *Under a Blood Red Sky*, a live album and video for which pretty much everything went wrong (and right) at the same time. The problem with playing outside is that you are beholden to the weather, especially when you are so high up. In the days before the concert it rained heavily, the mountain became covered in thick fog, a tornado blew through only forty miles away and at one point it started to sleet and snow. There was so much water around, and so much electrical equipment needed for the concert, that the whole thing was an accident waiting to happen.

Against the promoter's wishes, the band pressed ahead with the show, even though it was still raining, and even though only about a third of the audience turned up. For those who did turn up, though, the show was an against-the-elements triumph. The accompanying album, which collected all their hits to date, was not quite an accurate record of the night, in that the sound quality of the original recordings was not up to scratch: only two of the tracks on the record were actually from the Red Rocks concert, the others were from concerts in Boston and West Germany. Bono's shtick of freewheeling into other songs added hot water to the cold water of the setting: his segueing into an unauthorized 'Send in the Clowns' cost the band $50,000. None of which a young fan like me knew or cared about: the result was released as a low-budget album, which meant it was a pocket-money affordable, electrifying introduction to the band's music. At the same time, though, the band knew they'd sort of gone as far as they could in their current incarnation: hence the call to Brian Eno to shake things up.

Brian Eno – Brian Peter George St. John le Baptiste de la Salle Eno, to give him his full name – was the original keyboardist with Roxy Music, though 'keyboardist' doesn't quite do justice to it: for their famous first appearance on *Top of the Pops*, when Roxy Music performed their debut single, 'Virginia Plain', it was Bryan Ferry playing the song's opening chords on the piano while opposite him, like a sort of 'drag telephonist', stood Brian Eno, twiddling a few knobs on some strange-looking machine. That pretty much summed up the first couple of Roxy Music albums, with Eno and Ferry locking horns and making wonderful music, until – to the horror of young Kemps, Rhodeses and Edges everywhere – Eno left the band.

Eno grew up in East Anglia near a US Air Force base. He used to listen in to American Services radio (this was the mid-fifties) and the nascent rock and roll he heard sounded almost otherworldly compared with his rural surroundings – a conflict and contrast that stayed with him. Following his departure from Roxy Music, Eno continued his interest in music and strange sounds. In 1975 he invented what came to be known as ambient music: Eno was in bed after a car accident and couldn't get up to change the volume of the record of harp music a friend had put on. It was raining so loudly that Eno could hardly hear the harp – the combination of the two got him thinking about how sound, like light or colour, could create an ambience in a room. From this bedridden beginning, Eno starting talking about landscapes rather than songs, and created a number of experimental and influential albums such as *Before and After Science* and *Music for Airports*. As a result, he got the calls to produce the likes of forward-thinking acts such as Talking Heads (*Remain in Light*), David Bowie (*Low*) and now U2.

Initially Eno wasn't keen to work with U2 – and he wasn't the only person with reservations. Island Records boss Chris Blackwell was equally unsure: the Edge recounts how Eno had previously approached the label with 'a song called "Bird List", which was a recording of some very obscure beat over which Brian was reciting the names of birds. Osprey . . . Seagull . . . Thrush. Chris was terrified that Brian was going to [. . .] bury [us] under a layer of avant-garde nonsense.'[8]

Certainly Eno did things differently. The first thing was to get the band out of their usual studio (Windmill Lane in Dublin) and into somewhere with atmosphere and an interesting – you've guessed it – ambience. The venue chosen was Slane Castle, home of Lord Henry Mountcharles, who let the band take over to record. The gear was set up in the castle's Gothic ballroom, a commanding circular room with enormous arched windows, bookcases lining the walls, an intricately designed ceiling high, high up with a chandelier hanging down. Because it was originally designed for music its acoustics were excellent, allowing Bono's vocals and the Edge's guitar to really ring out. 'If Phil Spector was going to lie in state,' Bono said, 'it would be here.'[9]

Eno didn't just bring a new feel and space to U2's music; he also introduced them to new ways of working. The music of one song, 'Elvis Presley in America', consisted of the opening track, 'A Sort of Homecoming', played at half speed. Eno got Bono to improvise over the top and that initial stream of consciousness was the final product – as far Eno was concerned the moment was captured. Inspired, the band went for the big themes in the song's lyrics: 'Pride', a song that had started as a jam at a sound-check in Hawaii, was about the death of Martin Luther King (even if Bono got the time of day of his shooting wrong); the title track meanwhile, took its name from an exhibition called 'The Unforgettable Fire' the band saw at the Peace Museum in Chicago comprising artworks by survivors of Hiroshima and Nagasaki who used painting as a form of therapy. In the song itself, the city in question is Tokyo and drew on the band's Japanese publisher's account of escaping the fire-bombing there during the Second World War. Like 'Bad' being about Dublin heroin problems but also about suffering in general, 'Pride' was not just about Martin Luther King but also about love, and 'The Unforgettable Fire' was not just about Japan but also about grace and forgiveness (that nation's culture of not looking back, but moving forwards). Whether you knew the specifics or not didn't really matter: here was a collection of soaring songs that anyone could relate to.

The Unforgettable Fire wasn't U2's most successful album – its successor, *The Joshua Tree*, was the one with the bigger hits ('Where the Streets Have No Name', 'With or Without You', 'I Still Haven't Found What I'm Looking For') – but essentially it followed the formula set up by its predecessor: the combination of the band's passion and Eno's quiet sense of invention. *The Unforgettable Fire* was both the critical and commercial breakthrough that pushed U2 up and out of the pack, and set the template for other bands to follow. When Eno stepped back for U2's subsequent album, *Rattle and Hum*, the result was a bit rattly and humdrum: it was essentially a throwback, with the best bits being the passion of the live songs interspersed with Bono's antics (in the accompanying film, he sprays a statue with 'Rock and Roll Stops the Traffic'). The band ended the eighties needing to reinvent themselves again: this time it was back to Eno and a different setting (Berlin). The result was *Achtung Baby*, but that story is for another decade.

*   *   *

While U2 had Eno to thank for their breakthrough, for Simple Minds the helping hand came from Roxy Music's other Bryan. John Hughes, the king of American teenage comedies, was in the midst of putting together one of his finest works – *The Breakfast Club* – and the producers were looking around to find someone to record the film's closing number. The song, 'Don't You (Forget About Me)', had been written by Keith Forsey, a British songwriter and producer whose previous work included manning the mixing desk for punk-turned-LA-lip-curler Billy Idol.

Keith Forsey was one of Hollywood's go-to men for eighties soundtracks: he co-wrote 'Flashdance . . .What a Feeling', for which he shared an Oscar for best song, and was heavily involved in the *Beverly Hills Cop* soundtracks. Forsey's song for *The Breakfast Club* was written to close the film, where the five teenage misfits finish their Saturday detention, with Emilio Estevez and Ally Sheedy, and Molly Ringwald and Judd Nelson pairing off. Forsey's first choice to sing his song was Bryan Ferry, and if you listen to the verses in particular you can hear where he is coming from. Ferry, however, was recording his *Boys and Girls* album and turned it down. At which point Forsey turned to Simple Minds. Their response to this golden opportunity? 'When we heard it was for a teenage American movie,' Jim Kerr later explained, 'we just said, nah, no way, there's no chance [. . .] we knocked it back, I think, a handful of times.'[10] Forsey, however, was a fan of the band and refused to take no for an answer – he flew over to see them, and eventually twisted their arm. Simple Minds wanted to make the song more their own, so they added the intro (the 'Heys!' and throat-clearing 'oohs') and the end (the 'lahs') and rather crossly recorded the song in two hours flat in a studio near Wembley. The result was not just the band's first hit in America but also a Number 1, while in the UK it was their first Top 10 hit. Simple Minds had originally refused to release the record in Europe (partly on the grounds that it would confuse their audience, and partly I think because they were still a bit embarrassed about it), but then relented: 'as soon as people started to get immense enjoyment from it, I didn't want to say, "This is a piece of crap and we could do it with our eyes shut."'[11]

Simple Minds were now in the big league. Jim Kerr, who got married to Chrissie Hynde, was now one half of eighties rock's golden couple. The band played at the American end of Live Aid, with Kerr wearing a shiny olive-green roll-neck shirt, white trousers (with the bottoms rolled up) and espadrilles: a performance marred by him saying a farewell 'Thank you' and walking off as the band launched into 'Promised You a Miracle'. And there was *Once Upon a Time*, perhaps *the* archetypal stadium-rock album, with its sing-along choruses, drums sounding as though they'd been recorded in a cave and lyrics about doves and believing and never looking back. There are moments of Bono-style passion – towards the end of 'Ghostdancing' Kerr sounds knackered and out of breath, as if to show he has given it his all – but, for all their carping about 'Don't You (Put Parts of Titles in Brackets; It Really Annoys Me)', I think that the band had learnt something too from the Ferryesque nature of the original song: how being a rock band is not all about going full throttle, but also about knowing when to take the foot off the gas.

For the second half of the eighties – probably until U2 pulled away with *Achtung Baby* – Simple Minds and U2 sat together on top of their stadium-rock mountain. They had the sales to play the stadiums which required their 'big music' to work in. And as well as sharing a sound, they also shared an interest in politics and causes. In U2's film *Rattle and Hum*, the key moment is Bono's impassioned mid-song speech during 'Sunday Bloody Sunday', the day after the 1987 IRA Remembrance Day bombing in Enniskillen ('Fuck the Revolution'); a few days after the incident, an equally moved Jim Kerr came across the traditional Irish folksong 'She Moved Through the Fair', which he adapted into 'Belfast Child'. U2 headlined Amnesty International's 1986 'Conspiracy of Hope' tour; Simple Minds gave the charity the proceeds of their 'Ghostdancing' single. *Rattle and Hum*, meanwhile, contained a live recording of 'Silver and Gold', U2's anti-apartheid song; Simple Minds played the 'Mandela Day' concert at Wembley, and their song of the same name joined 'Belfast Child' and a cover of Peter Gabriel's 'Biko' to form their only UK Number 1, the 'Ballad of the Streets' EP. On top of this, Simple Minds also regularly performed another famous anti-apartheid number in concert, and one that might have hit a nerve with some of the other high-profile Live Aid acts: a song called 'Sun City'.

*　　*　　*

Aside from U2 and Simple Minds, the other star turn at Live Aid is generally considered to have been that of Queen. Taking the Wembley stage at just after six p.m., Queen delivered a tightly rehearsed twenty-minute set that squeezed in six of their hits ('Bohemian Rhapsody', 'Radio Ga Ga', 'Hammer to Fall', 'Crazy Little Thing Called Love', 'We Will Rock You' and 'We Are the Champions'), segueing from extract to extract like an eighties equivalent of the second half of *Abbey Road*. While some bands on the Live Aid bill had never played to an audience anywhere near as big as Wembley, Queen were old hands at concerts that size and even larger: on their 1981 tour of South America they played to audiences of 130,000 (Brazil), 150,000 (Mexico) and 300,000 (Argentina).

Re-watching the performance now, as back then, leaves one in no doubt that Freddie Mercury was a leading man at the peak of his powers. Like U2, Queen found a way of connecting directly with the audience, making Wembley for that twenty minutes feel as if it was their own gig. Prowling the stage left and right like a caged tiger in a white vest, Freddie Mercury gives a masterclass in how to do a call-and-respond sing-along with the crowd ('Dayyyyyy-oh!'). Then there are the hand-in-the-air movements: that triplet of claps in 'Radio Ga Ga', the punches in the air for 'We Will Rock You', the rather seventies swaying from side to side for 'We Are the Champions'.

The last of these was a curious, oddly triumphal note on which to end. Watching it live, it seemed to fit in with the moment, the band sweeping everyone along with their performance. Yet looking back on it one can't help feeling that its lyrics jar in the same way that U2's 'Bad' connected: this is a song about success, about not giving the time of day to 'losers'. The 'we' in 'We Are the Champions' comes across less as 'we' the successful band as it does 'we' the West, in full congratulatory mode. That's consistent with the way Queen said nothing during the performance about why they were there: they thanked the audience for making it a 'great occasion', flattering them instead by telling them they are 'beautiful' and saying 'We love you'.

Queen's inclusion on the bill had been controversial for some because of their decision to play the exclusive South African resort of Sun City the previous year. Sun City was a sort of racist's Las Vegas, a five-star luxury resort that offered its guests that Nevadan mix of casinos, topless dancing, boxing and high-profile pop stars. It was situated in Bophuthatswana, one of the Bantustans or black homelands that the South African government had set up: by making black people involuntary citizens of these mini-states, they stopped them being citizens of South Africa, and hence reinforced white rule. These homelands were also exempt from South African laws on, for example, gambling, with the result that resorts such Sun City could legitimately be set up 'within' the country. Although in theory Sun City was a multiracial venue, in practice its exorbitant prices made it a playground for South Africa's white elite.

Following its launch in 1981, Western music stars were offered a small fortune to play. Queen were not the only ones to accept the offer: Frank Sinatra, Rod Stewart, Black

Sabbath, Elaine Paige and Elton John were just some of the artists to perform there. Why Queen got it in the neck and, say, Elton John didn't is unclear: maybe it was because they were bigger; maybe it was because they had played their gigs only a few months before Live Aid. Queen's argument (which they'd used before to justify those huge Argentinian gigs while a military junta was in charge) was they weren't political and would play to anyone who wanted to turn up and watch. The payment for performing presumably more than covered the fine from the Musicians' Union (who had been running a cultural boycott of South Africa since the early 1960s) and cushioned the blow of being blacklisted by the United Nations. In 1986, Paul Simon visited South Africa to record *Graceland* with artists such as Ladysmith Black Mambazo: despite the fact that he didn't perform there, and made such groups international stars, the UN Special Committee Against Apartheid decreed that anyone who purchased the album was violating the cultural boycott on South Africa. It did little to deter the album's huge sales.

In 1985, a couple of months after Live Aid, Steve Van Zandt, guitarist in Bruce Springsteen's E Street Band and later a star of the TV show *The Sopranos*, put together Artists United Against Apartheid to record 'Sun City', a rather repetitive song that basically reiterated how the acts involved (including Bruce Springsteen and Bono) weren't going to play the venue. Certainly the international publicity the record created, and consequent notoriety the venue gained, served to put a lot of people off and the number of big artists playing there in the second half of the eighties was significantly fewer than before. Though the message didn't get through to everyone: I don't know if they chatted about it backstage, but Status Quo, who followed Live Aid by supporting Queen, then followed their headline act by performing ten nights there in 1987, as part of the not especially tactfully named 'You're in the Army Now' tour.

I was exactly the right age to become fascinated by South Africa and inspired by the anti-apartheid struggle. At home this led to a personal campaign against Cape fruit, which pissed my dad off no end as he really liked his grapes. As I was getting into bands like U2 and Simple Minds, I liked the fact that they had something to say, and would quote Bono and Jim Kerr at length, as though they were founts of wisdom. Being just in my teens, I was no doubt rich with self-righteousness, happy to lecture my elders and betters as though only I knew anything about the subject.

One person subjected to one of my overbearing lectures about how no one was doing anything to stop apartheid, and how we should all be thoroughly ashamed of ourselves, was my paternal grandmother, Granny Sweffling (so called because she once lived near Sweffling in Suffolk). So I was a bit taken aback when at the end of one such tirade my gran said she'd got a record I should listen to.

My instinctive thirteen-year-old reaction was to roll my eyes. You want me to listen to one of your records, Grandma? What speed is that going to play at? 78? The record my grandmother returned with was *Why I Am Ready to Die* by Nelson Mandela – the extraordinary speech he made in his 1962 trial, rendered by the actor Peter Finch. On the other side is a collection of what it calls 'Freedom Songs': Zulu, Xhosa and Sotho songs like 'We the African Nation', 'Forward to Victory Mandela' and 'Freedom is My Hope'.

Like a friend lending me the latest album by one of my favourite bands, my grandmother said I should have it. Many years later, I still do, and it remains one of my most treasured possessions.

Track Three

Like a Virgin

If I was asked to pinpoint a moment when I officially became a teenager it wouldn't be when I turned thirteen, at the end of 1985, but rather nine months earlier, when I put a new poster up on my bedroom wall. Up until then my room had been dominated by a poster that my parents had helpfully picked out for me: a promotional one for Boosey & Hawkes, a well-known manufacturer of musical instruments, featuring their latest range of flutes, French horns and other orchestral delights against a black backdrop.

By now I was an avid *Smash Hits* reader, a magazine that as well as its various features came with the occasional free pull-out poster. It was one such double-sided poster that came with an early 1985 edition. I can't remember exactly who was on the other side – I think it was Duran Duran – but the poster I chose to put up was a sepia-tinted, black-and-white picture of Madonna, a shot from the cover shoot for her second album, *Like a Virgin*, sat down and leaning back in what looked to my twelve-year-old self like some sort of fashion-ripped wedding dress.

Madonna's look was iconic and quickly copied by teenage girls everywhere: the arm-length white-lace fingerless gloves; the beauty spot on the chin; the large crucifix earring; the tulle skirt dotted with hearts; the belt emblazoned with the words 'BOY TOY'; the white bodice, for which the technical term is 'heaving'; the carefully, casually stacked hair and a look in her eyes saying something I was yet to fully understand.

As much as I liked Madonna's music, it was Madonna herself that I was particularly interested in. I'd had crushes on various people when I was younger – Doctor Who assistants called things like Leela (Louise Jameson) and Romana (Lalla Ward) – but these were always very simple, romantic fantasies. Madonna, though, was different. My interests in her were more, as Olivia Newton John might have put it, physical.

Teenage years are an awkward time of transition. Even recollecting them all this time later, the memories of that slightly sweaty, slightly sticky cocktail of embarrassment still carries a twinge of freshness. My particular experience wasn't helped by my complexion or my bashfulness either: I blushed fantastically easily, to the point that for a while my nickname at school was Beetroot Bromley. In those early teenage years, there was suddenly plenty for me to blush about. It wasn't just me who was changing shape: the girls in my class were, too. It was as if someone had flicked a switch and suddenly there were breasts everywhere: teachers, my parents' friends, newsreaders on the television (the female ones, not Trevor McDonald).

Learning about sex is difficult for an eldest child, but it's doubly so if you're a boy. Joe Jackson once sang about how it's 'Different for Girls', and nowhere was it more true than here. They have magazines to read, like *Just Seventeen* back then, with agony aunts and problem pages to answer all their questions and concerns. There's also the fact that girls actually talk to each other about this sort of stuff – swap tips and bits of information. Teenage boys just aren't like that.

Not only do boys not talk about this stuff, but we also didn't have a *Just Seventeen* equivalent to tell us what we needed to know – the magazines my friends and I read were all about *stuff*: music, or football, or cars. What we boys passed around instead, when we could get hold of them, were porn mags. The first time I saw one was when I was just finishing junior school and a friend had been given a rather crumpled issue by his father – I'm guessing as a sort of rites-of-passage thing. I can't remember which magazine it was, but it was probably *Mayfair* as the models were British: dowdy, slightly down-at-heel, and looking as uncomfortable pretending to play squash as I felt looking at them.

The problem with porn mags – well, there are *lots* of problems with porn mags, but let's stay focused here – is that, beyond a fairly intimate guide to the female body, they don't really give out any useful and practical information for a teenage boy to take away. Instead, I picked up a patchwork of knowledge from anywhere I could get hold of it: a passage from a novel here, an aside in a film there. Music, too, was once again a life saviour – although, given that my main guides in this area were Madonna and Prince, that knowledge was shot through with a confusing religious undertone. George Michael's 'I Want Your Sex' might have given me some helpful pointers, but was only allowed to be played after nine p.m., and John Peel was never likely to add it to his playlist. Jermaine Stewart, meanwhile, confused me something rotten with his claim that 'We Don't Have to Take Our Clothes Off to Have a Good Time'. I might not have known much about sex, but even *I* knew the taking-clothes-off bit was kind of crucial.

My friend with the porn-father went to a different secondary school, and we drifted apart, a separation that took my one reliable source of magazines with it. The eighties, though, was the video age, and I instead became reliant on a selection of films recorded off the television – usually American comedies with bit of gratuitous nudity thrown in for the rating. While one could pause and freeze-frame, say, Jamie Lee Curtis getting undressed in *Trading Places*, the problem with doing it too often was that the VHS tape became marked, and started wobbling awkwardly through the tell-tale part. At which point you had to record something else over it before anyone noticed, and hope that the erased film would be back on the television before too long.

In 1979 the editor of *Mayfair*, Kenneth Bound, gave an interview in which he claimed that 'recently I have detected signs that boobs could be making a comeback – more and more readers are asking for them. Not just any boobs, but big boobs.'[1] As the historian Alwyn Turner noted in his book *Rejoice!, Rejoice!* (his title refers to the Falklands War, not this trend), what occurred in the eighties was a vogue for 'extreme youth and for large-breasted models', none more so than Samantha Fox, who made her page-three debut in the *Sun* a couple of days after her sixteenth birthday.

If you look at the female pop stars of the early eighties, at dancers in troupes like Legs & Co., what you find is a complete proliferation of different-sized girls: how big their breasts were simply wasn't an issue, or a factor in their perceived attractiveness. Exactly when or why this changed I'm not entirely sure: my guess is that the growth of pornography has had something to do with this, via the arrival first of videos and then of computers. But changed I think things did: bigger breasts became a dominant part of what society deemed attractive (and, with the likes of Katie Price, still does). That shift was part of a sexualization of culture in the eighties, and one that the success of stars like Madonna and Prince both played on and tapped into.

I don't remember Madonna's earlier visit to Britain, when she came over to perform on *The Tube* the previous year, dancing and singing along to 'Burning Up' and 'Holiday' at Manchester's huge Hacienda club. Instead, I first clapped eyes on her in the video for 'Like a Virgin', in which she sauntered around a sunny Venice, either writhing about on a gondola, wandering about with a large lion, or wearing wedding gear and getting it together with a man wearing a lion mask. I wasn't really sure quite what any of that meant – the lion is apparently the symbol of St Mark, the patron saint of Venice. To be honest, I think the lion was a bit confused by it all as well: 'all of a sudden I felt this nudge up against my left hand side,' Madonna told *Smash Hits*, 'I looked down and the lion was right there with his head in my crotch! [. . .] I lifted up my veil and had a stare-down with the lion. We glared at each other for about three quarters of a minute. Then he opened his mouth and let out this huge roar.'[2]

The song itself was both open to interpretation and equally confusing for a twelve-year-old boy. As with the look Madonna was giving me from my poster, I was fairly sure it was rude but wasn't quite sure in what particular way. Was it, as some people suggested, about the experience of having sex for the first time? Or was it about having a new kind of sexual experience? The opening scene of Quentin Tarantino's film *Reservoir Dogs* includes a long discussion as to what the lyric is about. Mr Brown, played by Tarantino, holds forth with a theory that it is a 'metaphor for big dicks': 'one day she meets a John Holmes mother-fucker [. . .] when this cat fucks her, it hurts. It hurts like the first time.'[3]

Madonna apparently then sent Tarantino a signed copy of her album *Erotica*, writing, 'Quentin: It's about love, not dick.' Which perhaps would have been more conclusive if she hadn't written the message on an album called *Erotica*. Muddying the Venetian water a little further, Madonna complained in an interview that 'Everyone interpreted it as

I don't want to be a virgin anymore, fuck my brains out! That's not what I sang at all. "Like a Virgin" was always absolutely ambiguous.'[4] There was, however, little ambiguity in Madonna's performance of the song on her 1990 Blonde Ambition tour, which involved the singer simulating masturbation on a velvet bed.

Where the lyric actually originated is with the person who wrote it, songwriter Billy Steinberg. Steinberg – who also wrote, among others, the equally uncontroversial 'I Touch Myself' by the Divinyls – got the idea for the words driving a red pick-up truck around his father's vineyards in California. Steinberg had come out of an intense, difficult relationship, and was now going out with someone new. Life, for Steinberg, as he bumped along the dust-track, felt pretty good. He'd been through the wringer and, now dating his new girlfriend, everything was shiny and new: he was starting all over again; it felt like, like, oh if *only* there was a simile to describe this feeling.

Steinberg's choice of simile is (let's be honest here) a little odd. It's not the first comparison that springs to mind when it comes to the feel-good factor of a new relationship. That was clear when Steinberg and co-writer Tom Kelly sat down to write the music to the words. Kelly originally came up with a gentle, sensitive ballad, which sort of worked until the song hit the chorus and the title. However, rather than thinking, *You know what? Perhaps we ought to come up with a different analogy . . .* the pair instead decided to stick with what they were sure was a winning title and rewrite the song as an upbeat, poppy number. A little in the same way that

George Michael was tapping into Motown for 'Freedom', so 'Like a Virgin' begins with a bass line that is not dissimilar to 'I Can't Help Myself' by the Four Tops.

It feels, in retrospect, the perfect calling card for Madonna, though initially she was unsure about it – thought it a little throwaway and put it aside. Madonna was recording her second album with Nile Rodgers, whom she'd chosen because of his previous work with David Bowie: it wasn't just the British New Romantics who'd been wowed by seeing his Ziggy Stardust tour; his Detroit date was the first gig she went to as well. A couple of days after making the recording, Madonna came back and told Rodgers the song was still going round in her head, and so they went for it. Rodgers called in his former Chic drummer, Tony Thompson, to play the rhythm track, with the sixties Motown bass line and seventies disco drummer helping to deliver an eighties pop classic.

The other element in the mix is Madonna herself. If the lyrics weren't provocative enough, the combination of her name and title gave the song a religious connotation that was hard to miss. Then there was the fact that, as the poster on my wall proved, Madonna is female. Had a man been singing the song it might have sounded a little bit creepy. A woman singing the lyric, however, made it about not just sexual provocation but also sexual liberation: *I have had sex*, the lyric is in effect saying, *and it felt good*.

Society, especially conservative society, has always felt a little uncomfortable when it comes to sexually confident young women. Madonna consequently wound up Republican America something rotten and at the same time became a role model – *the* role model – for teenage girls everywhere. There was her dress sense, a criss-cross mix of crop-tops and leggings, jewellery and fingerless gloves, and there was that sliver of empowerment and sexiness too. And there were further hits, like 'Dress You Up' – a song that, rather than using sex as a metaphor, used dressing up as a metaphor for sex. Boy George had famously said how he'd prefer a cup of tea: Madonna, you got the clear sense, wasn't that thirsty.

There were other strings to Madonna's bow as well. 'Material Girl' was the next big hit off *Like a Virgin* – as if Madonna, rather than following sex with war, á la Frankie Goes to Hollywood, had gone for capitalism instead. In its way, this song is probably the more objectionable of the two – a celebration of eighties materialism without the notice-able irony of, say, the Pet Shop Boys' 'Opportunities (Let's Make Lots of Money)', it wasn't so much 'greed is good' as 'greed is fun'. This time round, it was probably left-lean-ing parents who were shaking their heads. But Madonna, as it turned out, could do sensitive, too: for all the upbeat numbers, perhaps it is her ballads that are better records. 'Crazy for You' was her strongest song from this period, with Madonna putting her emotional money where her mouth was rather than just sticking the tab on the credit card.

Madonna's third album, *True Blue*, is almost Nigel Lawson in its conservatism: there's 'Papa Don't Preach', with its 'baby not abortion' message; there's the title track, with its rather twee sixties feel; there's the equally banal message of 'Love Makes the World Go Round'. Had Madonna changed? Had she heck. Back to the simile cupboard she went, this time taking on religion and replacing 'virgin' with 'prayer'. Such was the size of her sponsorship with Pepsi that when the video for 'Like a Prayer' was ready an entire advert break was booked out to show it. The video depicted a statue of a black Jesus coming to life and getting on down with Madonna. Perhaps unsurprisingly, when she turned up in Rome the following year in her Jean Paul Gaultier bra for her Blonde Ambition tour, the Vatican helpfully gave her a quote to put on the poster: 'One of the most satanic shows in the history of humanity.'

Anything Madonna could do, Prince Rogers Nelson could more than match for sheer provocativeness (maybe that's inevitable, when given a middle name like that).

Take his song 'Head', which wasn't about the thing on the top of your shoulders. Or 'Bambi', which wasn't about his favourite Disney film (being instead his generous offer to 'turn' a lesbian). Or 'Sister', a touching tale (literally so) about an underwear-free teenage sibling. Or 'Jack U Off'. Or 'Soft and Wet'. Or 'Do Me, Baby'. Or 'Le Grind' . . . you get the idea. Prince, to quote the closing song from his notorious *Black Album* was 'Rock Hard in a Funky Place'.

However, his most successful song in this respect was 1984's 'Darling Nikki'. This sensitive character piece about a women with a penchant for pleasuring herself in hotel lobbies was never released as a single, but hit the Number 1 spot in an alternative chart called the Filthy Fifteen. The chart was put together by America's PMRC, or Parents Music Resource Center, and consisted of the songs this parental pressure group felt were particularly objectionable and dangerous for innocent young ears. 'Darling Nikki' probably got the top spot for sentimental reasons: that was the song that Tipper Gore, wife of then US Senator Al Gore, had discovered her daughter Karenna listening to, and led to the founding of the PMRC. Alongside Tipper on the starting committee was Susan Baker, wife of Treasury Secretary James Baker: her equivalent moment of fury was when she heard her seven-year-old daughter singing various Madonna lyrics she'd learnt.

I don't know if Madonna was disappointed to get only to Number 8 in the Filthy Fifteen with 'Dress You Up', particularly as Prince was all over the top of the chart. Just below 'Darling Nikki' was 'Sugar Walls', the song he wrote for Sheena Easton about what my twelve-year-old self was still embarrassingly calling her 'lady's area'. Just below that was Prince's (and Adam Ant's) former girlfriend Vanity, with 'Strap On Robbie Baby', a song about, well, it wasn't about Robbie Baby. What is striking now about all these songs (and Cyndi Lauper's 'She Bop' at Number 15) is the fact that they are all about *female* sexuality: there were the stereotypically male-heavy metal songs in the list (WASP's tender and heartfelt ballad, 'Animal (Fuck Like a Beast)') but primarily this was about female behaviour. It doesn't seem insignificant that the campaign was led by two mothers worried about what their daughters were listening to.

The PMRC led to those 'Parental Advisory' stickers on records, which for a certain kind of band were less a warning and more a badge of honour. Metallica, for example, helpfully added one of their own to their 1986 album *Master of Puppets*: '*The only track you probably won't want to play is "Damage, Inc." due to the multiple use of the infamous "f" word. Otherwise, there aren't any "shits", "fucks", "pisses", "cunts", "motherfuckers" or "cocksuckers" anywhere on this record.*' It also led to government hearings into what was called 'porn rock', which probably cheered up the senators no end as they spent their afternoons watching the videos for Van Halen's 'Hot for Teacher' and suchlike. The hearings also heard from an unlikely musical trio of John Denver, Frank Zappa and Dee Snider of Twisted Sister, who between them powerfully articulated the case against the sort of censorship of music that some were promoting.

Sex wasn't the only thing that Prince and Madonna had in common: the other key component in their careers was their interest in cinema, with both benefiting from a breakthrough film – albeit that they both also followed these up with a string of embarrassing sequels. In a way, this was the process that Michael Jackson had started being taken to its logical conclusion. With his videos for the *Thriller* album, Jackson had upped the stakes of the genre and created something that was not just about the music but about the dancing and performance as well – Prince and Madonna were the two artists who could offer listeners and viewers this sort of complete package.

The fourteen-minute video for 'Thriller' itself had been less of a pop promo and more of a short film. The logical extension of this was to make a full-length feature film, which Prince did with *Purple Rain* in 1984 and Madonna with *Desperately Seeking Susan* in 1985. In the same way that some people get confused over soap-opera actors, assuming they must be like their real-life characters, so the characterizations Prince and Madonna played in the films became the personifications of the stars themselves. So people presumed that the real-life Prince bombed around on a motorbike, made love to glamorous women and played a mean guitar at his local club; Madonna, meanwhile, *was* the wisecracking Susan in her film, all fun, flirty and footloose. The reason that both these films succeeded was that to an extent both Madonna and Prince *were* playing themselves – which, even with their limited acting skills, they could just about manage. Consequently people saw a glossy, glamorous version of them on the silver screen and these became the Madonna and Prince that they 'knew'.

Unfortunately, rather than leaving it there, both Madonna and Prince continued their acting careers. The only surprise about *Shanghai Surprise* was that Sean Penn agreed to be in it. In Prince's *Under the Cherry Moon* it was Kristen Scott Thomas who found herself wondering what she was doing being involved. *Who's That Girl* was a sort of broken-down *Bringing Up Baby*, while the less said about *Graffiti Bridge*, the sequel to *Purple Rain*, the better. Prince and Madonna weren't the only pop stars in the second half of the eighties to prove they should stick to what they were best at: also to be avoided at your local video shop were *Hearts of Fire*, which found Bob Dylan struggling to play a character that was essentially himself; *It Couldn't Happen Here,* the one false eighties move by the otherwise impeccable Pet Shop Boys; and *Jerusalem*, sort of *A Hard Day's Night* meets *Magical Mystery Tour*, except without the Beatles and with the Style Council. In the latter, the band end up in court, where they are accused of 'deliberately flaunt[ing] the laws of the popland' and of being 'articulate, intelligent and even well-bloody dressed'. (Were they found guilty? You'll never guess.)

Prince's acting skills might have left a little to be desired, but it was about the only thing that he *couldn't* do: not only was his dancing on a par with Michael Jackson's, and his provocativeness on a level with Madonna's, but his vocal range, songwriting skills and guitar pyrotechnics made him the most naturally talented music star of the era. While his films might not make it into many of the must-see lists of the decade, the soundtracks that went with them more than made up the difference: *Purple Rain* featured the likes of 'When Doves Cry' and this film's regal theme tune of the same name; the *Under the Cherry Moon* soundtrack, *Parade*, included such light-as-a-feather delights as 'Kiss'.

Rather than making a film with an album attached to it, the winning formula for Prince was making an album that came with an accompanying film. That was the case with *Sign o' the Times*, his glorious double album that was turned into a cinema-release concert movie – in other words, Prince predominantly playing his songs and keeping his acting around to a minimum. The songs themselves were more than good enough to stand up to such scrutiny: there was the title track, demonstrating a hitherto untapped interest in politics; pop gems like 'Starfish and Coffee'; pervy weirdness like 'If I Was Your Girlfriend'; and full-on funk wig-outs like 'It's Gonna Be a Beautiful Night'. I played that album to death, and it led to me becoming a lifelong fan – even to the point of paying good money for that album he did about the Jehovah's Witnesses.

That's payback, really, for the other thing Prince gave me in the eighties. For, as much as I fancied Madonna, and as much as I had fleeting flings with Nena (and her '99 Red Balloons') and Tiffany, my major crush was undoubtedly Susanna Hoffs from the Bangles – and it was a Prince penned-hit that gave the group its breakthrough single. The Bangles were an all-girl guitar group, also consisting of sisters Debbi and Vicki, and Michael, which, yes, I'd agree is a strange name for a woman. When 'Manic Monday' entered the charts, it was Susanna's deep-brown Californian eyes I fell for, dreaming about getting lost in the tangles of her tantalizing auburn curls. The group's success continued with the incorrectly tensed 'If She Knew What She Wants' (If She Knows What She Wants? If She Knew What She Wanted?), by which point I wasn't far off booking a flight and heading over to America on the thin pretext of offering Susanna some English lessons. Proving her class, Susanna has had the dignified decency to stay true to my teenage memories and avoided the subsequent Madonna-type embarrassments of publishing a *Sex* book or having candle-wax dripped on her in *Body of Evidence*.

All of which should be the natural point to end this chapter. Except that this is the one about Prince, and he is the man responsible for perhaps the greatest eighties end to a song. I'm referring, as if you didn't know, to 'Let's Go Crazy', the opening song on *Purple Rain*, which, after three and a half minutes of dearly beloved barkingness about going party mental, winds up for the big finish. At three minutes twenty-four the band go into their walking bass round-and-round riff, as if circling to land. At three minutes forty-four they get the landing gear out and hold down the heaviest low chord while Prince revs his guitar up. At three minutes fifty-three Prince hits that high note, the single soaring guitar squeal that lasts only three or four seconds but feels as if time is standing still. From that single guitar note tumble out all the others, this racing riffing segues into a spacey sonic squall, and back in come the band for a slowed-down electric-blues finish. At four minutes twenty-seven the drummer begins bashing any skin or cymbal he can reach, until at four minutes thirty-five Prince screams the cue for the finish and at four minutes thirty-seven, finally, here it comes: *Crash!*

Track Four

Every Loser Wins

In 1986 a group of teenagers in East London decided to get together to form a band. The driving force was keyboardist Simon, a good-looking market trader of a guy who called up his old friend, guitarist Eddie, with whom he had previously played in bands before some dodgy loan-shark deal got in the way. To complete the band Simon and Eddie pulled together what on the surface seemed a strange collection of friends: there was local caterer Ian doing his Phil Collins impression on drums, student Kelvin on vocals, along with Sharon, the daughter of a local publican. The group even had a manager in the shape of Harry – though frankly he appeared more interested in left-wing political agitation than the shameless capitalism of promoting the group.

The original name for the band was Dog Market, but on the night of their debut gig, at Sharon's dad's pub, their amplifiers blew the electrics, and Sharon's dad kicked them out, shouting, 'You're banned!' After that they ditched Dog Market: now they were the Banned instead. The group then entered a local battle-of-the-bands contest and that hoary old rock cliché, musical differences, reared its ugly head: manager Harry wanted the group to perform their song 'Something Outa Nothing' (and yes, that is the correct the spelling of 'outa'); Simon preferred the soppy little piece of balladry he'd written instead. Harry owned the gear, however, so the rest of the band decided to side with him. Harry (who by now the group should have seen was not the sort of guy to be managing a band) then decided to put the wrong cartridge in the keyboard to sabotage their perform-ance. He didn't really need to do that as the song was awful enough to lose on its own, but the Banned were a disaster, split up, and were never heard of again.

If this sorry tale sounds like something out of an *EastEnders* plotline, then that's because it was. The soap opera, still only a year old at this stage, had decided it would be cool to have a musical storyline (presumably to take the edge off the usual rut of murders, rapes and drug over-doses). What was less cool, perhaps, was the decision to cross over from fiction to reality, and these appalling ditties made their way into the charts. There was Sharon Watts (Letitia Dean) and Kelvin Carpenter (Paul Medford) sing-ing 'Something Outa Nothing' (now without Ian Beale's 'drumming', it has to be said). And there was Simon Wicks – Nick Berry – knocking Madonna off the Number 1 spot with 'Every Loser Wins'.

EVERY LOSER WINS

If eighties pop music was a pint of milk, then Nick Berry's Number 1 was the point when it was on the turn. This was the year when the big British names of the first half of the decade collapsed like a company's share price on Black Monday, and when the next generation of pop stars (a few notable exceptions aside) did their musical best (or worst) to drop the baton. 'Every Loser Wins' wasn't the most dreadful song of the eighties: as per my earlier 'Agadoo' theory of bad music, the really awful tunes were both terrible and forgettable. Something like 'Something Outa Nothing', in fact: a sort of Frank Butcher driving into Tiffany to music, it is right down there with the 'You can't sing, you can't dance, you look terrible' band in the KitKat advert of the time.

There is, however, another layer of musical ghastliness that I'm afraid that we must visit. Because even worse than a song as awful as 'Every Loser Wins', or a song that is both awful and forgettable like 'Something Outa Nothing', are the songs that never made it on to record in the first place. I'm sorry to say that it wasn't just teenagers in Walford who had the urge to get together and form a band. The same was also true in the suburbs of York.

The starting point for my musical career (if one can call it that) was when my friend Ed, who'd previously played the violin to my flute, switched to playing the drums. Drummers are always the key components of bands, much harder to find than two-a-penny guitarists, and Ed, with his brand-new Premier APK (Advanced Power Kit), was an opportunity I wasn't about to overlook. 'We should start a band,' I suggested, casually overlooking the fact that I couldn't play anything except a breathy version of 'Londonderry Air' on the flute. I decided that I really wanted to play the electric guitar, and asked for one of those budget black-and-white imitation Stratocasters for my birthday.

Even bad music, I discovered, brought credibility in the playground. There was Marie, local queen of the eighties flick, and friends, queuing up to be singers in the band (just as well as my own singing voice is only brought out to sing-out-of-tune hymns at weddings). The line-up was completed by friends Ben on bass and Oliver on keyboards. Oliver was particularly fascinated by the sound effects the school's Korg synthesizer could produce. That might make him sound like the band's Brian Eno, but in truth I suspect he found it funny to add a layer of what sounded like fart noises to proceedings.

All this musical endeavour needed some songs; and, having now learnt one and a half chords on the guitar, I decided I was up to the job. Enthused with a Live Aid sensibility that pop could change the world, I wrote what even my own diary at the time described as a 'depressing little jaunt', called 'Dictator'. Dictators, I'd decided, were bad, and I was going to stick it to the man big time by showing the world just how awful they were: *'There's bloodstains on your window'*, the song cheerfully began, *'Around you children cry/The streets are all deserted/The people weep and die'*. Who, I hear you cry? Just who is responsible for all this misery? *'In the middle of the chaos/No cash he ever owed/ The symbol of destruction/Dictator counts his gold'*. At which point the song unleashed its devastating chorus: *'Dictator!*

Dictator! Exterminator! He kills, he kills! He's a deadly threat! Dictator! Dictator! Exterminator! I Wonder . . .' cue pay-off and weird closing chord '*. . . if he ever regrets . . .!*'

Whether it was because of the mirrored sunglasses I thought I looked fucking cool in, or because through my hard-hitting lyrics I was revealing what the world was really like, we called ourselves Reflection. Our debut gig was at a school open evening, where about half the year was crammed into a tiny music room to watch us perform. During a set as short as Adam Ant's had been at Live Aid, we played 'Dictator' to impressed nods and surprisingly warm applause. Surprising in particular because we hadn't worked out that if you sampled the word 'dictator' into a keyboard and didn't hold down the subsequent note long enough, it played only the first syllable of the word. Consequently, my heartfelt and eloquent lyrics were complemented by the repeated sound of 'Dick! Dick!' bursting through the speakers, as though it had been remixed by Black Lace during their 'blue' period.

So, did pop music really go off the boil in the second half of the eighties? Well, the biggest-selling single in 1986 was not an original song, but a cover – the Communards' version of the old Harold Melvin and the Blue Notes hit 'Don't Leave Me This Way'. (The bestselling original song, I'm sorry to say, was the aforementioned 'Every Loser Wins'.) Secondly, at the following year's British Record Industry Awards, as the Brits were then pompously titled, the band awarded the title of Best British Group were Five Star.

Five Star were pitched hard as a sort of Essex version of the Jackson Five, even if the squeaky-clean family-fivesome were more virginal than vajazzled. The band consisted of brothers and sisters Denise, Doris, Stedman, Lorraine and Delroy Pearson, all managed by dad Buster, and offered up (this being the eighties) a poor facsimile of the original Jackson sound: a JL-less? With the sort of matching outfits and dance routines at which even Debbie Gibson might have balked, Five Star pulled off the difficult trick of making Shakatak seem like musical pioneers: soon they were having hits with songs like 'System Addict' and their need-the-toilet anthem, 'Can't Wait Another Minute'; further successes like 'Rain or Shine' and 'Strong as Steel' showcased the band's primary-school range of metaphor; as if to reinforce their wholesome image still further, they even recorded a song called 'Hide and Seek', which as far I can work out was about the pleasures of playing hide and seek. What stuck in the throat was their moneyed, ostentatious image: on albums with titles like *Silk and Steel* and *Luxury of Life*, the band lorded it in designer clothes in various bland, glossy settings. This was, in essence, Thatcherism on record; conservative with both a small and large C, Five Star delivered the unpleasant sound of the south enjoying its lion's share of Britain's by-now-booming economy.

I was with Eliot, the caller on *Going Live!* who got put through to the band and asked, live on air, 'why they're so fucking crap'. Five Star were symptomatic of slightly sappy, soulless soul that suddenly seemed to permeate much of the charts. While the north had found its voice in the expanse of stadium rock, the south, and London in particular, had responded by going all trendy wine bar on us, sprinkling its sounds with the sort of jazzy, funky pretensions that everyone thought had died a death with Blue Rondo á la Turk. This was the era when Level 42 broke through to the big time, with slap-bass singer Mark King supposedly insuring his thumbs for a million pounds and the band's stage set boasting a large pair of furry dice hanging from the ceiling.

Perhaps it was all Sade's fault: by far the most fashionable person at Live Aid in her backless top, her 'smooth operator' music had given hope to out-of-work saxophonists everywhere. But, while her music conjured up a glamorous 'Diamond Life', her successors lacked a similar sparkle. Instead what the music industry came up with was a watered-down pop with added – addled? – funk, jazz or soul. One such act were Wet Wet Wet, whose debut LP was knowingly titled *Popped In Souled Out* – and both album and band name sort of work as alternative names for this insipid genre.

In the early 1980s the 'wets' was the disparaging name given to the liberal end of the Conservative government (everything's relative): ministers like Francis Pym and Peter Ian Gilmour who weren't true blue believers and who Margaret Thatcher successfully undermined at every turn. In the late eighties, 'the Wets' was shorthand used by *Smash Hits* writers who couldn't quite be arsed to write the word 'Wet' three times in a row when having to do an article on Marti Pellow (the name comes from a Scritti Politti song, apparently). There's no doubt Pellow could sing (and the band would later go off to Memphis to try to prove their soul credentials), but a combination of that knowing smile and smug 'Mmmm!' on songs like 'Wishing I Was Lucky' was enough to melt or harden hearts accordingly.

Then there was Johnny Hates Jazz. Johnny, if you're interested, was the brother-in-law of the guitarist and apparently really did have a dislike of improvisational noodling: his hatred was stronger than that of the band itself, who were signed after a performance at Ronnie Scott's. 'I Don't Want to Be a Hero' was one of their biggest hits – an aspiration they more than succeeded in achieving. Swing Out Sister continued the jazz undercurrent by naming themselves after a forties film, *Swing Out, Sister*, in which an upper-class type secretly got a job in a jazz club without informing her parents. The only thing memorable about them was the cut of singer Corinne Drewery's striking dark bob. Similarly, my main recollection of the Blow Monkeys was not their music but the venom with which Dr Robert laid into milk during an interview with *Smash Hits;* 'rancid phlegm' he dismissed it as, with far more emotion that their music ever showed.

Curiosity Killed the Cat were one of a string of mid- to late-eighties bands who briefly looked like being contenders but failed to push on beyond their first album. Following the Kajagoogoo model of naming themselves after one of their songs, the band then took their name a little too literally and played it safe in terms of their music. They had a potential poster boy in their lead singer, Ben, who struggled valiantly against his surname (Volpeliere-Pierrot), his dancing (all rubber legs, and Ben-dy knees) and his fashion style (the Frank Spencer beret). They weren't all bad: I bought 'Down to Earth', I have to admit; later on, 'Name and Number' was a worthy addition to that canon of songs about telephone-answering machines. Unfortunately for Ben, when he did check his answerphone to see if the nation were still interested, the machine bleeped: 'You have . . . no . . . new messages'.

King were the other band with pretensions to pop royalty. Like Curiosity, their biggest hit was their first: in this case, the Number 2 hit 'Love & Pride'. The band broke through at the same time as Madonna, and lead singer Paul King told *Smash Hits* and anyone else who'd listen how he and Madge were the new monarchs of the music scene. Half points there, Paul. The band's gimmick, spraying their trademark Doc Martens with graffiti paint, didn't quite catch on, and neither did a succession of disappointing follow-up singles.

The one person who looked like they really might go on to bigger things was Terence Trent D'Arby. As with Ben Volpeliere-Pierrot, *Smash Hits'* response was to rechristen a tricky surname with a Bryan Ferry/Byron Ferrari equivalent. For them, and for readers like me, he was therefore Terence Trout Derby (Ben, I think, was Ben Vol-au-vent Parrot). In contrast to all the wet, sloppy soul whitewashing the charts, Derby sounded and felt closer to the real thing. There were proper songs ('If You Let Me Stay', 'Dance Little Sister', 'Wishing Well'), James Brown-style dance moves and oodles of confidence: his debut album, *Introducing the Hardline According to . . .* he compared to *Sgt. Pepper*; of his own ability, he declared, like a foul-mouthed Oscar Wilde, 'I'm a fucking genius.' Unfortunately, Terence turned out to be so brilliant that no one else knew what on earth he was on about. One can imagine the reaction of his record company when he delivered the follow-up album, *Neither Fish Nor Flesh*: 'relentlessly peculiar, wildly squiffy [. . .] sheer creative pigheadedness' was Q magazine's verdict of an LP with song titles as long as some of the tunes themselves ('To Know Someone Deeply Is To Know Someone Softly', 'You Will Pay Tomorrow For What You Do Today'). Still, at least it tried to match his best moment (inviting his grandmother to dance at the beginning of 'Dance Little Sister') with demands for listeners to find themselves a shovel – that being how much they were going to 'dig' his new record.

It is sometimes said that the music of the era is defined by the battles between its biggest stars. So the nineties is remembered for the Britpop battle between Blur and Oasis, the sixties for the rivalry between the Beatles and the Rolling Stones. In the early eighties, the main rivalry was either between Duran Duran and Spandau Ballet (if you were in Spandau Ballet) or Duran Duran and Wham! (if you were in Duran or Wham!). And for the late eighties? The contest that captured the paucity of its music was that between two rival American female teen stars: Tiffany and Debbie Gibson.

While I was feeling pretty chuffed at having come up with 'Dictator! Dictator! Exterminator!' the teenage Debbie Gibson was writing, singing and producing her debut album. Now, admittedly I don't believe that 'Shake Your Love' was an attempt to tackle the potential for gross human-rights abuses that can arise under a political system of totalitarianism, but Debbie was on *Top of the Pops* and I was playing a school open evening. I guess that if she'd been twenty-five I wouldn't have thought twice about it, but the fact that she was sixteen was a bit too close to home for comfort: she could have been in your class at school – and had she been, you'd have hated her for that head-girl 'I can't help it if I'm perfect' routine.

My personal dislike for Debbie Gibson was at least partly due to my feelings for her erstwhile rival. Tiffany, by contrast, was undoubtedly not head-girl material. With her hennaed hair, oversize jumpers and a teenage Stevie Nicks-style croak in her voice, Tiffany was the 'back seat of the class' girl you thought might have 'back seat of the cinema' potential. While Debbie Gibson spent no doubt countless hours practising her Disney dance routines until they were pointlessly perfect, Tiffany got famous by doing a tour of shopping malls. I'm struggling to think of a tackier way of becoming a famous pop star, but that was the key to Tiffany's charm: she hit Number 1 with her cover of the Rubinoos' 'I Think We're Alone Now' and I don't believe I was the only one thinking about being alone with her. As much as Debbie Gibson offered to 'shake your love', only Tiffany would know what that might euphemistically mean. If you asked Debbie, she'd probably give you some line about how it was a 'West Indian type of saucepan'. For a brief while, the two teenage starlets competed with each other tooth and nail extensions. Both had two Number 1s in the US; and, while only Tiffany hit the top spot in Britain, Gibson had by far the bigger number of hits.

There, one might think, this ramshackle rivalry might have ended. But while the couple left each other alone in the nineties, come the noughties the gloves (and pretty much everything else) were off all over again. In 2002, Tiffany agreed to pose nude for *Playboy*, a decision that took some explaining to her nine-year-old son (her argument was that it was a bit like having your photograph taken in *Elle*, except with slightly fewer clothes on). I'm sure the money was part of it, but the driving force behind the decision seems to have been the urge to shake off her teenage image: Tiffany, who was upfront (in more ways than one) about the fact that she'd had breast implants, wanted to show the world she'd grown up.

I'm not quite sure what I would have given as a teenager to have seen Tiffany, er, 'alone' – possibly a sibling or two – but seeing those images now (and I felt I should, for research purposes you understand) leaves me feeling like the J. Geils Band in their hit 'Centerfold'. This was the song where the singer discovers his former childhood sweetheart facing similar staple-chafing issues. I felt equally sullied, which I'll admit was probably just a touch on the rich side given the sort of impure thoughts my teenage self had been having in the first place.

One might – just – have expected the centrefold spread to be the sort of thing Tiffany would do, but I was somewhat surprised to find that, in 2005, Debbie Gibson had decided to follow birthday suit. For Debbie, her instincts were not dissimilar to her rival. It just so happened that she'd recorded a new song, 'Naked', and the photo-shoot seemed an ideal way to drum up some publicity, and shed that teenage image. Again, I felt I should be thorough in my research for your benefit, and the upshot has been telling my teenage self to find in himself just a little bit of patience as, twenty years on, his affections might just find themselves switching sides.

Here, once again, you might think that this rivalry had finally reached its squalid conclusion. But, having fought it out in the pop charts and on the pages of *Playboy*, Tiffany and Debbie (who was by now calling herself Deborah to match her new-found classiness) then slugged it out in round three, this time on the silver screen. By this point, both Debbie and Tiffany had started appearing in 'Mockbusters', almost deliberately bad pastiches of their bigger-budget cousins: the sort of films that make *Anaconda* seem like *Citizen Kane* in comparison. Here was Debbie Gibson starring in something called *Mega Shark versus Giant Octopus*. There was Tiffany with her name above the title in *Mega Piranha* – a film about mutant Piranhas that are, well, presumably a bit like normal piranhas but a little bit bigger.

Then some cinematic genius thought, How about if we got Tiffany and Debbie Gibson *together in the same film*? They could play bitter rivals and have an embarrassing cat fight that includes some *Dynasty*-style slapping and some rubbing of each other's faces into a cream cake, finishing up with some thrashing around in the water? I know that sounds like the figment of my sordid imagination, but that's what happened in 2011's *Mega Python vs. Gatoroid* ('*Screaming. Scratching. Biting . . . And That's Just the Girls!*'). In the film animal-rights activist Debbie and Florida park warden Tiffany do battle in a thoroughly preposterous plot that includes mutant snakes, scientifically enhanced alligators and a severe loss of dignity all round.

Karl Marx once famously declared that history repeats itself, first as tragedy and then as farce. He was actually referring to Napoleon I and Napoleon III, but I'd like to think that, had he been alive today, he'd have found similar inspiration in this tale of two former eighties pop stars.

Track Five

What Have I Done to Deserve This?

It is Boxing Day 1985 and a man is walking into a launderette. A launderette? On Boxing Day? Has the guy spilt
cranberry sauce on his shirt or something? It's not a *real*
launderette, of course, but a fictional one: it's the first showing of a new advert on television. And in this advert, we're
not in 1985 but – in a *Back to the Future* vibe – actually in
the 1950s. At least, I think it's the 1950s, though Marvin
Gaye's 'I Heard It Through the Grapevine' is playing in the
background, and that wasn't released until 1969, so maybe
the DeLorean stopped off on the way or something.

The man walking into this 1985/1969/1953 launderette
is the model Nick Kamen. And the reason he is heading into
the launderette is to show off his bronzed, beefcake body
and stonewash his new pair of jeans. Depending on who
you listen to, there is a whole lot of things going on in this

advert. For some, there is something newly 'new mannish' about proceedings: like the Athena poster of Adam Perry, the similarly good-looking male model holding a baby, here Kamen is a man in a traditionally female role (i.e., doing his washing). For others, this is the start of men being ogled as sexual objects in mainstream culture: in the advert, the viewer is 'watching' Kamen through the eyes of the two giggling women – one wearing 3D glasses, presumably for a closer look. For some cultural commentators, the images are less to do with female emancipation – presuming female emancipation is objectifying the opposite sex in the way men do – and more about homoerotica: the opening shot of Nick Kamen features his crotch, framed by a young boy with his head at the same height; the same boy (and his brother) then watch Kamen get undressed, until they're shooed away by their disapproving mother. Perhaps the whole construction is to depict a man's man: jeans were famously given out to GIs during the Second World War and the Korean War. To own a pair in the early fifties was the symbol of a man who'd been places and seen action. He was doing his own washing not because he was being girly, nor because he was a new man, but because he was his *own* man. Grrr. Or maybe the advert was just a cleverly shot update of those phallocentric Cadbury's Flake adverts, with the whole commercial centred around the contents of Nick Kamen's button fly.

The Nick Kamen advert was one of a number for Levi's 501s with this retro-sexual, fifties-Americana setting. But it was the Nick Kamen one that everyone remembered and the one most instrumental in revitalizing Levi's fortunes:

the advert increased UK sales of its jeans by 800 per cent; so successful was the campaign, in fact, that at one point the adverts were even taken off the air because the company couldn't cope with the demand they were creating.

A few months later, a similar process was taking place in a completely different setting. The Labour party, having been badly mauled by Margaret Thatcher in the 1983 General Election, was now under the leadership of Neil Kinnock. In 1985 he appointed the young, moustachioed Peter Mandelson as his Director of Communications. One of Mandelson's first acts was to change the party's logo, which for many years had been based around the red flag. Mandelson's replacement was the red rose: '[it] evoked England's gardens. It suggested growth in fresh soil. Sunlight. Optimism.'[1] The new image was launched at the 1986 party conference, with Kinnock throwing roses into the audience like a latter-day Renato from Renée and Renato fame.

What did Nick Kamen and Neil Kinnock have in common? The answer was branding. In the mid-1980s, branding was the big new business idea of management theorists – the way to get audience recognition and draw in loyal punters for your product. Whether it was the Red Tab or the red rose, the logo was everything. Nowhere was this truer than in fashion. In the early eighties, this was all about buying clothes in the right shops: the 'right shops', as far as I was concerned, being York's newly opened C&A (especially their day-glo Avanti collection) and Chelsea Man (later recast as the intellectually confused Concept

Man). In the late eighties, it was all about the labels. Levi's Red Tab was just one of the must-haves: at my school it was also about Lacoste, with its trademark crocodile logo, which did battle (like a Tiffany and Debbie Gibson movie) with Paul & Shark's shark (or at least a knock-off 'le croc' and 'le shark' approximation of the real thing); later on, it was all about the OP of Ocean Pacific, despite the fact that surf-boarding beachwear was not the most appropriate clothing for the icy temperatures of a northern winter.

What does anything of this have to do with pop music? The problem with a lot of the acts in the second half of the eighties was that a lot of them felt a bit samey. It didn't really matter which band you bought – Johnny Hates Jazz or Living in a Box or Climie Fisher – they were each as clean and dull as the other. But, at the same time as the Levi's commercials hit and advertising changed up a gear, the more successful pop bands of the time were the ones who, deliberately or not, were echoing these new marketing ideas. If the winning formula in the early eighties was the marriage of music and video, the focus in the later eighties was on creating a brand for the music you made: coming up with a Red Tab equivalent for fans to wear and be identified by. The first of these 'brand' bands – to the consternation of my parents and no doubt Nick Kamen himself – encouraged taking a pair of scissors to your newly purchased pair of 501s . . .

In 1981, two members of the Scandinavian band Poem arrived in London with hopes of getting a record deal. Poem had originally been school band Bridges, who attempted (and probably failed) to fuse seventies art rock with a love of the Doors. Not everyone in the band was convinced about the chances of the London trip being a success: their most commercial tune, a light and bouncy number called 'The Juicyfruit Song', was felt to be out of kilter with the band's more serious pretensions, and was left unfinished. The Poem members (Poets?) who stayed home were proved right: Oslo school friends Pål (guitar) and Magne (keyboards) ended up playing in a Queensway pub for a pound an hour before heading back to Oslo. Back in Norway, Pål and Magne found themselves a new lead singer: Morten Harket, the long-haired front man of soul-and-blues band Souldier Blue. Morten, Pål and Magne then decamped to a cottage at Nærsnes, a small village on the rugged, windswept Norwegian coast, to write songs. It was here, over the autumn and winter months of 1982, that the band's melancholic pop sound came together, 'The Juicyfruit Song' became 'Lesson One', and Poem, after a lyric Pål had written and Morten liked, morphed into a-ha.

A-ha (whose lower-case name doesn't trump the normal rules at the start of a sentence) returned to London to try their luck again. This time their attitude was the opposite to Poem's seriousness: 'When you came from Norway in those days,' Pål remembers, 'you had just one single chance. So we were as commercial as we could be. We had to be uber-commercial, uber catchy.'[2] Uber-commercial meant returning to 'The Juicyfruit Song', which was about to change again: soon it wasn't called 'Lesson One' but 'Take On Me'.

In the autumn of 1984 the original version of the song was released to a less than ecstatic response. The single sold 300 copies, and the group didn't exactly figure in Bob Geldof's subsequent Band Aid plans. The video, featuring the band playing in a plain blue studio with a female dancer doing silhouetted handstands in the background, was not exactly the sort to get MTV's taste buds tingling. The record company, however, were convinced that they were on to something and decided to remix the song. In came Alan Tarney, whose production credits included Squeeze, Leo Sayer and Cliff Richard's 'Wired for Sound' (he'd also written Cliff's 'We Don't Talk Anymore'). Tarney's version took the song back towards its slightly sparser demo version, beginning with just the drum beat, a flash of a sparkly, spooky keyboard chord, a bit of synthesized bass, and finally that famous Casio-esque riff that Poem had been sniffy about all those years before. Then there were Morten's vocals: a smattering of melancholy, the clipped edge of English-as-a-second-language, and a soaring range to match that of any Norwegian mountains. It's a distinctive voice: while the George Michael of 'Freedom' or Tony Hadley of 'True' are very clean, pure English pop voices, the way Morten Harket sings hints at something else.

'Take On Me' (the Alan Tarney version that you'd be familiar with) was released in spring 1985 and flopped again – at which point you might have thought their record company would have given the band up for a dead loss. Instead they decided to give things a third go and spunked a hundred grand on bringing in Steve Barron to direct a new video for the song. Barron's take on 'Take On Me' was comic-book stuff with a girl sat in a café reading the comic-strip adventures of motorcyclist Morten. Before you knew it, his black-and-white sketched hand was coming out of the magazine and inviting her in: there followed three and a half minutes of animated shenanigans involving a nasty-looking man with an equally nasty-looking spanner, before first the girl and then Morten escape back into the real world.

Third time round, everything fell into place: the video was picked up by MTV and 'Take On Me' went to Number 1 in the US. On the back of that, 'Take On Me' was re-released again in the UK and became the band's first huge hit. The follow-up, 'The Sun Always Shines on TV', gave them their first Number 1. From here, a-ha quickly established themselves as the biggest pop band of the late eighties, interspersing their more moody, Norwegian-noir numbers ('Hunting High and Low', 'Stay On These Roads') with the occasional cheesy counterpart (the terrible 'Touchy' and the howler 'Cry Wolf', complete with lupine impressions).

A-ha were the heartthrob band to take advantage of Duran Duran disappearing into side projects and Spandau Ballet heading off on their tax break abroad. There's no doubt the band were strikingly good-looking. Morten was a man with cheekbones: with his leather jackets and Brylcreemed hair, he came across as a sort of Scandinavian Elvis but with a brooding sense of mystery. Magne – or Mags, as *Smash Hits* called him – was similarly good-looking but in a softer, less intense way. Pål (whose name, *Smash Hits* helpfully informed readers, was pronounced like Paul rather than like the dog food) was, frankly, not quite in the same league looks-wise; he did, however, write most of the music and so was the choice of the more serious female fan. While the girls in my schoolyard were happily dividing the band up between them on some fictional triple-date, boys like me were buying their records too. A bit like Duran Duran a few years earlier, a-ha were the sort of pop band it was OK for both sexes to like – one of the final few (possibly even the last) to which this rule applied.

All of which meant that both boys and girls were improvising their own version of the a-ha look. 'You can't go around in that stuff if you want to pull women,' Morten told Pål about his appearance early on, and set about revitalizing the band image.[3] Top of this list was the ripped jeans, a brand look that started by accident: 'we had jeans that were starting to fall apart, and we [. . .] took it from there,' explained Pål.[4] The other element to be quickly imitated was the thin leather straps wrapped around the wrists like Gothic bracelets. If you worked out, you could then add the final Morten touch: layer upon layer of thermal undershirt, with sleeves pulled up or ripped off to reveal muscular arms. Morten packed a punch here – I reckoned it wasn't just me he could have in an arm-wrestle, but maybe even Sylvester Stallone in *Over the Top*, too – so I stuck to the straps of leather and feeling chilly around the thighs and knees.

Ripped a-ha jeans and leather wrist straps aside, what any self-respecting pop fan needed for the full mid- to late-eighties look was a VW badge on a chain around their neck and (for the girls) a Grolsch-bottle top attached to their shoes. These were the emblems chosen by the Beastie Boys and Bros – or, more specifically, the emblems of Volkswagen and Grolsch as appropriated by the Beastie Boys, Bros and their respective fans.

In the case of the Beastie Boys, the VW emblem wasn't so much the borrowing of a brand as the wholesale theft of one. The VW badge, the one from the middle of the radiator grill, was worn by Beastie Mike D. He did so in a slightly mocking way, in response to the number of American rappers who wore the Mercedes-Benz logo as part of their look. Such playful New York satire was very quickly lost in translation in places like old York. Here there were few Mercedes-Benz cars around to take emblems from (and few records sold by the rappers who wore them). There were, however, plenty of Beastie Boys fans and Volkswagens to attack. Volkswagen, who presumably had never really considered people wanting to steal badges from their radiator grilles, had left them fantastically easy to remove. If you were unlucky you might need a screwdriver, but usually (apparently) you could just slide the thing out.

It's difficult to say how many of the badge stealers were actual Beastie Boys fans and how many were just teenage toe-rags who actually preferred Wet Wet Wet but thought it'd be a right laugh. Certainly in 1987 the Beastie Boys were big news in the UK. In the same way that Michael Jackson had rung up Eddie Van Halen and added a rock element to get on MTV, so the most successful rap bands of the time strapped themselves to a succession of thumping guitar riffs: Run DMC had teamed up with Aerosmith for 'Walk This Way', while the Beastie Boys' debut album *Licensed to Ill* sampled Black Sabbath and Led Zeppelin (when I say most successful, I'm talking in terms of the charts: in terms of influence, the real rap action was with the likes of Public Enemy and groundbreaking albums such as *It Takes a Nation of Millions to Hold Us Back*).

In 1987 Run DMC and the Beastie Boys went out on the road together as the Raising Hell tour, first in the US and then in the UK. The Beasties' portion of the show involved plenty of dicking about – literally, with the unfurling of a giant inflatable penis onstage. That, coupled with scantily clad women dancing in cages, was plenty enough to whip up a typical British tabloid storm: 'Depraved' was the *Daily Star*'s verdict of the band, a comment the newspaper wrote without any apparent trace of irony. Then there was the notorious *Daily Mirror* headline 'Pop Idols Sneer at Dying Kids', beneath which it was claimed that the band had shouted 'Go away, you fucking cripples' at a group of hand-icapped children staying at their hotel. This incident itself was apparently the work of a journalist who was cross about not getting an interview with the band: 'because she [the journalist] was snubbed,' Mike D later remembered, 'she made the whole thing up. We got a small retraction printed much later but the damage had been done.' By the time the tour hit Liverpool the band were met by an audience not so much ready to fight for their right to party as to party for their right to fight the band. The crowd threw cans and bottles at the Beasties; the Beasties knocked them back with baseball bats. One fan alleged she had been hit by one of the returning cans and Ad Rock was arrested and charged with grievous bodily harm (in the subsequent court case, once the tabloid hysteria had died down, he was cleared).

There was undoubtedly an element of shock value to what the Beastie Boys were doing, but most of the reaction was down to a (deliberate?) misunderstanding of the band's playfulness by the tabloid press. The same was true with the appropriating of the VW emblem: when Mike D saw his ironic statement had become mass-market theft, he stopped wearing his badge. What he'd started, though, was more difficult to shut down: in Yorkshire there were still cases of VW-badge theft as late as the early noughties. Back in the eighties Volkswagen tried to defuse the situation by offering badges not just to disgruntled owners but also to young rap fans: adverts in the likes of *Smash Hits* tried to play the 'Hey! We like music too!' card, punningly claiming that they'd 'invented the Beetles'. Of course, once you could get a badge for free it didn't quite have the same kudos as it would if you'd stolen it, and the craze died down. It reminded me a bit of the fashion at school for wearing the 'thin' end of your tie, rather than the traditional kipper end: my school responded by producing a thin tie: 'Hey! We understand fashion too!' Almost overnight the trend became to wear your tie as fat as possible.

One of the mysteries of eighties pop was just how all the Bros fans – Brosettes – got hold of those Grolsch-bottle tops. The original idea had come to Matt Goss by chance: 'I was bored one day and was playing around with some bottle tops that were lying around, and for some reason I whacked them on my shoe. It wasn't premeditated in any way, it was just something to do really.'⁵ A couple of days later he was driving through West London when he saw girl after girl wearing said Grolsch accessory. Like the VW badge for Beastie Boys fans, and ripped jeans for a-ha acolytes, if you didn't have a Grolsch-bottle top on your shoes you weren't a proper Brosette. Despite most such fans being under-age, sales of Grolsch went up by a third.

I was probably fifteen when I started getting served in pubs. I say pubs. *Pub* would be more accurate: like most towns, York had its one boozer lax enough to turn a blind eye to your age because it needed the custom. I spent Friday and Saturday nights out drinking the sweetest things I could find, these being the only things I could manage to keep down. Cider was an obvious choice, or a succession of sickly combinations – usually Archers and lemonade – which I would sip pretending to be sophisticated. The alternative was to visit a wine bar. York's solitary wine bar was a safe haven for idiots such as me who couldn't hold down their lager, as they didn't have any beer on the premises.

Perhaps I was too busy hamming it up to notice all the girls drinking Grolsch, but I certainly have no recollection of them doing so and pocketing the tops. Something along those lines must have been going on, though, because Bros' album *Push* was the fastest-selling debut album their record company had ever had. The fact that Bros had a brand logo for their fans to wear summed up the fact that the band were aware of the reasons behind their rise to fame: 'It's called marketing,' a twenty-year-old Matt Goss explained at the time. 'It's the same as with everything. A tin of baked beans or tomato sauce needs marketing [. . .] it's a bit like a band; it's nothing to be ashamed of.'[6] This might have been coincidental, but even the title of the album was an advertising term – used to describe exactly the sort of marketing campaign Bros were embarking on, bottle tops and all.

Bros were an odd musical line-up, consisting of a singer (Matt Goss), a drummer (his drummer Luke) and a bassist (Craig Logan). What you got through your radio, therefore, was predominantly a lot of drums and Matt doing his trademark throat-clearing growl, while Craig's bass got lost in the medium-wave mix. Craig was later famously told to get lost himself, leaving the band on the grounds of suffering from ME, or 'yuppie flu' as it was then called, though Matt rather cattily commented in his autobiography that it was difficult to notice that Craig had gone as he had never really done that much in the first place. What Craig did do was to take a large pay-off, a move that looked particularly canny when the remaining duo became better known for their financial problems than for their music. It might have just been good timing, but it was not Craig's last astute reading of the music scene: he went on to become a successful A&R man and manager of Pink, among others.

For a brief moment, though, Bros enjoyed a Beastie Boys level of hysteria, of a teenage rather than tabloid sort. Forgiving the band for some particularly wonky metaphors (the ballad 'Cat Among the Pigeons', the opening line in 'I Owe You Nothing' comparing an ex's breakdown to the crumbling of 'a very old wall'), the band's fans were undoubtedly devoted. There were the Brosettes who were so desperate to see the band they managed to rip the door off their limousine; the ones who kicked and punched Jonathan King after he wrote a less than flattering review in the *Sun*; then there were the ones who sent the band animal hearts and entrails in the post (one particular fan professed her love by posting Matt cans of meatballs). Not everyone was quite so friendly in the letters. It goes without saying that one can't condone a person who sent Bros death threats, but at the same time the 'fan' who mailed a series of coordinated hate letters from the four furthest geographical points of the British Isles has to be applauded for their attention to detail.

While Bros, a-ha and the Beastie Boys all had images and identities that their fans could copy and follow, the most successful branding of late-eighties pop acts was probably the group that didn't have a brand at all: the Pet Shop Boys. It was the perception of their not playing the game, of standing apart, of being detached, dry and ironic that became their powerfully anti-brand brand.

In contrast to the missed irony of Mike D's VW badge, the Pet Shop Boys were assumed to be so cool and knowing that irony and cleverness were ascribed to them even when they weren't there. So when keyboardist Chris Lowe cited Kylie Minogue's 'I Should Be So Lucky' as one of his favourite records of 1988 the assumption was that he was taking the George Michael (the band actually had a genuine love of pop music). When the duo didn't move on stage this was assumed to be a carefully planned statement against, I don't know, the big dance numbers of a Debbie Gibson. In fact, the band had turned up to do what they thought was a radio interview in Belgium and found themselves on the telly. Chris was wearing his 'BOY' hat at the time, and there was only one keyboard there, so he stood behind it and mimed playing the bass part with one finger. What started out as an accident became the band's early stage 'show', with them unintentionally benefiting from the fact that if you stay still on TV the camera zooms in on you to compensate for your lack of movement.

Then there was the group's name itself. The truth behind the Pet Shop Boys was that Chris Lowe knew three lads who worked in a pet shop in Ealing and had said, as a joke, that they should form a band, play 'How Much is that Doggie in the Window?' and call themselves the Pet Shop Boys in a spoof hip-hop way. Later, after the group had taken the name for themselves (they were previously called West End), the rumours started to fly around about what the name *really* meant: *apparently,* the word went round the playground like wildfire, *it referred to gay men in New York who got their kicks by putting hamsters up each other's bottoms!* It wasn't, and no such term actually existed, but, as singer Neil Tennant explained, 'people assume that it's an incredibly clever in-joke that Tennant and Lowe thought of'.[7] The more they denied it, the more people assumed it must be true.

Perhaps part of the perceived archness came from Neil
Tennant's previous career; in the early eighties he had been
assistant editor of *Smash Hits*. It was therefore presumed
that he knew the system better than anyone and could
manipulate things to his advantage. While it can't have hurt
for Tennant to have met pop stars and got a sense of what
being famous might be like, perhaps the biggest perk of the
Smash Hits job was that he'd been able to claim back the cost
of the records he bought and thus had a pretty eclectic bank
of musical influences. One artist Tennant particularly liked
was Bobby O, the American producer he worked with in
New York on, among others, 'West End Girls'. The Bobby
O version is a bit like the original 'Take On Me' single by
a-ha: it's almost there but not quite. In this case, everything
sounds a little too plastic (lots of cheesy keyboard hand-
claps) and a little too fast. Back in the UK Tennant and
Lowe reworked the song with producer Stephen Hague,
who slowed things down and added that atmospheric
street-noise start to set the mood. I've always taken it as a
London song, even if there are possible references to some
sort of Western (Tennant apparently got the idea for the
opening lines after seeing a film starring James Cagney)
and Lenin (the journey from Geneva to the Finland Station
in St Petersburg is the one Lenin took to start the October
Revolution in 1917).

The element of the Pet Shop Boys that people often
underestimate is the surprising warmth of the music. If the
duo really were as ironic, detached and calculated as cari-
catured, then they would never have been successful: the

songs would have been simply too cold to engage. This was pop music that was intelligent rather than clever: in a pop landscape that had become more troughs than peaks, they stood out a country mile.

Track Six

Love Changes (Everything)

Among the celebrity and success of the Duran Durans and the George Michaels, the Bonos and Bruce Springsteens, the Madonnas and Michael Jacksons, there is another, less well-known but equally influential musician whose work also made the eighties what it was: the American country singer Bobby Goldsboro. For, in 1973, Goldsboro had a Top 10 hit with 'Summer (The First Time)', one of those 'western' songs about a teenager's first sexual experience on a hot sultry June evening. The song's narrator was seventeen: the women he met, sipping on her julep on her front porch, was thirty-one. She suggested a walk to the beach; he went there a 'boy' and came back (Tom Jones cough) a 'man'.

So far, so seventies. But in the summer of 1980 a young lady called Susan from Manchester went on holiday to Bournemouth. Susan had recently finished school and was just starting to make her way in the world as a secretary. And, although holidays in this country can be hostage to the weather, that fortnight Susan got two weeks of the British seaside at its very best: clear blue skies, hot sunshine and glorious sunset evenings.

And then Susan met Stephen. She met him in a wine bar, and liked him instantly. He told her he was from near London, a place just outside Twickenham, and as they talked . . . Susan realized . . . just how funny, how kind and how . . . *attractive* he was. Her holiday became . . . *their* holiday . . . sunbathing together . . . romantic walks on the beach . . . visits in Stephen's car to the . . . nearby New Forest. (Can you hear that classical music in the background, by the way? I think it's the love theme from Franco Zeffirelli's *Romeo and Juliet*.)

Then came that . . . painful day . . . when the holiday was over. Stephen drove Susan to the station . . . and as the train got ready to depart . . . there was just time . . . for one last . . . farewell embrace . . . on the platform. Susan . . . as you can imagine . . . was distraught. But as she made her way . . . back to her parents' house in Manchester . . . at least . . . she had the comfort of Stephen's promise . . . to stay in touch . . . to telephone and write to her. But then came . . . *that* day . . . when *that* letter . . . came through Susan's letterbox. It can't have been . . . easy for Stephen to write . . . because he had to tell Susan . . . the truth. For what Stephen . . . hadn't told her . . . as they drove down to the New Forest . . . for another one of their 'walks' in the countryside . . . was that he was an officer in the army.

Stephen . . . was being posted to Germany . . . and this letter was to be his last.

Susan . . . as you can imagine . . . was heartbroken. So Susan wrote a letter . . . Not to Stephen, but to the . . . one man . . . Susan knew she could rely on . . . Radio One DJ Simon Bates. And, at about eleven o'clock . . . one weekday morning . . . Bates read her . . . letter out . . . and played . . . their song . . . the one that would always remind Susan . . . of that . . . special fortnight . . . on the south coast. And *that* record . . . the first-ever 'Our Tune' . . . was 'Summer (The First Time)' . . . by Bobby Goldsboro.

The beginning of 'Our Tune' was as simple and spontaneous as that. Without even a suggestion that Susan had been taken for a ride by a soldier getting his end away on leave (come on, you thought that too), Simon Bates read out her letter, played her song, and asked his listeners if anyone else had any summer-romance stories that they'd like to send in. Within days he'd received 2,000 letters: my personal favourite of this early batch was from the woman who went on holiday to Tenerife with a friend, fell for some guy and, as they were sitting down in a restaurant together, spotted her boyfriend from home at another table . . . having a romantic meal with another girl. Apparently this couple eventually ended up getting married, though history sadly doesn't reveal for how long.

What started out as a short radio feature (Bates originally tried to end it after six weeks only for the switchboard to become jammed) ended up a national institution. In the UK it seemed that everyone stopped what they were doing at eleven o'clock to listen to that day's 'Our Tune': whether or not the classic image of weeping truck drivers pulling over into the nearest layby is to be believed, the feature regularly pulled in a quite staggering eleven million listeners. That's an astonishing number, and so was the number of people who wanted to pour their heart out to the nation and hear Simon Bates play 'I Want to Know What Love Is' by Foreigner again: over the following decade, more than 200,000 people sent in letters for inclusion; that's 400 per week that Bates had to sift through.

What letters they were – and what love lives the nation led. There was the classic young love dilemma of Merchant Navy officer Matt meeting Susan (a different one, I think): 'On the way home, Matt got the first inkling that all was not well. Matt's sister was in the same year as Susan at school . . . and that made Susan fourteen. It raised all sorts of questions.'[1] I'll bet it did, Matt. Mary, meanwhile, went on an 18–30 holiday against her boyfriend Bill's wishes: she hadn't realized she was pregnant and miscarried when she got back, to which Bill reassuringly 'said that going on holiday had killed our baby. He called me a murderess'.[2] You old romantic, Bill. Vera told the nation about her meeting with Malcolm: 'I was nineteen, and he was thirty-seven, and married.'[3] You knew instantly that wasn't going to end well. We heard Tessa's description of a difficult patch she had been going through with her husband: 'Ben is a long-distance lorry driver, and I was bored and lonely.'[4] If that isn't a put-the-kettle-on-Mike-we're-in-for-a-right-cracker-here of a beginning, then I really don't know what is.

The letters weren't all about romance: there were tales about adoptions, car accidents, abusive relationships and even suicide attempts (on a couple of occasions, people even rang the studio threatening to end it all, leaving Simon Bates the tricky balancing act of talking them down while simultaneously playing the new single from Living in a Box). The first half of the eighties, as unemployment rocketed, was dominated by stories of broken marriages as families splintered under the effects of no work and no money. The second half was marked by the sprinkling of AIDS stories, and young men unable to tell their family about their sexuality (eleven million strangers, though, not a problem).

Whatever the theme, what united the letters was that each correspondent had a song that reminded them of their illicit affair, or whose lyrics somehow pulled them through the dark times. If you'd managed to pluck up the courage to turn back from Beachy Head, but had done so without the assistance of the latest Phil Collins single ringing in your ears, then frankly it wasn't worth your while writing in. The nation needed to hear that saccharine three and a half minutes of soppy balladry to pull themselves together before going back to find out they'd been laid off, or whatever it was that workers did in the eighties: 'Miss You Like Crazy' by Natalie Cole, 'Suddenly' by Billy Ocean and 'Together We Are Beautiful' by Fern Kinney were just some of the various 'Our Tune's selected. More often than not, though, the songs were sung by small women with big voices and an even bigger drum sound behind them: if music was the food of love, then that eleven-o'clock biscuit being dunked in the tea was from a packet of McVitie's Power Ballads.

The power ballad is, by any standards, a curious hybrid of a musical genre. Even its very name is contradictory: a ballad, by definition, is quiet, soft, lyrical and thoughtful; adding power into that mix can only shatter any atmosphere or ambience the songwriter has created. I can't think of any other musical genre that attempts to fuse together two such contrasting elements – it's like someone coming up with quiet thrash metal, low-NRG dance, or progressive punk. The essence of the power ballad is that the emotions of the singer are so strong that they can't be held back and, despite the gentle accompaniment, have to be unleashed with full velocity.

In the same way that *Once Upon a Time* by Simple Minds is the archetypal stadium-rock album, then the archetypal power ballad is Phil Collins's 1984 hit 'Against All Odds'. April of that year was not a good time to be listening to music if you were lovesick: in that brief hiatus between Frankie singles you had Phil at Number 2 and Lionel Richie's 'Hello' at Number 1. Presumably the latter won out on the grounds that it had a better video. Obviously by 'better video' I mean *weirder* video – it still seems almost perverse that the video for a song about looking for love features a blind sculptor who replicates Lionel's head in a sort of spooky *Close Encounters of the Third Kind* manner.

It might seem odd to pick out Phil, given that his receding hairline goes against the grain of almost every other singer in this genre, but he is the power balladeer par excellence for three reasons. Firstly, Phil lived and breathed what he was singing; this was a successful rock star whose first wife left him for their painter and decorator (a fact that Phil ruefully 'celebrated' by leaving a tin of paint on top of his piano during a performance on *Top of the Pops*). From here, it was a veritable merry-go-round of divorce followed by remarriage, followed by divorce by fax machine (as one does) followed by another remarriage, followed by another divorce. When Phil sang about breaking up, you knew it was coming from personal experience.

Then there are the lyrics themselves. 'Against All Odds' is precisely the sort of phooey sentiment that the power-ballad lover is after. Here Phil is essentially singing about how slim the chances are of him getting back together with a painted and decorated partner: it's time to move on and find a new wife to divorce (in the film of the same name that the song is from, the lovers don't end up together). Yes, there might be some who take Phil's words at face value, but the thought ringing through the deluded heads of most lovesick listeners is: You mean there's still a chance? Of course, you say it's against the odds – we're talking odds of Loch-Ness-Monster-existing proportions – but *isn't that what love's all about*? The fact that the possibility of it happening is so close to zero is all but proof that it must be the real thing!

Thirdly, there are the drums. That Phil doesn't unleash the beats until the song hits its second verse, a minute and a half in, is positive restraint on his behalf. Once the drums do come in, though, it's with a wallop, a bang and a crash

– the sort of solid thump that, should you be feeling on the edge of tears during the song's quieter beginning, would be enough of a jolt to tip you over into a full-blown soba-thon. The technical term for this sound is 'gated reverb': essentially, to get a big drum sound you need a lot of echo or reverb, but what they worked out in the eighties was a way to 'gate' or stop this – so rather than everything boom-ing about like it had been recorded in a cave, you get the big sound the reverb brings as the stick hits the skin, but then close it off before it all gets a bit 'echo-y'. This sound, found by accident in the studio when Phil was playing drums on a Peter Gabriel album, is what underpins a lot of these songs: on first listen the drums sound as though they've been put too high in the mix, but actually they just sound enormous because of the effects they've gone through. And possibly because Phil is imagining catching up with the decorator as he's playing.

The drums, however, were just one part of the 'power' that fuelled these ballads. The other part was the voices: predominantly full-throated, glass-threatening perform-ances from women with hair as big as their lung capacity. Historians may argue over when the power-ballad era occurred, but my own theory is that it can be marked by the performances of three such singers: beginning in 1983 with Bonnie Tyler's 'Total Eclipse of the Heart', ending in 1987 with T'Pau's 'China in Your Hand' and reaching its peak in 1985 with Jennifer Rush's 'The Power of Love', then the UK's highest-selling single by a female artist of all time. These are the standout Number 1s, backed up by a triple-play of American soft-rockery: the aforementioned Foreigner's 'I Want to Know What Love Is', Berlin's *Top Gun* theme 'Take My Breath Away' (which I don't think is an invitation to be strangled) and Starship's 'Nothing's Gonna Stop Us Now'.

Whatever you think of the song, 'Total Eclipse of the Heart' is a great title for a pop song – brilliantly overblown to the point that you can't help imagining looking up at the sky to see that not only has the moon somehow morphed into a heart shape but somehow the sun has too (otherwise the eclipse would not actually be total). I might be taking this lyric a little too literally, a charge that can also be levelled at my belief that the song's opening verse is ruined by the fact Bonnie was facing the wrong way in the studio ('Turn around' is the producer's repeated, plaintive direction). Following this is what sounds like a pitched battle between Bonnie and her drummer as to who can sing/play the loudest, a contest that Bonnie just about wins, though it leaves her in serious need of some Strepsils. Quite what the freaky video is about, with its eerie schoolboys with lights instead of eyes, is anyone's guess (it has been suggested that the boy at the end is a young Gianfranco Zola but sadly this is an urban myth, though he does look similar).

'China in Your Hand' is another classic power-ballad metaphor that this time the video director decided to portray a little more literally: Oh look! There's a piece of china – a small figurine – in singer Carol Decker's hand! Oh look again, it's just fallen from her grasp, on its way to be smashed in slow motion on the floor as the saxophone solo starts! In 2011 *X Factor* judge Gary Barlow bizarrely criticized Carol Decker's vocal performance on the record, preferring the version of one of the show's contestants: bizarre because Carol's version is clearly soaringly peerless, and the only china the hapless *X Factor* contestant was going to get in her hand was when she went back to washing dishes. There is one criticism of the song that stands up, and that's the premature interjection of the T'Pau drummer after a mere thirty-seven seconds. In power balladology, that's far too early in the song to be giving the kit its emotional going-over.

In between the blonde Bonnie and copper-curled Carol was the brunette Jennifer Rush, a singer whose power-ballad credentials were clear from sharing a name with an American AOR band: if Jackie Collins was writing one of her bonk-busters about an eighties singer, Jennifer Rush is exactly the sort of moniker she'd be given. Rush by name Jennifer might have been but rush by nature she most certainly wasn't: unlike T'Pau's thirty-seven-second itch, she waited a full two minutes and seventeen seconds before allowing her drummer to let rip. Jennifer was careful with her choruses, too: after the first verse, there's that half-primal/half-Athena-lady/man section about how she is yours and you are mine. This, however, isn't the chorus proper but mere lyrical hors d'oeuvres to wet your romantic taste buds. Maybe it takes a while for Jennifer to warm up: it isn't until almost three minutes in that she finally hits the chorus, lets rip those high notes she has been holding back and brings herself to speak of the awe-inspiring power of love.

Jennifer Rush was the third act to have a hit called 'The Power of Love' in less than a year, the others being Frankie Goes to Hollywood and Huey Lewis. It might have been the biggest seller, but Rush's effort was the furthest away in managing to capture what real romance is all about. Frankie, for once without a euphemism in sight, attempted to explain love by giving it a religious spin. Huey Lewis, by contrast, portrayed the whole love thing as some sort of good-fun fairground rollercoaster. Actually, a rollercoaster was about the only thing Huey Lewis didn't compare love to – sticking instead with, among other things, a dove, a train, diamonds and a big seventies hit by Boston.

What insight did Jennifer offer? If there was an award for the vaguest chorus of the eighties, 'The Power of Love' might just win it. Any couplets that include the words, 'something', 'somewhere' and 'sometimes' are unlikely to offer much in the way of philosophical fulfilment: even if you somehow managed to stay away until the end of the song (maybe that's what those big drums were about after all?) you weren't going to come away any the wiser. Howard Jones once asked 'What is Love?' but Jennifer Rush's answer was about as intelligible as a routine by Jed, his bizarre, be-chained mime dancer.

The reason that 'Our Tune' was so successful as a radio feature – aside from the fact that it acted as a sort of national therapy session – was that it recognized the power that pop music can have in capturing a moment in your life. One can mock Jennifer Rush's 'The Power of Love', but if you fell in love while it was Number 1 the chances are that your reservations about it went of the window and that it instead holds a cherished place in your heart as the song that summed up your heady rush of romantic abandon. While the rest of the nation was reaching for the 'Off' button on their radio dial, you were turning the volume up ready to wallow in that emotion. Maybe even the chorus made some sort of sense.

In the same way that your first single wouldn't be a reliable pointer towards your ultimate musical taste, so these 'Our Tune' records don't necessarily have anything to do with your preferences. Hence the inclusion of the quite terrible Climie Fisher in my record collection. Climie Fisher were a fairly nondescript musical duo (Simon Climie and Rob Fisher, or was it Rob Climie and Simon Fisher?) and would have no place in this book were it not for the fact that my relationship with my first proper girlfriend, a girl from school called Emma, lasted for pretty much the same length as their brief and undistinguished musical career.

On Wednesday 11 May 1988 – I can verify the date because I was keeping a diary at the time – Emma asked me out. *'Cute is the best way to describe her. As for her personality, I don't think it is possible to be depressed in her company.'* Presumably she'd given up any hope of me ever making a move. *'This lunchtime she asked me out. Funny thing was, only moments earlier she asked if I was going out with someone else. I replied, "No, so I'm still available Emma." Yeuchh! I had no idea she was going to ask me until she did. And you know what? I sort of accepted.'*

Our (my) first date was two days later, on Friday the 13th, a fact that probably summed up my romantic luck at the time. We went to see *Three Men and a Baby*. Even on this first evening, Climie Fisher reared their heads:

Emma and I had been having one of those faux flirty arguments about whether or not their first hit, 'Rise to the Occasion', started with someone shouting 'Hey! I know you're gonna dig this!' and whoever was wrong was paying for the popcorn. As it turned out, there were *two* versions of the song, the original and a remixed 'hip hop' version (it wasn't really), and so we symbolically split the cost of the bucket. *'All the time,'* my diary noted, *'my mind was wondering how far to go. All the way, nowhere at all?'* You'll be as relieved as the cinema audience, and probably Emma as well, that I didn't suggest a 'Sly Fox', but instead went for a bit of draping my arm around her chair and even, after a further ten minutes, Emma herself. *'That's as far as it got, honest!'*

Screen One of the York Odeon ended up being mine and Emma's spiritual home. A few weeks later we went back to see *The Last Emperor* and had our first kiss. What did my fifteen-year-old self make of snogging? *'The whole process was gentle, relaxing and very pleasing,'* was my slightly clenched-buttocks conclusion. At which point it would appear I lost all sense of proportion: *'Love is a gift from God,'* I continued, a view I'd ascribe to Frankie Goes to Hollywood rather than any religious conviction. I found myself channelling Huey Lewis: *'You don't have to be young or old, handsome or ugly.'* Then, *'It's there for you to take,'* I

pompously concluded, before signing off: *'Remember that.'*
Quite who I thought I was talking to, goodness knows.

The relationship began with 'Rise to the Occasion'
but it was Climie Fisher's second hit, 'Love Changes
(Everything)', that was all over the airwaves while we were
going out, and was 'our tune'. For those few short weeks,
every time I heard the song it put a spring in my step and
an equally clichéd smile on my face. *Rob Climie and Simon
Fisher (or is it Simon Climie and Rob Fisher?) are so right,* I
thought. *Love does indeed change everything.* I was so happy
that, for once, I even overlooked the fact that they'd need-
lessly put a pair of brackets in the song title.

It didn't last, of course. As Climie Fisher slid down the
charts, so my relationship dwindled. I followed my first
kiss with my first experience of being dumped, something
I responded to in the only way I knew how: getting cross
with brackets in song titles all over again. Looking back,
though, and from what I can bear to read of my diaries
through the cracks between my fingers, what comes across
is not the fall-out of breaking up, hurtful though that was,
but how happy Emma had briefly made my fifteen-year-old
self. Essentially, I probably needed to loosen up a bit. OK,
I probably needed to loosen up quite a lot – and that brief
relationship with Emma helped me to do that.

After Emma, I found success with a small and very specific
niche of girls – ones who were big fans of another eighties duo, Hue and Cry. Hue and Cry weren't actually their
real names, that was Pat and Greg Kane (they were brothers). They had a succession of alliterative hits called things

like 'Labour of Love' and 'Looking for Linda' and had just the right mix of soulful rock, lyrical wordplay and political touches (the 'Labour' in the song being Neil Kinnock's party) to attract a certain type of female fan. In 1989 the band released *Bitter Suite*, a double album that boasted a live recording alongside their second album, *Remote*. Any proper Hue and Cry fan, as a string of my girlfriends turned out to be, already owned *Remote*. Therefore, as a sign of their love, they gave me this additional copy to treasure. This happened to me on several occasions in succession – and, while I still might not have known much about women, I was smart enough not to say, 'Oh God, you're not about to give me another bloody Hue and Cry album, are you?'

Track Seven

Who Wants to be the Disco King?

Having successfully seen off dictators in my sensational songwriting debut, I continued my personal lyrical journey of putting the world to rights. The band might have had a new name (the Pulse), a new singer and keyboardist (Celia and Lee), and a new rival (the strangely named Brockley Haven), but the song remained depressingly the same. There was a 'Two Tribes'-style take on the Cold War called 'King of the Cowboys', in which I reimagined the nuclear conflict as a battle between cowboys and Indians. The cowboy section was all guitars, the Red Indian section all drums; and the last part saw a sort of nuclear 'confrontation' between the two, with the world ending and the audience whimpering for the noise to stop. There was 'Tears' – *'another depressing ballad'*, as even I noted in my diary. *'Staring defeat in the face,'* I optimistically wrote,

'*Last generation of the human race/This sums up all my fears/Too late to stop the tears.*'

When I wasn't being doom-laden to point of making the listener want to slit their wrists to end it all there and then, I went completely the opposite way – sounding so cheerful and optimistic that you had to tie me down to stop me floating away. One song, 'World Without a Cloud', took its inspiration from Live Aid, the glorious weather of the day symbolizing for me that anything was possible: '*We don't want your stormy weather,*' I declared, '*It should be allowed/I want the sun to shine forever/I want a world without a cloud.*' Apart from the fact that rhymes like that should be forbidden, I hadn't really thought things through for my carefully crafted metaphor. After all, one of the reasons that Bob Geldof and everyone else had been standing up to sing in the first place was that the sun had been shining for far too *long*, creating the sort of baking-dry conditions that had led to crop failures and the subsequent famine. My 'world without a cloud' philosophy was only going to exacerbate these appalling conditions yet further.

Looking back through the sort of lyrics I was writing, I think it's a wonder that I bothered to get up in the morning. It's a wonder, too, that anyone ever turned up to one of our gigs – I can only apologize to the various friends who must have somehow found the courage to sit through another evening of teenage meanderings about the sheer pointlessness of it all. The first of these gigs was as part of a local band competition called Rockstage. The occasion wasn't helped by the compère, who took one look at our name and introduced us by saying, 'They're nothing to do with lentils . . . Here are the Pulse.' I think someone must have had a word with me about keeping it light, because our miserable set was actually interspersed with a few upbeat numbers: we opened with Katrina and the Waves' 'Walking on Sunshine' and had a passable attempt at Aztec Camera's 'Somewhere in My Heart'. *'I looked out at the audience,'* I later wrote in my diary. *'People had got up and were dancing. They were dancing to us. US!'* It was, according to this impartial teenage correspondent, a blinding performance. *'I would have stayed up there and played all night if I could've.'* Given that that would have involved giving 'Dictator' a dusting down, it was probably best that we left the crowd hungry for more.

You might think, given my attempts to write songs and their not always over-optimistic feel, that the music of Morrissey and the Smiths would have been tailor-made for me. Yet, while the group were undoubtedly the darlings of all the cool kids at school (the far hipper Brockley Haven, for example, were already covering them while I was still working out the chords to 'Walking on Sunshine'), I remained curiously resistant to their charms. Not only that, but I am surprised to discover just how much vitriol I had for Morrissey in my diary: one entry during a particular uneventful weekend reads: 'I'd hate to be Morrissey, I mean he sings "Everyday is Like Sunday". Poor guy. But then he is a depressing bastard.' On another occasion, writing about a friend's party, I describe being given an earful for fifteen minutes after innocently suggesting that Morrissey was 'the most depressing boring sod in the entire world'.

The girl who bit my head off was quite right to do so, because the Smiths were one of the true original bands of the time. One of the results of the charts becoming more poppy, and then more pappy, and rock becoming more stadium in size was the rise of 'indie' music. This was made by predominantly guitar-led bands who released their records on independent labels such as Postcard, Factory, Go and Rough Trade. The 'indie' moniker therefore worked twofold – it described not only the sound but also the labels the bands were signed to.

If indie music had a moment where it came together as a scene, it was in 1986 – when the *NME* put together its *C86* compilation cassette, in association with Rough Trade. Five years earlier, the music magazine had put together *C81*, a similar celebration of independent music. The original cassette, however, had enjoyed a far more eclectic track listing: artists included Scritti Politti, the Beat, the Specials, Cabaret Voltaire and Robert Wyatt. The *C86* cassette was far more uniform in its sound: the Mighty Lemon Drops, the Pastels, the Shop Assistants, the Wedding Present and pre-*Screamadelica* Primal Scream all offered the same sort of flower-shirted, jangly-guitar worldview.

The music papers came up with an indie chart from which the Simple Minds and U2s of the world were excluded. This helped foster an alternative scene, a parallel universe to the proper charts, where the Smiths went in at Number 1 and stayed there for week after week. In the second half of the eighties, as the likes of Stock, Aitken and Waterman took hold of the real charts, more and more people bought in to and identified with the indie scene – a splintering of the ways that probably changed only when Britpop came along and the whole scene went mainstream again.

I think the reason I didn't really get into the Smiths properly until after the event was partly that they were what the cool kids were listening to. Which sounds a slightly odd thing to say, as you would have thought that credibility was *exactly* the sort of thing my teenage self would have been after. However, the Morrissey fans at school had the zeal of real believers. (When I went to see Morrissey in concert, many years later, I was struck by how many people had brought small children with them to the gig, so determined were they for them to see the great man.) This zeal, along with the passion they felt, left me feeling a little excluded. 'Meat is Murder' was one such dividing line: the proper fans all went vegetarian; at the same time, I was excited about the opening of the first McDonald's in York. Then there was Band Aid: while I was moved by Bob Geldof and his actions, Morrissey dismissed the record as 'absolutely tuneless [. . .] one can have a great concern for the people of Ethiopia, but it's another thing to inflict daily torture on the people of England.'[1]

The other reason for my 'protests too much' dislike of Morrissey was the great degree to which I liked the music the band was making. As a wonky guitarist myself, I could only begin to appreciate just how brilliant Johnny Marr was, with his silky, spidery arpeggiated runs, sparkly sixties Byrdsian licks and wall-of-sound vibrato on the likes of 'How Soon Is Now?'. If you shut out the singing and listened to the backing of songs like 'This Charming Man' and 'Heaven Knows I'm Miserable Now', what you heard was some of the sweetest, most delicate guitar playing around. Songs like 'London', meanwhile, offered flashes of the rock band the Smiths could be. All of which, I concluded, Morrissey had systematically ruined with his 'woe is me' warblings over the top.

I guess, too, that what Morrissey was singing about wasn't striking a chord with my own particular teenage vulnerabilities: my concerns were more overtly political, about whether we were all going to die in a nuclear war or when Nelson Mandela was going to be freed from prison – Morrissey and the Smiths never went for the same sort of pronouncements and moralizing that you got from a Jim Kerr or a Bono. My main insecurities were more to do with having a girlfriend – or, rather, not having one: I wanted songs to reassure me, to reaffirm my belief that love was the answer. Again, this wasn't particularly Morrissey's boat: songs with the romantic sweep of 'There Is a Light That Never Goes Out' felt few and far between – and even then I wasn't completely certain that Morrissey wasn't mocking what I believed in anyway.

The eighties was a very straight decade. This wasn't the nineties, with its *Loaded* magazine and laddism and everything swathed in irony and everyone pretending they didn't really mean a thing they said. The eighties didn't have that same knowing sense of humour, or much of a sense of humour at all in fact: things felt serious, at least to me, and everyone meant what they said. Which meant that the humour and the subtlety in Morrissey's lyrics passed me by. I was too busy trying to work out what Johnny Marr was playing to notice the Wildean brushstrokes beneath what Morrissey was singing about: I mistakenly took what he was saying at face value, as if I was listening to Bono. I was too literal, and not literary enough, to really get what he was singing about at the time.

By contrast, an indie band who hit closer to home for me were the Cure. The Cure were the sort of band that everyone seemed to like. What engaged here was Robert Smith's wearing of his heart on his sleeve. Nowhere was this more so than on 'Boys Don't Cry' – a rallying cry to teenagers like me: yes, I might be male, but I have feelings too! The song's message was reiterated by the record sleeve, which was turned into a hugely popular poster: this featured the semi-silhouetted figure of Robert Smith and guitar shot from behind, with his shoes pointing inwards like an awkward, self-conscious adolescent from York. In a way, Robert Smith wasn't coming from a dissimilar place to Morrissey, but the way he went about it was completely the opposite: his response to his insecurities was to be straight up about them, whereas Morrissey's was to come up with some biting, melodramatic quip. Even though the Cure's music was more Goth by nature, their sound felt somehow warmer and more uplifting.

Another indie band who I played to death were the Housemartins. The self-professed 'fourth-best band in

Hull' continued the Robert Smith feet-in modesty, their greatest-hits album mockingly called *Now That's What I Call Quite Good*. I certainly liked the fact that finally there was a decent band from down the road. I liked, too, the passion and political anger that underpinned both *London 0 Hull 4* and *The People Who Grinned Themselves to Death*. The title track of the latter was a typically sharp anti-royalist diatribe, which must have shocked the people who liked 'Caravan of Love' because it sounded a bit like the Flying Pickets: the band might have been wearing cardigans, but they had plenty of sharp implements hidden in the pockets. They were like a super-group in reverse, with star members singer Paul Heaton and bassist Norman Cook going on to be two of the biggest acts of the nineties in the somewhat different shapes of the Beautiful South and Fatboy Slim.

The lyricist who I really liked was Shane McGowan of the Pogues. His songs had just the right mix of romanticism and politics to tickle my teenage taste buds. While the band were most famous for ramshackle punk-fuelled folk thrashes like 'Fiesta' and the 'Irish Rover', on their albums were softer delights like their ballads 'Misty Morning, Albert Bridge' and 'Rainy Night in Soho'. There was the political bite of 'Birmingham Six', which got banned for suggesting that the imprisoned might be innocent, and the lament of 'And the Band Playing Waltzing Matilda', about the effects of war through the eyes of a Gallipoli survivor. Then there was 'Fairytale of New York', the greatest Christmas Number 1 that never was, which Shane McGowan and Kirsty MacColl performed their duet like a Den and Angie of downtown New York.

In fact, the Pogues were the first proper band I went to see in concert, on their If I Should Fall From Grace with God tour in 1988. With no chance of them coming to York, I somehow persuaded my dad to take me and fellow band-mates Ben and Ed to the Manchester Apollo to see them play. It was probably for my own safety that we ended up watching the show from the balcony upstairs: I looked on at the melee of bodies downstairs, crashing about full of Christmas spirit. I'm referring to the audience but could equally have meant the band, whose stage set included pints of Guinness lined up all the way across the front of the stage. By the end of the gig, Shane and band had made their way through all the drinks and were as inebriated as the rest of the audience. It was fortunate I knew the words to the songs, because the longer the gig went on the more intelligible Shane's pronunciation became. Certainly there was a noticeable different between his clarity and that of Kirsty MacColl, who joined the band for 'Fairytale of New York'. I remember coming out of the gig reeking of alcohol, stinking of cigarette smoke and having a strange new sensation of a ringing sound in my ears – I was almost disappointed when it faded the following day.

While my first proper gig was a 'Fairytale of New York' affair, my own musical career was very much more set in the reality of old York. That meant the somewhat smaller confines of the backroom of the Spotted Cow, a fairly nondescript pub just outside the City Walls near the town swimming pool. While the Pulse's debut performance had won critical acclaim in my own diary, it was getting this backroom swinging that was the real test in making headway on the York scene.

Beating us to the punch were Brockley Haven, who were the first to get their own headline slot at the Spotted Cow. Despite the rivalry (which, the more I think about it, was increasingly of Spandau vs Duran dimensions), we had an agreement whereby we'd get into each other's gigs for free. Which meant I got the kudos of being on the guest list – a good move for my credibility, seeing as when I turned up at the Spotted Cow pretty much half the school year was crammed in there, and the cool half of the year at that. The atmosphere was thick with people trying their first ciga-rette – I remember one friend frustratingly trying to light his cigarette in mid-air – and attempting to convince the barman they were older than fifteen.

Brockley Haven, it was clear, had better taste in music than we did. Rather than covering Aztec Camera and Katrina and the Waves, their choices were the Smiths ('London') and the Housemartins ('Sheep'). Rather than writing doom-laden songs about the end of the world, they wrote songs called things like 'Button Moon' and 'Girlfriend in My Soup'. And while musically they might not have been that much better (or any worse) than we were, in terms of perform-ance they were in a different league: they *looked* rather than played the part. I remember at another gig of theirs, a short while later, watching the singer climb on to the table at the side that the PA was on, causing the whole stand to start wobbling precariously. It was sort of stupid and captivating at the same time. It would never have crossed our minds to have done anything like that: my goodness, we politely thought, someone could have got hurt.

Not that I had any intention of giving up the fight. The Pulse rejigged in response, dropping the keyboards and becoming a straight-guitar, more indie-influenced four-piece. We changed our name again (of course): this time plumping for the November Criminals, which was the name the Nazis labelled the German government who signed the armistice that ended the First World War. OK, so it's not the greatest name in the world, but I was doing GCSE Modern History at the time – and, anyway, it was pretty much guaranteed to avoid any more hilarious lentil-based introductions (as well as heading off any Spandau Ballet-type fascism quips). Out went 'Walking on Sunshine' and in came covers by the Wonderstuff ('Wish You Were Here') and the Smiths ('Cemetery Gates'). I couldn't quite drop the doomy lyrics, however, though I was at least varying the subject matter a bit. Probably our best song was 'Lady in Waiting', about a German teenager called Silke Bischoff who was taken hostage after a bank robbery, paraded in front of the press with a gun against her throat and shot to death in the subsequent police shootout. I can't believe there were many people who read that particular story and thought, 'Oh boy! Have *we* got a hit on our hands.' Equally uplifting was 'Quite Depressed', about a father who sexually abused his daughter but was let off on the grounds that his wife was pregnant and he was feeling frustrated.

Rather surprisingly, the local newspaper decided to review the new line-up's debut gig at the Spotted Cow. 'In Praise of the Criminal Tendency' declared the *Yorkshire Evening Press*: 'It seems like the lunatic fringe of music fans are starting to follow the November Criminals. Although the turnout wasn't very high, the group went down a bomb.' I think we can all translate that as 'played to their mates'. The article went on to describe 'Celia's near-perfect vocals, Tom's stunning guitar playing, Ben's thudding bass line and frantic drummer Eddie', before concluding that 'for 50p, the evening was great value'. Which made us sound like a sort of bargain-bucket indie band – which, to be fair, we probably were.

The starting point of the Smiths' single 'Panic' was when Morrissey was listening to Radio One and the DJ followed a newsflash about the Chernobyl nuclear disaster by playing the sombre, respectful sound of 'I'm Your Man' by Wham! Morrissey, who had previously got it in the neck from 'in the afternoon' DJ Steve Wright, who regularly took the George Michael out of him on the show, decided to get his revenge. 'Panic' involves the repeated refrain calling for a disc jockey to be hanged, with a Steve Wright-emblazoned T-shirt on the subsequent Smiths tour making clear at whom his ire was aimed. However, some people interpreted the song more widely. The rallying cry of the chorus to set fire to the disco was nothing to do with cheesy Radio One DJs, but could be taken as a wider criticism of dance music in general. This was coupled with other statements Morrissey had made about how 'reggae is vile', and how the work of, among others, Whitney Houston and Janet Jackson was 'vile in the extreme [. . .] this music doesn't say anything whatsoever'.

Morrissey and electronic sounds were not exactly bedfellows. The Smiths had originally chosen their name for its ordinariness, a riposte to the stylized names of the synthesizer bands of the early eighties. In the same way as Queen had their 'no synthesizers' policy in the seventies, so part of the Smiths' musical manifesto was to keep their records similarly electronically free: 'there is nothing more repellent than the synthesizer,' Morrissey told *Sounds* magazine in 1983. So, while the music of the early eighties had seen an attempt to bring dance and rock together, the indie scene (of which Morrissey was the de facto leader) was very much for keeping the two separate: dance bad, guitar good was the basic mantra. With the exception of New Order, who dug their particular dance-rock furrow with the likes of the brilliant 'Blue Monday', most indie music was very straight, very white guitar music: plenty of rock but not much roll, with the main black element being the clothes worn by many of its followers. It was, ironically enough given its political stance, essentially a very conservative type of music. As laudable as the post-punk purity might have been, it came with an anti-technology luddism attached. If the early eighties had been like punk had never happened, this music was a little like the early eighties had never existed.

Which was a shame, partly because of the restrictions that it placed on the music you could make, and partly because it kept people away from what was happening in dance music

– which by this point was culturally far more interesting, challenging and radical. Once again technology had played a key role: first, there was the development of sampling, which led to a succession of monster hits from the likes of M/A/R/R/S ('Pump Up the Volume') and Bomb the Bass ('Beat Dis'). These were as much pop-culture collages as traditional songs, creative in their pulling together, and on the edge in terms of the copyright laws.

Then there was the arrival of acid house, a cocktail of an old piece of kit (the Roland 303) and a new drug: ecstasy. The Roland 303 had been around in the early eighties as a small side unit for keyboardists or guitarists to programme bass lines on, so they had something to play along to at home. The machine hadn't sold, and was discontinued. By 1986 the couple of thousand in existence had started find their way into second-hand shops, and could be picked up for forty or fifty quid. What someone then worked out (that someone being Marshall Jefferson and Nathaniel 'DJ Pierre' Jones) was that if you messed around with the resonance knobs ('wanging it', as one user described it), you got this fantastic new sound – a 'crazy buzzing noise that churned and writhed and twisted like a mainframe malfunction'.[2] You might not recognize the sound from that description but you would if you heard the wibbly-wobbly bass line thumping through your speakers: this was the sound that would become the basis of all acid house music. The term 'acid' came from the first track to use the sound, 'Acid Tracks' by DJ Pierre's Phuture. Where Phuture got the term 'acid' from depends on who you listen to: there were stories about people putting LSD in the water at one club; another version is that the sound reminded the record-label boss of acid-rock music. Wherever it came from, this offshoot of the burgeoning Chicago house-music scene quickly became a genre of its own. Overnight the Roland 303 became the sound that defined acid house – the machines that no one had wanted were suddenly changing hands for thousands of pounds.

The other element in all of this was ecstasy, which first started being around in the UK in 1985: the drug meshed perfectly with acid house, bringing out the music, giving you the energy to stay up all night feeling at one with those you were dancing with. Having taken over Ibiza in summer 1987, acid house and ecstasy became the sound of London's clubs the following year. Even this was not enough to house – if you'll pardon the pun – the phenomenon. Over the summer of 1988, raves started sprouting in disused warehouses and carefully coordinated out-of-town locations – farmers' fields, aircraft hangars, you name it (Pulp's later hit 'Sorted for E's & Wizz' was Jarvis Cocker's astute recollection of one such night out). By that autumn, acid house and its smiley-face T-shirts were everywhere: you could buy them in Top Shop and even the *Sun* was selling them ('Trend-setting Bizarre has come up with some far-out T-shirts to help you keep way ahead of Britain's latest dance craze').

The BBC, though, were a little more jumpy about the drug element. They might not have got what 'Pass the Dutchie' was about, but even they were fairly sure about D

Mob's Top 5 hit, 'We Call it Acieed'. I'm saying that was the reason they banned it: it could of course have been to do with not wanting to hear that 'Acieeeed!' shout ever again. In one of those classic tabloid about-turns, the *Sun* stopped selling its T-shirts and started telling its readers about the dangers of taking E: togetherness? All-night dancing? How about hallucinations, biting the heads off pigeons and death?

Rave culture rapidly became counter-culture, and confrontations with the police and government grew. In the wake of the infamous Castlemorton Common rave in the Malvern Hills, in 1992, the Conservative government passed a Criminal Justice Act outlawing such gatherings: turning music critic, the law defined such music as 'sounds wholly or predominantly characterized by the emission of a succession of repetitive beats'. Although the gatherings were clamped down, dance music as we know it today was just beginning, with the super-clubs such as the Ministry of Sound and Cream becoming the places to be.

My own experience of the so-called Second Summer of Love? It wasn't to be the first or the last time that a cultural event passed me by. I was just a touch too young, to be fair. I was still trying to wean myself off Archers and lemonade on to something slightly less sweet. The thought of taking something illegal was well off where I was at. Also I wasn't a fan of the music: by this point I was firmly a member of the orthodox indie church and, despite having my disagreements with Morrissey, was down on the dance scene by definition. And lastly, while the raves were regular happenings off the M25, the York ring road, the A64, was somewhat less crowded with clubbers: it was a bit too bloody cold, frankly, to consider standing in a field near Tadcaster at three in the morning.

My own musical career had one final act to play, one final shuffling of the school pack. I was in the sixth form when Celia sensibly decided she had had enough of having to learn my morose lyrics. Meanwhile, over in Brockley Haven, a classic case of musical differences led to guitarist Paul 'Banksy' Banks leaving, and coming over to join us as both guitarist and lead singer. Banksy was a properly good guitarist, much better than me, and somewhat better than he was as a vocalist. But he made up for that with confidence – his attitude at school was that he didn't give a flying fuck because he was going to be famous – and, working on the theory that two guitars were better than one, we really rocked.

You'd have had to look hard to have found any evidence of ecstasy culture in this new line-up. Rather, it was stadium rock in name (Heartland) and in sound: big expansive music that we thought mixed the best of U2 with Simple Minds but that ended up coming across like a poor man's Then Jericho.

The thing about stadium rock is that you need a stadium to play it in: in the backroom of the Spotted Cow it just seemed a bit vague and empty. It all sounded a bit better on tape – we went into the studio and cut a demo that the local music press (YourK Music – do you see what they did there?) compared favourably to Deacon Blue: 'Is anybody in York making better pop songs?' the review asked, one of those comments that could go two ways.

The band in York who *were* making better pop songs were Brockley Haven, who had got themselves a new guitarist and were now performing under the name Shed Seven. Heartland, after a few gigs, drifted apart as A levels and exams reared their heads. As the rest of us went off to university and started thinking about the real world, Banksy continued playing in bands, convinced that stardom was still just around the corner. Before long, the inevitable reconciliation occurred and he took his rightful place in Shed Seven. The next time I saw him it was at one of their gigs, at the Jericho Tavern in Oxford, and the group had just scored what would be their first of many hits with 'Dolphin'. *Didn't I tell you so?* his welcoming handshake seemed to say.

Track Eight

Fools Gold

By the end of the 1980s the love affair I'd had with pop music was coming to an end. Partly, to use the classic break-up formula, this wasn't about them; it was about me. I was a different person to that of ten years earlier, and not just in that literal all-your-cells-change-every-seven-years sort of a way. The difference between being seven and seventeen is a lot bigger than the difference between being seventeen and twenty-seven, or twenty-seven and thirty-seven (I could go on; I probably have). Those formative teenage years are full of first-time experiences and, at plenty of times, excruciating embarrassments. Being a teenager is all about switchbacking between cocksure self-belief and a crushing lack of self-confidence.

Looking back, what's amazing is how much you thought you knew – especially considering how little you actually did. Flicking through my teenage diaries, it's as though I thought had the answers to pretty much everything: politics, love, culture, morality . . . Like an early television set, it's all there in black and white. These days I might know a lot more, but among that is the understanding of how little I actually do. What would my teenage self think of that? He'd probably write a vituperative diary entry about how I'd lost it, gone soft, sold out.

There's a cliché about British politics that if you don't vote Labour when you're twenty you've got no heart and if you don't vote Conservative when you're forty you've got no head. I certainly had heart when I was young: I might (might?) have been innocent and naïve but there is something admirably pure about the belief that I had. I'm sure that's why Bob Geldof and Band Aid made such an impact on me at the time: as a teenager, I could understand Bob's simple response that something was wrong and something needed to be done. I'm sure that's also why bands like U2 and Simple Minds meant so much to me. Ian McCulloch, in one of his waspish asides, dismissed such bands as 'music for teenagers'; but, as a teenager myself at the time, the straightforwardness of their passion hit home. It might have been a clanging chime, but it struck a chord.

These days I might not vote Conservative, as my teen-age self would be glad to hear (he'd probably have written another song about suicide if he knew that was coming, before it was too late), but, though I still vote the way I have always done, it's without much enthusiasm: without any, well, heart. I might be talking specifically about politics here, but the point I'm really trying to make is something more fundamental, about the process of getting older and getting old: you wouldn't be human if you didn't sometimes look back at your youth and think, I miss that. Where did it all go?

The word nostalgia comes from the Greek *'nostos'*, meaning 'return home'. The term was originally about homesickness, about a longing to get back to a particular, familiar place. These days, of course, nostalgia is all about time, about a harking back to a particular, familiar era. For some, the sense of sickness is now a sense of sickliness – a sign of people clinging to the past rather than making the most of the present day. They dismiss such people as sad and – you know what? – maybe we are, but in a different, softer way than they're dismissively suggesting. That, at least, is how I feel when looking back to my own childhood. Rather than it feeling like a malaise, it actually feels healthy to remind myself of where I came from once in a while.

What has happened over recent years is that these individual memories have become part of a collective nostalgia industry, as companies have cashed in on this instinct. The writer Simon Reynolds writes about this in his book *Retromania*: there is now so much looking back, he argues, that there is a danger of contemporary culture being suffocated. It's certainly true that researching this book has been a different experience to researching the ones I wrote even ten years ago. Compared to scrabbling around libraries and second-hand record shops, the availability of material on the Internet now is quite extraordinary: footage you never thought you'd see again has been transferred from VHS cassette on to YouTube. These days, if you want to wallow in your decade of choice, there are eighties-only radio stations and even eighties festivals where the line-up comprises once-famous stars dusting down their hits for one last payday. For some, all this is the opposite of growing up: it's a refusal to let go, an infantilizing of culture.

Once upon a time, such nostalgia simply wasn't an option. Cavemen and -women didn't sit around going, 'Do you remember the time we caught that woolly mammoth?' or, 'That last Ice Age, now that were proper cold!' or, 'Cliff Richard's really gone downhill since "Move It", hasn't he?' People didn't survive long enough to be able to look back in the way we do now. But as lives have got longer (at least for those of us lucky enough to live in the first world), so the idea of being young has stretched, and so have what Strawberry Switchblade called our 'thoughts of yesterday'. While technological changes might have accelerated this process – digital radio, the Internet – the impulse this draws on isn't new. It doesn't strike me as coincidence that punk, with its nods both musically and stylistically to fifties rock and roll, happened at the same time as Tim Rice and friends had the idea to put together the first *Guinness Book of Hit Singles*; these were two very different musical ideas, but both had their roots in returning to and reclaiming the past.

Previous generations showed a marked if not stronger nostalgia for their own younger days. Anyone who has ever had a conversation with an elderly relative banging on about the war should be in no doubt that we are all shaped by past events. Yet if Great Uncle William unwinds about the latest book he has read about El Alamein, or gets out his old letters from the front, no one ever accuses him of wallowing in the past or being culturally infantilized. The difference between his generation and mine is that, thankfully, the decade in which I grew up wasn't shaped by being at war: I blather on about old Duran Duran singles because that's what was happening when I was growing up. But if a hypothetical Great Uncle William and I swapped places, in some sort of Hollywood-type time-travel plot, then it would me recounting the Blitz and him going on about Tears for Fears. Yes, you could argue the experiences are qualitatively different, but that ignores the point that you can be nostalgic only for the time you have been lucky or unlucky enough to have lived through.

For me, that time was the eighties, and what gets my emotional juices flowing was the music that mattered to me. There's a line from the *Born in the USA* song 'No Surrender' about how Bruce Springsteen learnt far more from a 'three-minute record' than from the education he got at school. Bruce's point is that when it comes to the important things in life – love, friendship, beliefs, identity – it is the singers and songwriters you listen to growing up who are your real teachers. I think as an eldest child I probably felt that acutely: pop music was my guide, my surrogate elder sibling.

As already said, as the eighties drew to a close, my romance with pop did the same. I also said it was partly about me, not them – partly, but not entirely. Partly it was indeed about them. I was listening to different things – rock, indie, jazz, folk, even bits of African music – not just because my musical palate was becoming (marginally) more sophisticated, but also because pop music, the stuff that got a front cover of *Smash Hits* and a barbed comment from John Peel on *Top of the Pops*, was not what it once was. In fact, it wasn't just not what it once was: it was becoming as bad as it had been in (whisper it) the mid-seventies.

By one of those quirks of pop fate, both the first and second halves of the eighties finished with a band having achieved the hallowed chart goal of getting their first three singles to Number 1, and both also ended with the same record at Number 1. In 1984, it was Frankie Goes to Hollywood who saw 'Relax', 'Two Tribes' and 'The Power of Love' all reaching the top spot: three great pop songs that each stand the test of time. In 1989, the same feat was achieved by Jive Bunny and the Mastermixers – and, by contrast, if you can recall their three Number 1s, let alone name them, I'd be 'impressed' ('Swing the Mood', 'That's What I Like', 'Let's Party'). I'm ashamed to say that, like fellow irritating novelty act Black Lace, the band also hailed from Yorkshire (Rotherham). Or at least the real-life members were: I can't vouch for the rabbit who grooved along to their seventies-style 'Stars on 45' medley of old hits and TV theme tunes, occasionally encouraging listeners to 'Come on!' like the crummy local DJ the man in the suit probably was. I'd like to think that if there was ever a symbolic fight between Jive Bunny and that cartoon compilation-album pig, the latter would punch the rabbit to the floor, oinking triumphantly, 'Now *that's* what I call music.'

Back in Christmas 1984 the original Band Aid single was Number 1 – having pulled in Duran Duran, Culture Club, Wham! and Spandau Ballet, the song brought together all the big names of the first half of the decade, and served to sum up that particular generation of pop stars. Five years later, Christmas 1989 saw 'Do They Know It's Christmas?' back at Number 1. This time, however, the song was sung by the not-quite-so big names of the second half of eighties British pop. And rather than having had its mixing-desk knobs twiddled by Midge Ure, this new version was produced by the three men many held responsible for the sorry decline in British music: Mike Stock, Matt Aitken and Peter '*The Hit Man and Her*' Waterman.

'What I think about Stock, Aitken and Waterman,' offered Neil Tennant in 1990, 'is that it's like in 1984 when all the proles have that ghastly cheerful music [. . .] [Stock, Aitken and Waterman]'d say, "We're just making records for people to have a good time to." They are utterly and totally Thatcherite and their records are utterly and totally Thatcherite records. In which sense they are perfect pop because they are totally records of their time.'[1]

The music of Stock, Aitken and Waterman has been called many things over the years, not least by the trio themselves: they were the 'Hit Factory', the self-styled 'British Motown', a sort of Holland–Dozier–Holland with a Casio keyboard and a South London accent. Their record label,

PWL, even had a slogan that would not have been out of place on the backdrop of a political-party conference – 'The Sound of a Bright Young Britain'. I think, looking back, it was this attitude that possibly riled people as much as the music itself. It wasn't just that there was something quite un-English about boasting about your success – after all, they wouldn't be the only songwriters ever to make claims to greatness (Oasis, for example). It wasn't just that they were distrusted pop Svengalis, pulling the strings on their musical puppets – people have always been suspicious of such people, from Malcolm McLaren to Simon Cowell. It wasn't even just the fact that PWL was an independent record label, which meant that Kylie kept the Wedding Present off the top of the indie charts and royally pissing off *NME* readers.

I think it was a combination of all these points, but added to a touch of the Gerald Ratner. Gerald Ratner was a hugely successful businessman in the eighties, whose chain of jewellery stores made him both huge profits and won him plaudits from the Conservative government. In 1991, Ratner made some misjudged comments in a speech to the Institute of Directors: his golden earrings were 'cheaper than an M&S prawn sandwich but probably wouldn't last as long'; he could sell a set of six glasses and sherry decanter for under a fiver 'because it's total crap'. Overnight, the British public stopped shopping at his stores, and the chain collapsed.

Stock, Aitken and Waterman never made such foot-in-mouth comments, but there were occasions when they weren't far off: Kylie Minogue's 'I Should Be So Lucky', they proudly claimed, was written and recorded in forty minutes. Compare that to the six months Trevor Horn spent on recording and re-recording Frankie Goes to Hollywood's 'Relax'. Compare that to Neil Tennant's theory that 'good pop music has got a sort of magical quality to it, a fabulous quality'. Of Stock, Aitken and Waterman he suggested: 'I don't think when they make a record they make any attempt to make it fabulous.'[2]

To spend forty minutes creating a hit single that goes on to sell millions is, on a business level, a triumph: that little input can create that much financial reward. 'Relax', on that score, is a folly: six months and six-figure costs for one five-minute record? Artistically, however, the situation is the other way round. A bit like a partner getting ready to go out, it takes more than forty minutes to add those fabulous touches. Six months might be a touch on the extreme side (I'm talking about records now, not getting ready to go out), but there's no denying the quality of the end product and consequently how much it still holds up.

Calling themselves the Hit Factory probably didn't help perceptions either. A factory, after all, is designed to reproduce the same thing again and again. Certainly there was an element of interchangeability at times: 'Got to Be Certain', for example, was written for the young Mrs Wyman, Mandy Smith, but ended up being recorded by Kylie Minogue; Rick Astley's 'Whenever You Need Somebody' had previously been written for O'Chi Brown. But more than that, the trio were victims of their own success: in 1989, their most successful year, Stock, Aitken and Waterman had seven Number 1 singles and fifteen Top 5 hits. On one estimate, their small, independent record label, PWL, had a 27 per cent share of the market. Thoughts about the music aside, that is a phenomenal level of success for a record company that size. The problem was, though, that that many hits resulted in a lot of airplay, to the point where it felt like Radio One was playing nothing else. The Stock, Aitken and Waterman sound became ubiquitous, and the more you heard it, the more you realized it was all rather similar. By the end of the decade, Stock, Aitken and Waterman records were the equivalent of Gerald Ratner's golden earrings, whose welcome lasted about as long as the metaphorical M&S prawn sandwich.

It would be hasty to dismiss everything Stock, Aitken and Waterman did. In the earlier years of their reign the trio did deliver some decent tunes. Their earlier hits were more rooted in a Hi-NRG feel, none more so than 1985's quite splendid 'You Spin Me Round (Like a Record)' by Dead or Alive, a song on which, like Frankie and 'Relax', only singer Pete Burns ended up on the final version. The following year, too, the charts remained refreshingly unburdened with the Stock, Aitken and Waterman sound: Bananarama had liked 'You Spin Me Round', so worked with them on their cover of 'Venus'; then there was Princess, with the sub-Galaxy soul of 'Say I'm Your Number One' (she had a '1' earring, just in case you couldn't remember); then there was 'Showing Out (Get Fresh at the Weekend)', the house-leaning debut single of duo Mel and Kim. Whatever you thought of the music, what there wasn't at this point was a distinctive 'SAW' sound: they were just essentially another team of young producers on their way up in the world.

The following year was where things really begin to take off. Now the stable didn't just have Mel and Kim, Bananarama and Dead or Alive scoring huge hits with the likes of 'Respectable' and 'Love in the First Degree'; they also produced hits for Sinitta, former Wham! singers Pepsi & Shirlie, Samantha Fox, and Rick Astley. Astley, one of life's perennial nice guys, was from Newton-Le-Willows in Lancashire, and was a van driver by day and singer with local band FBI at night. He was spotted by Pete Waterman's then girlfriend, Gaynor, who came back saying his voice 'makes me go all funny'. So Pete went to watch FBI play in Warrington, and made what seems now like an odd offer: come down to London, we'll give you a job as a studio assistant (or tea boy, depending on your point of view), and make a record.

Neither of Pete Waterman's partners was as enamoured with Rick's voice: 'Neither Matt [Aitken] or I were certain about his voice,' recalled Mike Stock. 'There was something unusual about it. Sure, he had a BIG voice, but it was either on or off [. . .] there was no subtlety [. . .] we wondered whether it was really an *attractive* voice.'[3]

They tried a cover of the Temptations' 'Ain't Too Proud to Beg' (a song that, nothing wasted, would end up on Rick's second album). Then there was an attempt to launch Rick as part of a duo – Rick and Lisa – whose song 'When You Gonna' found the couple moaning about when the other was 'gonna' return home, all over a Mel and Kim-style house beat. Lisa (Fabien) could also sing, but with her voice so high, and Rick's so low, they didn't really gel. It sounded, frankly, a bit of a mess.

It also wasn't very Rick. He was a nice guy and not the sort to leave women wondering where he had got to: this was someone who'd been going out with the same girl since junior school. One day, Pete Waterman had been chatting with Rick about his girlfriend, and Rick said, 'You're never gonna give her up, are you?' That was a light-bulb moment for Waterman: Stock and Aitken then wrote the song around that and Rick's childhood relationship: that old-fashioned ideal of staying 'Together Forever', to quote another Rick hit along the same lines. The music, meanwhile, took its cue from 'Trapped', a 1985 hit for Colonel Abrams. Colonel Abrams is not a real colonel (it's his name), which is probably why the trio felt comfortable 'adapting the bass line rhythm'[4] without facing attack from some sort of house-music SWAT team. 'Never Gonna Give You Up' worked because it successfully matched artist and subject: you can always tell when the singer means it, and Rick did here.

A similar sort of matching of subject occurred with Kylie Minogue's debut hit, 'I Should Be So Lucky'. The story behind the recording was cock-up all round: Kylie turned up at the Hit Factory studios in Borough, South London, which had been arranged by Pete Waterman but without anyone telling Stock or Aitken; not only that, but Kylie had a flight to catch back to Australia late that afternoon. That explains why the song was written and recorded so quickly.

A brainstorm between Matt and Mike came up with the idea that Kylie must be so busy, what with *Neighbours* and flying around and everything, that she couldn't have any time for a relationship – Mike remembered the saying, 'lucky at cards, unlucky in love', and everything unfurled from there. Matt, like with Rick Astley, wasn't sure about her voice ('too tremulous' was his verdict this time), but in true professional mode Kylie did her vocals and left to catch the plane.

Hard as it is to think this now, but at the time Kylie wasn't a household name: I remember a comedian on *Friday Night Live* making a joke about how Kylie Minogue sounded like the sort of obscure Eastern European football team that Liverpool would face in the European Cup (presuming English clubs hadn't been banned from Europe, as they were at the time). 'I Should Be So Lucky' was huge, and became the first of many *Neighbours*-related hits. If Kylie hadn't been successful, we'd never have suffered the likes of mop-head Craig McLachlan and his band Check 1-2 (so called after what roadies say when testing microphones). We'd also have been spared the sight of a thrusting Stefan Dennis, whose 'Don't It Make You Feel Good' sounded less of a come-on and more of a threat. Kylie's hits continued (though she made them come to her in Australia, rather than hanging around in London again), and was joined at the Hit Factory by Jason Donovan, Scott to her Charlene, both on screen and, briefly, in real life. To mix fiction and reality still further, Kylie and Jason then released 'Especially for You', a quite appalling duet, just as Scott and Charlene were getting married on *Neighbours* (or at least when the episode was finally shown on UK TV). In the days before Kylie met Michael Hutchence and Jason Donovan found himself fending off accusations from the *Face*, both singers (and their soap characters) were still on the squeaky side of clean: when they left *Neighbours*, their characters weren't killed off but were left to live happily ever after in Brisbane. Both, meanwhile, had Number 1s with covers that wouldn't have been out of place on *Heartbeat* ('Tears on My Pillow', 'Sealed with a Kiss').

Despite all their success, Stock, Aitken and Waterman felt they weren't getting the credit they deserved. When 'Never Gonna Give You Up' won Best Single at the Brits, only for Rick Astley to be elbowed out to make way for the Who, it felt symbolic of the rest of the industry's attitude to them. Their response to their records not being played on the radio (an opinion that seemed at odds to my perception of the Radio One playlist) was the Reynolds Girls' 'I'd Rather Jack', in which the duo criticized DJs for playing, among others, Fleetwood Mac, the Rolling Stones, Pink Floyd and Dire Straits. I don't know about that – maybe the girls had tuned into Capital Gold by mistake – but their comment about how the DJs were twice as old as them rang very true and did presage the end of the 'Smashy and Nicey' era in the early 1990s. After Stock, Aitken and Waterman weren't even nominated for best producer at the 1990 BPI Awards, the trio printed an ad in the industry paper *Music Week*, listing all 100 of their hits like it was a singles chart: the headline read 'Your Worst Nightmare Come True'.

It wasn't just a lack of industry respect that got Stock, Aitken and Waterman's proverbial goat: the dance community, too, was similarly unimpressed by their work. The trio turned up to receive an award at the Disco Mix Club event at the Royal Albert Hall in 1987 and were bottled, with some DJs taking the time and effort to fill their projectiles with urine: 'I hope you get your needles stuck up your arses,' was Pete Waterman's oil and water response to the jeering protagonists. Rather than take it lying down, Stock, Aitken and Waterman decided to send the dance community up in revenge. The result was 'Roadblock' – a seventies-sounding funk jam that the trio put out anonymously as a white-label release. Before long, the DJs who had jeered Stock, Aitken and Waterman were unwittingly playing it as part of their set: until, that is, they revealed who it was by. That might have been it, except for another white-label release also doing the rounds: M/A/R/R/S' sample-heavy hit 'Pump Up the Volume', which included a seven-second section from the DJ-mocking 'Roadblock'. Did Stock, Aitken and Waterman take their inclusion alongside samples of James Brown and Public Enemy as the credibility they'd been searching for? Not quite: Waterman called the move 'wholesale theft' and SAW took out an injunction to get the sample removed.

'Roadblock' aside, Stock, Aitken and Waterman stuck religiously to their chart-topping formula of relentlessly cheerful inoffensiveness, all sung by a roster of harmless, clean-cut acts. Take Rick Astley: you couldn't argue that this was someone with an extraordinary voice, but in every other aspect he was just an ordinary guy; he was perfectly nice, came from a normal background, was still going out with his childhood sweetheart, wasn't particularly trendy (suits not ripped jeans for him), was OK-looking and couldn't dance to save his life. Rick was the type of person who today would be plucked out of the audition queue on the *X Factor* to actually sing in front of the judges. Would he have been told he had the X Factor? He'd probably have been told he needed to sort out his dance moves and would end up crashing out during a choreographed disaster on Rock Week.

It was this sort of everyman everydayness that became the trio's Stock (Aitken and Waterman) in trade. The street plucking continued with the likes of Sonia ('You'll Never Stop Me Loving You') and the Reynolds Girls: none of them really had any star quality, just the nerve to knock on Pete Waterman's door and tell him they wanted to be famous. I can't help thinking back to Neil Tennant's comment about how pop music should be fabulous: I agree and so, I think, should its stars. Pop, for me, is about fantasy, not reality. It feels instructive that a young A&R executive called Simon Cowell saw Stock, Aitken and Waterman at first hand, via his act Sinitta, and also through his licensing of the Hit Factory compilation albums. Even though their own musical success faltered as SAW splintered apart – the hits dried up as Matt Aitken left in 1991, then Mike Stock in 1993 – the formula they created retains, sadly, its hold over pop music today.

As 1989 and the eighties drew to a close, Stock, Aitken and Waterman's influence remained absolute. Which was why Bob Geldof gave them a ring to re-record 'Do They Know It's Christmas?'. I don't actually know if he added, 'And could you get every single terrible artist from the second half of the eighties on board?' but he might as well have done. The video to the song featured a message from Michael Buerk about that year's situation: 'It isn't the same as the great famine of 1984,' he began. He could also have added, 'And the version you are listening to is not a patch on the original record either.'

Everything, and I mean *everything*, is a pale shadow of the first Band Aid single. There sitting in Phil Collins's drum seat was Luke Goss. There singing Paul Young/ David Bowie's moody opening line was Kylie. There, *given actual lines of their own to sing*, were Sonia, Big Fun and Bananarama, the latter perhaps still hanging around from the first recording in the hope of finally getting near a microphone. There was Wet Wet Wet, with the video director choosing to have a shot of Marti Pellow smiling and winking as he sang his line about 'clanging chimes of doom'. As for the line Bono had had such problems singing five years before, any feelings of awkwardness were got round by splitting it meaninglessly into two – Kylie and Jason Donovan harmonizing the first half, Matt Goss growling the second.

And there, in his big round Mike Read glasses, clutching his 'cans' for all he was worth, was Mr 'Wired for Sound' himself, Cliff Richard. Cliff, who'd had the Christmas Number 1 in 1988 with 'Mistletoe and Wine' and would have it again in 1990 with 'Saviour's Day', was doing his best to sing on three Christmas Number 1s in a row. The fact that he had seamlessly assimilated himself into this new generation of *Smash Hits* stars said much about how far pop had fallen. The early-eighties stars had looked up to the likes of David Bowie and Bryan Ferry; this new generation, either covering songs from the late fifties and early sixties (Kylie and Jason) or splicing them together (Jive Bunny), had their very own grandfather figure to share vocals with. If the first half of the eighties were as if punk had never happened, the pop stars of the second half were winding the clock back to before even the Beatles had begun.

It could have been Gary Davies, but he presented the week after. It could have been Mark Goodier, but he did it the week after that. It could have been Bruno Brookes, Anthea Turner or Andy 'Broom Cupboard' Crane, but it was their turn the week before. Instead, it was the turn of Jenny Powell, whose other TV credits at the time included *No Limits*, the Jonathan King pop-music programme, and various children's shows on Saturday morning. Jenny was joined this particular Thursday evening – 23 November 1989, to be precise – by Radio One DJ Jakki Brambles, and it was Jakki who got given the following link to read out: 'The Stone Roses are one of two Manchester bands playing on *Top of the Pops* tonight. They've just finished their Japanese and European tour, and have a new entry at thirteen . . .'

Life, to quote Jeff Goldblum's character in *Jurassic Park*, finds a way. As with dinosaurs, so with music. For just as it seemed as though the charts were hitting the worst kind of mid-seventies malaise, so the previously isolated tribes of indie rock and dance came together to create a brilliant new alternative. As Pete Waterman was flicking through his Rolodex to find out if Cliff Richard was available to record Band Aid II, *Top of the Pops* was featuring debut performances from both the Stone Roses ('Fools Gold') and the Happy Mondays ('Hallelujah' from their *Madchester Rave On* EP). It might have been sheer coincidence that the two bands had new entries in the chart that week, but their combined presence felt deliberate, seismic: an iconic pop moment.

For the Stone Roses, it was the culmination of a year that had seen them rise from Manchester secret to proper contenders. They might have gained a large following in their home city, but as late as February they'd still been playing to tiny audiences around the country: when they played Brighton's Escape Club, essentially the upstairs room of a pub, fifty-two people turned up; at Middlesex Polytechnic, meanwhile, only thirty people attended. In May, the band's eponymous debut album was released. For what is now regularly hailed as one of great records of all time, not all the reviews were adulatory. The *NME* only gave it seven out of ten, not over-enthusiastically describing it as 'an aural Big Mac laced with a psychedelic drill [. . .] living proof that acid is good for you. Just.' *Q* magazine, in a month when recommended albums included new releases by Deacon Blue and Fine Young Cannibals, awarded it three stars out of five: it disliked the 'strangely monotone production' and concluded that 'what could have been great instead merely bulges with promise'. Record buyers appeared initially to agree with this assessment: the highest chart position the album reached in 1989 was a lowly Number 19.

As the year went on, however, the love began to spread. Part of that was probably to do with good old-fashioned word of mouth as people heard the record. Part of that, too, was the proliferation of ecstasy use: that undoubtedly helped break down barriers between dance and indie. The latter, previously puritanical angst-ridden souls in black clothes, were now chilling out to music about which they'd once have written a searing critique in green Biro, and were swapping their drainpipe jeans for brightly coloured T-shirts and flares. Essentially they cheered up a bit and stopped being quite so up themselves. The bands who benefited most from all of this were those with a foot in both camps: the Happy Mondays and the Stone Roses.

In August 1989 the Stone Roses played the Empress Ballroom in Blackpool. This time, rather more than thirty people turned up. The performance was extraordinary, not just for the way the band played but also because of the audience's reaction: this was a shared moment of ecstasy-fuelled euphoria; adulation and sweat poured down the walls in happy unison. Everything about the concert – from its location to the music, the fashion to the influences – was a long way from London: it was the south that was, to borrow a phrase from *Going for Gold*, having to play catch-up. That moment occurred in mid-November, when 7000 people watched the band sell out Alexandra Palace – a remarkable achievement when you consider that at this point they'd only had one Top 40 hit ('She Bangs the Drums' reaching number 36) and the album had barely broken the Top 20.

All that, though, was about to change: when guitarist John Squire and Ian Brown dropped in to Manchester record shop Eastern Bloc to sign some copies of the 'She Bangs the Drums' single, the owner let them have some records on return. One that Squire picked out was a compilation of break beats: songs that feature DJ and sample-friendly drum breaks. There's differing opinion as to precisely which song the Roses created a drum loop from: it's been suggested that it was 'Bra' by Cymande or a James Brown song; more likely, to my ears at least, is 'Hot Pants', a song by James Brown acolyte Bobby Byrd. Whatever the origin, that single-bar drum loop became the starting point for the band's breakthrough single. Lyrically, the song's starting point was *The Treasure of the Sierra Madre*, a 1940s Humphrey Bogart film about prospectors in 1920s Mexico. The title, meanwhile, came from a present John Squire's girlfriend had brought him back from holiday: a lump of the mineral pyrite, more commonly known as 'Fool's Gold' (with an apostrophe, unlike the single title).

The full song, clocking in at nine minutes fifty-three seconds, still sounds as box fresh as the first time I heard it: lithe and slinky, it's a funkily controlled coming together of three great musicians and a singer whose reserved vocals oozes confidence. After completing the record, the band somewhat bizarrely decided that it should be the B-side to their next single, 'What the World Is Waiting For'. It was only after the record company were getting such positive feedback to the B-side of the promo copies that the single became officially a double-A-side, and 'Fools Gold' became the track everyone played.

The band's *Top of the Pops* performance was actually the group's second television appearance of the week. The previous night the Stone Roses had appeared on *The Late Show*, BBC2's then post-*Newsnight* culture programme. That show, however, is remembered for somewhat different reasons: about a minute into the band's performance of 'Made of Stone', a power cut killed their amplifiers. Presenter Tracey McCleod did her best to keep the show going, introducing a piece about some photographer or other, while in the background Ian Brown could be seen pacing about, shouting, 'Amateurs, amateurs . . . We're wasting our time here, lads.'

The *Top of the Pops* performance, by contrast, is remembered for the right reasons: Ian's Brown request to sing live was turned down, resulting in a mimed performance during which he sang into his microphone half the time and waved it around in the air like a maraca the rest. The band had earlier spent a pleasant afternoon in the BBC garden, chewing the fat with the Happy Mondays: at one point the two bands even considered swapping drummers for the night. While the Stone Roses bassist Mani was still wearing the same red top from the *Culture Show* appearance, the Happy Mondays were wearing new clothes after persuading their record company to give them £1000 each to get something to wear (size: baggy).

The Mondays' appearance, with Shaun flanked by Bez on one side and (somewhat incongruously) Kirsty MacColl on the other, echoed the Stone Roses' in that it wasn't, in itself, a great performance: miming to a group of half-interested teenagers was never going to be the same as playing live to a packed-out Blackpool ballroom. The greatness lay in the sheer presence of their being there, that sartorial and sonic gap between them and everyone else on the programme. This was a week in which the 'Lambada' was rocketing up the charts, Milli Vanilli had mimed their way into the Top 10 and New Kids on the Block were at Number 1.

One of the things that scientists have noticed about evolution is the fact that species don't gradually evolve on a smooth, linear upwards curve: instead what actually happens is that things bumble along at the same level for a while and then – bang – everything suddenly jumps up a gear. It's the same with babies: they take an age to learn to walk and speak, and then suddenly they're running about with a whole range of words for different farmyard animals. What happened on that *Top of the Pops* was a similar sort of evolutionary musical jump – the moment stood out because overnight everything seemed different and new.

Madchester, as the catching-up press inevitably dubbed the scene, wasn't the only new sound to be heard that November. The other was a 'chink, chink, chink' as hammers were taken to the Berlin Wall. All year, regimes had been tumbling in Eastern Europe: in Poland, Hungary and Czechoslovakia, Bulgaria and Romania. But it was events in East Germany, with the symbolism of the Berlin Wall, that seemed to sum up the historic transition most distinctly. The fall of the Berlin Wall began on 9 November and over the next six weeks it was reduced to rubble. A decade that had begun musically in Britain with Pink Floyd adding another brick in the wall was ending with Berliners knocking the whole construct down.

There's nothing that immediately links the fall of the Berlin Wall and the Stone Roses and Happy Mondays appearing on *Top of the Pops*, the close proximity of the timing aside. And yet these events share an equivalent sense of mood: both felt celebratory; both felt as though the people were back in control; both offered huge promise and possibilities for a new decade that was just over a month away. A few weeks later, I celebrated my seventeenth birthday and started thinking seriously about life beyond school – what I wanted to do, where I might want to go. Had I reached that age earlier in the decade I might have been thinking about these things with trepidation. Instead, though, with walls tumbling down like a Style Council video, and with that Stone Roses groove going round and round in my head, anything and everything seemed possible.

Outro

September 2011. It is a warm and balmy late-summer/early autumn evening, and my wife and I are in the south-coast town of Bournemouth. We're in the Old Fire Station, to be precise, a smallish venue that doubles up as a Union bar during university term time. There's no one of student age here, however, except behind the bar. Instead the capacity crowd is a specific mixture of late thirty-somethings and early forty-somethings: groups of girlfriends or husbands chaperoning wives, each having made the dash across from putting the children down and showing the babysitter how the remote control for the television works. There's a ripple of excitement from the sheer fact of being let out for the evening, but mainly because of who we've all turned out to see: Duran Duran.

Earlier in the year, Duran had postponed the British leg of their European tour after Simon Le Bon had had throat

361

problems. With the American part of the tour about to start, and as a way of saying thank you/sorry, the band were doing a couple of small 'fan club' gigs to warm them up. Which was how I found myself watching the group in the sort of venue they probably hadn't played since they'd started out thirty years earlier. No big fancy light show. No special effects. Not even a backdrop. Just a band and their instruments, all within touching distance of the fans down the front.

To a cheer and a roar that bounced off the walls, and a scream or two from those who had briefly forgotten which decade it was, the Duran bounded on stage: Roger slipped quietly behind the drums with a cheery wave, Nick Rhodes slipped behind his stack of keyboards looking *exactly* the same, as though he had a Dorian Gray picture among his art collection; John Taylor, with a swish of white robe, looked a little too thin, the ghost of *Smash Hits* past; Simon Le Bon, by contrast, looked full of life – tanned, bearded and beefed-up. He's a big guy anyway, but on the small Bournemouth stage his presence felt enormous.

About halfway through the set, Duran launched into their mid-eighties James Bond theme, 'A View to a Kill'. Uh-oh, I thought. This was the song that they'd played at Live Aid, their last eighties appearance as the original line-up, the song left off the subsequent DVD on account of Simon Le Bon's famous failure to hit that high note. There's no hiding place here, I thought, no tour to have warmed up the tonsils: this *was* the warm-up. As this small south-coast venue reverberated to the sound of several hundred sardined fans heartily singing every one of the song's wonky lyrics about naked kisses, I wondered briefly whether Simon would play it safe, hold the microphone out and lead the singalong instead. But, a few feet up onstage, this was a man enjoying the occasion as much as his audience, and he wasn't about to duck the challenge.

And you know what? He was note perfect.

You're still here? It's over. Go home. Go . . .

Sleeve Notes

The Fourteen Songs that went Straight in at Number 1 in the 1980s

The Jam, 'Going Underground' (1980)
The Police, 'Don't Stand So Close to Me' (1980)
Adam and the Ants, 'Stand and Deliver' (1981)
The Jam, 'Town Called Malice' (1982)
The Jam, 'Beat Surrender' (1982)
Duran Duran, 'Is There Something I Should Know' (1983)
Frankie Goes to Hollywood, 'Two Tribes' (1984)
Band Aid, 'Do They Know It's Christmas?' (1984)
David Bowie and Mick Jagger, 'Dancing in the Street' (1985)
Ferry Aid, 'Let It Be' (1987)
Christians, Holly Johnson, Paul McCartney, Gerry Marsden and Stock, Aitken and Waterman, 'Ferry Cross the Mersey' (1989)
Jason Donovan, 'Sealed with a Kiss' (1989)
Jive Bunny, 'Let's Party' (1989)
Band Aid II, 'Do They Know It's Christmas?' (1989)

WIRED FOR SOUND

The Ten Bestselling Singles of the 1980s

Band Aid, 'Do They Know It's Christmas?'
Frankie Goes to Hollywood, 'Relax'
Stevie Wonder, 'I Just Called to Say I Love You'
Frankie Goes to Hollywood, 'Two Tribes'
Human League, 'Don't You Want Me'
Wham!, 'Last Christmas'
Culture Club, 'Karma Chameleon'
George Michael, 'Careless Whisper'
Jennifer Rush, 'The Power of Love'
Dexys Midnight Runners, 'Come On Eileen'

The Bestselling Singles of the 1980s, Year by Year

1980: The Police, 'Don't Stand So Close to Me'
1981: Soft Cell, 'Tainted Love'
1982: Dexys Midnight Runners, 'Come On Eileen'
1983: Culture Club, 'Karma Chameleon'
1984: Band Aid, 'Do They Know It's Christmas?'
1985: Jennifer Rush, 'The Power of Love'
1986: The Communards, 'Don't Leave Me this Way'
1987: Rick Astley, 'Never Gonna Give You Up'
1988: Cliff Richard, 'Mistletoe and Wine'
1989: Black Box, 'Ride on Time'

SLEEVE NOTES

The Greatest Song of the Eighties

Culture Club, 'Do You Really Want to Hurt Me'
Culture Club, 'Karma Chameleon'
INXS, 'Need You Tonight'
a-ha, 'Take On Me'
Michael Jackson, 'Thriller'
Michael Jackson, 'Beat It'
Ultravox, 'Vienna'
Bon Jovi, 'Living on a Prayer'
Adam and the Ants, 'Prince Charming'
Madonna, 'Like a Virgin'

(2011 Absolute 80s, MTV and Viva Poll)

The Greatest Song of the Eighties

Frankie Goes to Hollywood, 'Two Tribes'
Human League, 'Don't You Want Me'
Pet Shop Boys, 'West End Girls'
The Specials, 'Ghost Town'
Michael Jackson, 'Beat It'
The Stone Roses, 'Fools Gold'
Prince, 'Sign 'o' the Times'
Tears for Fears, 'Everybody Wants to Rule the World'
Billy Idol, 'White Wedding'
Propaganda, 'Duel'

(My Own Humble Opinion)

WIRED FOR SOUND

The Bestselling Albums of the 1980s, Year by Year

1980: ABBA, *Super Trouper*
1981: Adam and the Ants, *Kings of the Wild Frontier*
1982: Barbara Streisand, *Love Songs*
1983: Michael Jackson, *Thriller*
1984: Lionel Richie, *Can't Slow Down*
1985: Dire Straits, *Brothers in Arms*
1986: Madonna, *True Blue*
1987: Michael Jackson, *Bad*
1988: Kylie Minogue, *Kylie*
1989: Jason Donovan, *Ten Good Reasons*

The Ten Bestselling Albums of the 1980s

Dire Straits, *Brothers in Arms*
Michael Jackson, *Bad*
Michael Jackson, *Thriller*
Queen, *Greatest Hits*
Kylie Minogue, *Kylie*
Whitney Houston, *Whitney*
Fleetwood Mac, *Tango in the Night*
Phil Collins, *No Jacket Required*
Madonna, *True Blue*
U2, *The Joshua Tree*

SLEEVE NOTES

The Greatest Albums of the Eighties

U2, *The Joshua Tree*
Guns N' Roses, *Appetite for Destruction*
Michael Jackson, *Thriller*
Bruce Springsteen, *Born in the USA*
Prince, *Purple Rain*
AC/DC, *Back in Black*
The Smiths, *The Queen is Dead*
The Clash, *London Calling* (UK release, 1979)
The Cure, *Disintegration*
Metallica, *Master of Puppets*

(*Rolling Stone* Readers' Poll)

The Greatest Albums of the Eighties

Human League, *Dare*
ABC, *Lexicon of Love*
Prince, *Sign 'o' the Times*
U2, *The Unforgettable Fire*
The Stone Roses, *The Stone Roses*
The Pogues, *If I Should Fall from Grace with God*
ABBA, *The Visitors*
Tears for Fears, *The Hurting*
Kraftwerk, *Tour de France*
Dexys Midnight Runners, *Searching for the Young Soul Rebels*

(My Own Humble Opinion Again)

WIRED FOR SOUND

Band Aid Line-Up, 1984

Adam Clayton, Phil Collins, Bob Geldof, Steve Norman, Chris Cross, John Taylor, Paul Young, Tony Hadley, Glenn Gregory, Simon Le Bon, Simon Crowe, Marilyn, Keren (Bananarama), Martin Kemp, Jody Watley, Bono, Paul Weller, James Taylor, Peter Blake, George Michael, Midge Ure, Martin Ware, John Keeble, Gary Kemp, Roger Taylor, Sarah (Bananarama), Siobhan (Bananarama), Peter Briquette, Francis Rossi, Robert 'Kool' Bell, Dennis Thomas, Andy Taylor, Jon Moss, Sting, Rick Parfitt, Nick Rhodes, Johnny Fingers, Boy George, David Bowie, Holly Johnson, Paul McCartney (last three recorded phone messages on the B-side)

The Live Aid Running Order in Full, 13 July 1985

Status Quo, Style Council, Boomtown Rats, Adam Ant, Ultravox, Spandau Ballet, Elvis Costello, Nik Kershaw, Sade, Sting, Phil Collins, Howard Jones, Bryan Ferry, Paul Young and Alison Moyet, Bryan Adams, U2, the Beach Boys, Dire Straits, George Thorogood and the Destroyers, Queen, Simple Minds, David Bowie, the Pretenders, the Who, Kenny Loggins, Elton John and George Michael, Madonna, Freddie Mercury and Brian May, Paul McCartney, Band Aid ensemble, Tom Petty and the Heartbreakers, Black Sabbath, REO Speedwagon, Crosby Stills and Nash, Judas Priest, the Cars, Neil Young, Thompson Twins, Power Station, Eric Clapton, Led Zeppelin, Phil Collins again, Duran Duran, Patti LaBelle, Hall and Oates, Mick Jagger and Tina Turner, Bob Dylan with Keith Richards and Ron Wood, USA for Africa finale

SLEEVE NOTES

Music Retail Sales in the UK (£millions)

Singles Sales
1980: 72.2
1981: 83.6
1982: 94.9
1983: 97.6
1984: 123.9
1985: 137.6
1986: 127.9
1987: 126.9
1988: 137.1
1989: 131.5

LP Sales
1980: 266.7
1981: 244.0
1982: 241.8
1983: 233.4
1984: 228.8
1985: 250.9
1986: 239.5
1987: 256.9
1988: 287.2
1989: 223.3

Cassette Sales
1980: 100.3
1981: 104.0
1982: 125.6
1983: 157.2
1984: 189.4
1985: 243.3
1986: 277.9
1987: 335.5
1988: 395.8
1989: 424.1

CD Sales
1980: –
1981: –
1982: –
1983: 2.6
1984: 7.2
1985: 33.5
1986: 97.1
1987: 195.2
1988: 287.7
1989: 434.7

(Source: BPI Yearbooks)

WIRED FOR SOUND

The 1980s Presenters of the Top 40 Chart Show

1979–1982: Tony Blackburn
1982–1984: Tommy Vance
1984: Simon Bates
1984–1986: Richard Skinner
1986–1990: Bruno Brookes

The 1980s Presenters of the Radio One Breakfast Show

1978–1980: Dave Lee Travis
1981–1986: Mike Read
1986–1988: Mike Smith
1988–1993: Simon Mayo

Eighties Sales Figures of Music Magazines

Smash Hits: 786,886
Q: 133,975
Number One: 130,721
NME: 95,849
The *Face*: 74,357
Kerrang!: 60,126
Melody Maker: 59,962
Sounds: 49,201
Record Mirror: 41,089

(Source: Audit Bureau of Circulation, January–June 1989)

SLEEVE NOTES

The Ultimate Smash Hits Readers' Poll of the 1980s

I believe I am right in saying that I have created the first definitive *Smash Hits* readers' poll of the decade. As was done for the collating of the first-ever singles chart back in 1952, I have given ten points for being first in a particular year, going down to one point for being tenth. I have then added the results together to produce the following charts, as voted for by *Smash Hits* readers.

Best Group of the Eighties
Duran Duran
Pet Shop Boys
Wham!
a-ha
U2
Madness
Wet Wet Wet
Spandau Ballet
Five Star/Bros
The Police/Adam and the Ants/the Jam

Best Male Singer of the Eighties
Simon Le Bon
George Michael
Michael Jackson
Paul Young/David Bowie
Gary Numan/Adam Ant
Boy George
Rick Astley
Prince/Morten Harket
Bono
Midge Ure

Best Female Singer of the Eighties
Annie Lennox
Madonna
Alison Moyet
Kim Wilde
Kate Bush
Toyah
Siouxsie Sioux
Whitney Houston
Hazel O'Connor/Kylie Minogue
Tracey Ullman

Most Fanciable Male of the 1980s
John Taylor
Simon Le Bon
George Michael
Morten Harket
Adam Ant
Marti Pellow
Boy George
Matt Goss
Jason Donovan
Sting/David Sylvian

Most Fanciable Female of the 1980s
Kim Wilde
Madonna
Toyah
Samantha Fox
Kate Bush
Kylie Minogue/Clare Grogan
Whitney Houston
Debbie Harry
Debbie Gibson
Olivia Newton John/Jay Aston

SLEEVE NOTES

The Smash Hits Readers' Best Singles of the 1980s
1980: The Police, 'Don't Stand So Close to Me'
1981: Soft Cell, 'Tainted Love'
1982: Duran Duran, 'Save a Prayer'
1983: Culture Club, 'Karma Chameleon'
1984: Duran Duran, 'Wild Boys'
1985: Duran Duran, 'A View to a Kill'
1986: Duran Duran, 'Notorious'
1987: Rick Astley, 'Never Gonna Give You Up'
1988: Bros, 'I Owe You Nothing'
1989: Bros, 'Too Much'

The Smash Hits Readers' Best Albums of the 1980s
1980: The Police, *Zentatta Mondatta*
1981: Human League, *Dare*
1982: Duran Duran, *Rio*
1983: Wham!, *Fantastic*
1984: Duran Duran, *Seven and the Ragged Tiger*
1985: Madonna, *Like a Virgin*
1986: Madonna, *True Blue*
1987: Michael Jackson, *Bad*
1988: Wet Wet Wet, *Popped In Souled Out*
1989: Jason Donovan, *Ten Good Reasons*

Most Horrible Thing
Spiders
Margaret Thatcher
AIDS
George Michael
School
Michael Jackson's face
Madonna
Prince
Samantha Fox
Nuclear weapons

(1987 list: runners up included spots, brothers, Bernard Manning, blood sports, toes, earwigs, unhappiness, puff-ball skirts, Lilt, and vases.)

Notes

Side One

Track One: Another Brick in the Wall (Part 2)

1 'Goodbye Blue Sky', *Guitar World*, October 2009.
2 'Le Freak' started life as 'Fuck Off', written by the band in fury after they were refused entry to the legendary club Studio 54. Pure conjecture on my part, but I like the image of Erzin sat in his own studio wondering what's going on as Chic swear away next door.
3 Fiddler's Dram weren't the only ones guilty of such bracket abuse in song titles at the time: I must refer you to Coast to Coast, whose one entry in the *Guinness Book of British Hit Singles* is the equally execrable '(Do) the Hucklebuck'. Come *on*, guys . . .
4 Assuming they haven't all shut down by the time this is published.
5 *George Michael: Bare*, George Michael and Tony Parsons, pp. 30–1.

6 *Duran Duran: Notorious*, Steve Malins, p. 5.

7 *Wham! Confidential*, Johnny Rogan, p. 7.

8 *Take It Like a Man: the Autobiography of Boy George*, with Spencer Bright, p. 37.

9 *A Bone in My Flute*, Holly Johnson, p. 30.

10 Ibid., p. 36.

11 *I Know This Much: from Soho to Spandau*, Gary Kemp, p. 45.

12 Ibid., p. 59.

13 *Take It Like a Man*, p. 30

14 BBC website interview with Chris Nolan, author of *I Swear I Was There*, June 2006.

Track Two: Vienna

1 Ooh ooh ooh ooh, aieeya.

2 Actually, the very first chart was a Top 15, with records tying for Numbers 7, 8 and 11 respectively.

3 I had to go online to discover that, at the time of writing, it's the X Factor Finalists – which pretty much says it all, really.

4 If you go by the 'official' charts. In the sixties there were lots of different competing charts, which the BBC collated into one overall chart, their 'pick of the pops'. However, when the *Guinness Book of Hit Singles* was launched, in 1977, just one of them (the Record Retailer chart) was used for the sixties. This created occasional discrepancies with the charts that people remembered watching on *Top of the Pops*. An alternative collation suggests that there were actually more like eight or nine Number 1 straight-ins during that decade.

5 Even something as potentially exciting as the Blur/Oasis Britpop battle in 1995 came down to marketing – Blur's record label proved that bit cleverer with formats and pricing and consequently got bigger multiple sales.

NOTES

Track Three: Fade to Grey

1 *To Cut a Long Story Short*, Tony Hadley, p. 58.
2 *I Know This Much*, p. 101.
3 Spandau Ballet weren't the only ones to find themselves wandering unwittingly into such territory. When Duran Duran played their first gig as the five-piece they would become famous as, the music they chose to come on to was 'Tomorrow Belongs to Me' from the film *Cabaret*. Again the song choice left something to be desired: as it plays in the film, the camera slowly pulls back from the singer's face to reveal that he's a member of the Hitler Youth.
4 *Duran Duran: Notorious*, p. 14.
5 Ibid., p. 19.

Track Four: Computer Love

1 It didn't do Men at Work's actual bank balance much good either: in 2010 it was ruled that the flute riff was a little too close to 'The Kookaburra Song'.
2 *Q* interview, January 1990, p. 35
3 *MTV Ruled the World: the Early Years of Music Video*, Greg Prato, loc. 5761–68.

Track Five: Wired for Sound

1 *New York Times* interview, 17 December 2005.
2 'We Don't Talk Anymore' was, incidentally, written by songwriter Alan Tarney, who went on to be the producer behind a-ha.
3 *Rip It Up and Start Again: Postpunk 1978–1984*, Simon Reynolds, loc. 6017.

Track Six: Do You Really Want to Hurt Me

1 *Top of the Pops Mishaps, Miming and Music*, p. 60
2 Ibid., p. 41.
3 Ibid, p. 136.
4 *Take It Like a Man*, p. 149.
5 Ibid., p. 159.
6 Ibid., p. 181.
7 Ibid., p. 177.
8 Ibid., p. 198.
9 *Top of the Pops: Mishaps, Miming and Music*, p. 145.
10 Ibid, p. 53.

Track Eight: Thriller

1 *MTV Ruled the World*, loc. 2582.

Track Nine: Club Tropicana

1 http://www.guardian.co.uk/culture/2002/mar/08/artsfeatures.popandrock
2 Ibid.
3 *George Michael: Bare*, p. 69.
4 *Like Punk Never Happened: Culture Club and the New Pop*, Dave Rimmer, pp. 180–1.

Track Ten: Relax

1 *Q*, January 1989, p. 19.
2 *Rip It Up and Start Again*, p. 279.
3 *Sun*, 1 March 1984.

NOTES

Track Eleven: Do They Know It's Christmas?

1 *Is That It?*, Bob Geldof, p. 269.
2 Ibid., p. 270.
3 Ibid., p. 281.
4 Ibid., p. 274.
5 *If I Was . . .*, Midge Ure and Robin Eggar, p. 132.
6 Ibid., p. 133.
7 Ibid., p. 134.
8 *Is That It?*, p. 277.
9 *Smash Hits* interview, 8 November 1984.
10 *True: the Autobiography of Martin Kemp*, p. 93.
11 *U2 by U2*, with Neil McCormick, p. 158.
12 *XS All Areas: the Status Quo Autobiography*, Francis Rossi and Rick Parfitt with Mick Wall, p. 222.
13 *U2 by U2*, p. 158.
14 Ibid.
15 *If I Was . . .*, p. 142.

Side Two

Track One: A View to a Kill

1 *A Bone in My Flute*, p. 215.
2 *Is That It?*, p. 377.
3 *Take It Like a Man*, p. 314.
4 *Smash Hits*, 6 December 1984.
5 *A Bone in My Flute*, p. 248.
6 *Take It Like a Man*, p. 265.
7 Ibid., p. 339.
8 *Smash Hits*, 22 October 1984.
9 *I Know This Much*, p. 229.
10 *Duran Duran: Notorious*, p. 163.
11 Ibid. (both quotes), pp. 186–7.

Track Two: Alive and Kicking

1 *U2 by U2*, p. 164.
2 *Unforgettable Fire: the Story of U2*, Eamon Dunphy, p. 239.
3 *U2 by U2*, p. 162.
4 Ibid., p. 147.
5 *Smash Hits*, 3 January 1985.
6 *Rock: The Rough Guide*, Mark Ellingham and Jonathan Buckley, p. 73.
7 *Simple Minds*, Adam Sweeting, p. 143.
8 *U2 by U2*, p. 149.
9 Ibid.
10 *Simple Minds*, p. 154.
11 Ibid., p. 155.

Track Three: Like a Virgin

1 Quoted in *Rejoice, Rejoice! Britain in the 1980s*, Alwyn Turner, p. 200.
2 *Smash Hits*, January 1985.
3 *Reservoir Dogs: Screenplay*, Quentin Tarantino, p. 4.
4 *Madonna: the Complete Guide to Her Music*, Rikki Rooksby p. 17.

Track Five: What Have I Done to Deserve This?

1 *The Third Man*, Peter Mandelson, loc. 1717.
2 *A-ha: the Swing of Things 1985–2010*, Jan Omdahl, p. 25.
3 Ibid., p. 114.
4 Ibid.
5 *More Than You Know*, Matt Goss, p. 66.

NOTES

6 Q, January 1989, p. 72.
7 *Pet Shop Boys, Literally*, Chris Heath, p. 110.

Track Six: Love Changes (Everything)

1 *Our Tune: the Heartwarming Letters from Britain's Most Popular Radio Programme*, Simon Bates, p. 26.
2 Ibid., p. 143.
3 Ibid., p. 129.
4 Ibid., p. 125.

Track Seven: Who Wants to be the Disco King?

1 *Morrissey & Marr: the Severed Alliance*, Johnny Rogan, p. 209.
2 *Altered State: the Story of Ecstasy Culture and Acid House*, Matthew Collin, p. 21.

Track Eight: Fools Gold

1 *Pet Shop Boys, Literally*, pp. 238–9.
2 Ibid., p. 239.
3 *The Hit Factory: the Stock, Aitken and Waterman Story*, Mike Stock p. 43.
4 Ibid., p. 46.

Sources and Bibliography

Music and DVD

My starting point was to return to the music, either to dust down the original albums or put an equally dusty VHS cassette into the video player. To list everything that I have listened to and watched while researching this book would take up many more pages than I am allowed here. If you are interesting in investigating further, I have created a number of public playlists on Spotify. Each is entitled 'Wired for Sound' and includes all the songs I have discussed in any particular chapter. In terms of music video from the era, YouTube remains a remarkable resource.

Magazine and Newspapers

I have also spent many a happy hour going back through back issues of the various magazines from the decade. *Smash Hits* has been my primary source here, because of the book's pop focus, but I have also looked at relevant issues of other periodicals, particularly those of the *NME*, *Melody Maker* and *Q*. In terms of newspapers, my main sources have been the *Guardian*, the *Sun* and the *News of the World*.

Books

I have read widely around the subject, and list my main resources below. For those interested in reading further I would recommend four particular titles: Simon Reynolds's *Rip It Up and Start Again* is a wonderful account of the post-punk scene in the late 1970s and early 1980s; Dave Rimmer's *Like Punk Never Happened* is an excellent contemporaneous account of the early 1980s pop scene; Daniel Blythe's *Encyclopaedia of Classic 80s Pop* and Richard Evans's *Remember the 80s* are two more fascinating reads for those who like their eighties-pop knowledge.

Ant, Adam, *Stand and Deliver: the Autobiography* (Pan, 2007)
Bangay, Joe, *The Roxy Book* (Sidgwick and Jackson, 1987)
Barfe, Louis, *Where Have All the Good Times Gone? The Rise and Fall of the Record Industry* (Atlantic, 2004)
Bates, Simon, *My Tune: an Autobiography* (Virgin, 1994)
Bates, Simon, *Our Tune: the Heartwarming Letters from Britain's Most Popular Radio Programme* (Arrow, 1990)

SOURCES AND BIBLIOGRAPHY

Blacknell, Steve, *The Story of Top of the Pops* (Patrick Stephens, 1985)

Blythe, Daniel, *The Encyclopaedia of Classic 80s Pop* (Allison and Busby, 2002)

Bono, Edge, The, Clayton, Adam, and Mullen Jr, Larry, *U2 by U2* (HarperCollins, 2006)

Bordowitz, Hank, *Turning Points in Rock and Roll* (Citadel, 2004)

Bromley, Tom, *All in the Best Possible Taste: Growing Up Watching Telly in the 80s* (Simon and Schuster, 2010)

———— *We Could Have Been the Wombles: The Weird and Wonderful World of One-Hit Wonders* (Penguin, 2006)

Buckley, Jonathan and Ellingham, Mark, *Rock: the Rough Guide* (Rough Guides, 1996)

Burchill, Julie, *Love it or Shove It: the Best of Julie Burchill* (Century, 1985)

Cauty, Jimmy and Drummond, Bill, *The Manual (How to Have a Number One the Easy Way)* (Ellipsis, 1998)

Cavanagh, David, *My Magpie Eyes are Hungry for the Prize* (Virgin, 2000)

Chippindale, Peter and Horrie, Chris, *Stick It Up Your Punter: the Rise and Fall of the Sun* (Heinemann, 1990)

Chronicle of the 20th Century (Dorling Kindersley, 1995)

Cloonan, Martin, *Banned! Censorship of Popular Music in Britain: 1967–1992* (Arena, 1996)

Collin, Matthew, *Altered State: the Story of Ecstasy Culture and Acid House* (Serpent's Tale, 1997)

Dennis, Chris, *British and American Hit Singles 1946–1997* (Batsford, 1998)

Doggett, Peter, *You Never Give Me Your Loving: the Battle for the Soul of the Beatles* (Vintage, 2010)

Du Gay, Paul, Hall, Stuart, Janes, Linda, Mackay, Hugh and Negus, Keith, *Doing Cultural Studies: the Story of the Sony Walkman* (Open University, 1997)

Dunphy, Eamon, *Unforgettable Fire: the Story of U2* (Viking, 1987)

Easlea, Daryl, *Everybody Dance: Chic and the Politics of Disco* (Helter Skelter, 2004)

Evans, Richard, *Remember the 80s: Now That's What I Call Nostalgia* (Portico, 2008)

Frith, Mark (ed.), *The Best of Smash Hits* (Sphere, 2006)

Geldof, Bob, *Is That It?* (Sidgwick and Jackson, 1986)

George, Boy with Bright, Spencer, *Take It Like a Man: the Autobiography of Boy George* (Sidgwick and Jackson, 1995)

Garfield, Simon, *The Nation's Favourite: the True Adventures of Radio One* (Faber and Faber, 1998)

Gittins, Ian, *Top of the Pops: Mishaps, Miming and Music – True Adventures of TV's No.1 Pop Show* (BBC Books, 2007)

Goss, Matt, *More Than You Know: the Autobiography* (HarperCollins, 2005)

Hadley, Tony, *To Cut a Long Story Short* (Sidgwick and Jackson, 2004)

Harding, Phil, *PWL from the Factory Floor* (Cherry Red, 2010)

Harris, John, *The Last Party: Britpop, Blair and the Demise of English Rock* (Fourth Estate, 2003)

Harry, Bill, *Whatever Happened To . . .? The Ultimate Pop and Rock 'Where Are They Now?'* (Blandford, 1999)

Heath, Chris, *Pet Shop Boys, Literally* (Viking, 1990)

Hewitt, Paolo, *Paul Weller: the Changing Man* (Bantam, 2007)

Johnson, Holly, *A Bone in My Flute* (Arrow, 1995)

Johnstone, Nick, *Melody Maker: History of 20th Century Popular Music* (Bloomsbury, 1999)

Jones, Liz, *Slave to the Rhythm: the Artist Formerly Known as Prince* (Warner, 1997)

Jovanovic, Rob, *George Michael: the Biography* (Piatkus, 2007)

Kemp, Gary, *I Know This Much* (Fourth Estate, 2009)

Kemp, Martin, *True* (Orion, 2000)

Kent, Nick, *Apathy for the Devil* (Faber and Faber, 2010)

———*The Dark Stuff: Selected Writings on Rock Music 1972–1993* (Penguin, 1994)

Klein, Naomi, *No Logo* (Flamingo, 2000)

Long, Pat, *The History of the NME* (Portico, 2012)

McSmith, Andy, *No Such Thing as Society* (Constable, 2010)

Malins, Steve, *Duran Duran, Notorious* (Andre Deutsch, 2005)

Mann, Brent, *99 Red Balloons and 100 Other All Time Great One Hit Wonders* (Citadel, 2003)

Michael, George and Parsons, Tony, *Bare* (Michael Joseph, 1990)

Napier-Bell, Simon, *Black Vinyl White Powder* (Ebury, 2001)

SOURCES AND BIBLIOGRAPHY

————*I'm Coming to Take You to Lunch* (Ebury, 2005)

Ogg, Alex, *Top Ten: the Irreverent Guide to Music* (Channel 4 Books, 2001)

Omdahl, Jan, *A-ha: the Swing of Things 1985–2010* (Forlaget Press, 2010)

Parker, Martin, *Reading the Charts: Making Sense with the Hit Parade* (Popular Music, May 1991, Cambridge University Press)

Prato, Greg, *MTV Ruled the World: the Early Years of Music Video* (Greg Prato, 2011)

Reynolds, Simon, *Retromania: Pop Culture's Addiction to its Own Past* (Faber and Faber, 2011)

————*Rip It Up and Start Again: Postpunk 1978–1984* (Faber and Faber, 2005)

————*Totally Wired: Postpunk Interviews and Overviews* (Faber and Faber, 2009)

Richard, Cliff, *Which One's Cliff? The Autobiography* (Coronet, 1981)

Rideout, Ernie, Fortner, Stephen and Gallant, Michael (eds.), *Keyboard Presents the Best of the '80s: the Artists, Instruments and Techniques of an Era* (Backbeat, 2008)

Rimmer, Dave, *Like Punk Never Happened: Culture Club and the New Pop* (Faber and Faber, 1985)

Roach, Martin (ed.), *The Virgin Book of British Hit Albums* (Virgin, 2009)

Robb, John, *The Stone Roses and the Resurrection of British Pop* (Ebury, 1997)

Roberts, David (ed.), *British Hit Singles* (Guinness World Records, 2002)

Rodgers, Nile, *Le Freak: An Upside Down Story of Family, Disco and Destiny* (Sphere, 2011)

Rogan, Johnny, *Morrissey & Marr: the Severed Alliance* (Omnibus, 1992)

————*Wham! Confidential: the Death of a Supergroup* (Omnibus, 1987)

Rossi, Francis and Parfitt, Rick with Wall, Mick, *XS All Areas: the Status Quo Autobiography* (Sidgwick and Jackson, 2004)

Savage, Jon, *England's Dreaming: Sex Pistols and Punk Rock* (Faber and Faber, 1991)

Scaping, Peter (ed.), *The BPI Year Book 1982* (British Phonographic Industry, 1982)

————*The BPI Year Book 1984* (British Phonographic Industry, 1984)

————*The BPI Year Book 1985* (British Phonographic Industry, 1985)

————*The BPI Year Book 1987* (British Phonographic Industry, 1987)

————*The BPI Year Book 1988/89* (British Phonographic Industry, 1988)

————*The BPI Year Book 1989/90* (British Phonographic Industry, 1989)

————*The BPI Year Book 1991* (British Phonographic Industry, 1991)

Shore, Michael, *The Rolling Stone Book of Rock Video* (Sidgwick and Jackson, 1985)

Smash Hits Yearbook 1984 (Emap Publications, 1983)

Smash Hits Yearbook 1985 (Emap Publications, 1984)

Smash Hits Yearbook 1986 (Emap Publications, 1985)

Stock, Mike, *The Hit Factory: The Stock Aitken Waterman Story* (New Holland, 2004)

Simpson, Paul (ed.), *The Rough Guide to Cult Pop* (Rough Guides, 2003)

Sullivan, Paul, *Sullivan's Music Trivia* (Sanctuary, 2003)

Sweeting, Adam, *Simple Minds* (Sidgwick and Jackson, 1988)

Taylor, Andy, *Wild Boy: My Life in Duran Duran* (Orion, 2008)

Tennant, Neil (compiler), *The Best of Smash Hits* (Emap, 1985)

Turner, Alwyn, *Rejoice, Rejoice! Britain in the 1980s* (Aurum, 2010)

Ure, Midge and Eggar, Robin, *If I Was . . .* (Virgin, 2004)

Vail, Mark, *Vintage Synthesisers* (Miller Freeman, 2000)

Virgin Book of Top 40 Charts, The (Virgin Books, 2009)

Wall, Mick, *Bono In the Name of Love: the Unofficial Biography* (Andre Deutsch, 2005)

Warburton, John with Ryder, Shaun, *Hallelujah! The Extraordinary Story of Shaun Ryder and Happy Mondays* (Virgin, 2003)

Welch, Chris and Soar, Duncan, *One Hit Wonders* (New Holland, 1993)

Werner, Craig, *A Change is Gonna Come: Music, Race and the Soul of America* (Canongate, 2002)

Whitburn, Joel, *The Billboard Book of Top 40 Hits* (Billboard, 2000)

Yetknikoff, Walter, *Howling at the Moon* (Abacus, 2004)

Young, Hugo, *One of Us* (Macmillan, 1989)

Acknowledgements

Many thanks to the following, each of whom have been, as Wham!'s debut album would put it, fantastic: Mike Jones (Brilliant Mind), Simon Trewin (Church of the Poison Mind), Daniel Blythe (Wonderful Life), Will Hodgkinson (Our Lips Are Sealed), Michael Moran (Move On), Richard Evans (The Model), Dave Roberts (Only You), Helen Mockridge (Take on Me), Monica Hope (I Can't Wait), Emily Husain (Like a Prayer) and Joanna Bromley (Walking on Sunshine), Carol Decker (Hold Me Now).

Wired For Sound . . . with Sound

If you are signed up to Spotify (www.spotify.com) you can find a dedicated selection of playlists to accompany the reading of the book. There is a playlist for each individual chapter, featuring the songs discussed, or alternatively there is one overall playlist ('Wired For Sound Complete'). To find the playlists, simply type 'Wired For Sound' into the Spotify search box.

Index

INDEX

INDEX

INDEX

About the Author

Tom Bromley was born in Salisbury in 1972 and grew up in York. A writer and editor, he is the author of seven previous books, including the novels *Crazy Little Thing Called Love* and *Half A World Away*, and the non-fiction works *We Could Have Been The Wombles* and *All In The Best Possible Taste*. He lives in Salisbury with his wife, two daughters and his record collection.

www.tombromley.co.uk